"Not many academic books are touching; *Plato's Bedroom* is. Reading it, you hear the voice of the college lecturer — and what a lecturer! At turns folksy, poetic, passionate, and sometimes all three at once. This inquiry into love is the work of a penetrating thinker who is himself in love — in love with Plato, Shakespeare, and a surprising range of more contemporary literature and movies. The ideas are deeply informed by the author's religious faith, but even more by his faith in the value of philosophy, especially the kind of philosophy that can be taught through literature and art. The result is both powerfully illuminating and a joy to read."
— G.R.F. Ferrari, philosopher and classicist, University of California Berkeley

"*Plato's Bedroom* is an appropriately seductive study of the pleasures, pains and educational potential of love and makes a compelling case for the study of philosophy as a means to illuminate and foster it. Through argument and rich example, David O'Connor seeks to restore love to its rightful place in our physical, emotional and intellectual lives. He calls Plato's *Symposium* a 'potion against disenchantment'; the same could be said of this book."
— Angie Hobbs, Professor of the Public Understanding of Philosophy, University of Sheffield

"In *Plato's Bedroom*, David O'Connor shows himself to be a master of the telling observation. His readings of Plato's dialogues on love will reward students and specialists alike."
— Gabriel Lear, philosopher, University of Chicago

CONTINUED ON THE REVERSE SIDE.

"*Plato's Bedroom* is a book on an enchanting topic written to people of a disenchanted age. It is both an analysis of and an encomium to love. David O'Connor praises the beauty and wonder of Eros without neglecting to remind us of its dangers. He explores the depth of feeling that love inspires in us while carefully avoiding the cheapening sentimentalism characteristic of our age. He explores the exhilaration of sexual desire while eschewing the contemporary culture of pornography. In short, *Plato's Bedroom* manages to elevate Eros without divinizing it."

— John Houston, philosopher and national arm wrestling champion, College of St. Benedict and St. John's University

"*Plato's Bedroom* is one of the great surprises of the year, and perhaps of the decade — a masterful and engaging study of love, desire, romance, and sex, built on the wisdom of the ages. We all need wisdom about love. And we get it in abundance through this remarkable book, a masterful tapestry of insights into the core element of our lives, woven from deep and original readings of Plato, Shakespeare, the Bible, and a wide range of captivating modern films. David O'Connor is one of the most insightful living philosophers to devote his attention to ancient wisdom for modern life. You will find an immense wealth of insight in this book. Love yourself; Read *Plato's Bedroom*!"

— Tom Morris, philosopher, public speaker, and author of *True Success*, *If Aristotle Ran General Motors*, and *The Stoic Art of Living*

CONTINUED ON THE INSIDE BACK ENDSHEET.

PLATO'S BEDROOM

Other Books of Interest from St. Augustine's Press

Peter Kreeft, *Socrates' Children* (in four volumes):
Ancient, Medieval, Modern, and *Contemporary*

Peter Kreeft, *Summa Philosophica*

Gerhart Niemeyer, *The Loss and Recovery of Truth*

Stanley Rosen, *Essays in Philosophy* (in two volumes):
Ancient and *Modern*

Stanley Rosen, *Platonic Productions:
Theme and Variations: The Gilson Lectures*

Gabriel Marcel, *The Mystery of Being* (in two volumes):
I: *Reflections and Mystery* and II: *Faith and Reality*

Seth Benardete, *The Archaeology of the Soul*

Philippe Bénéton, *The Kingdom Suffereth Violence:
The Machiavelli / Erasmus / More Correspondence*

Rémi Brague, *On the God of the Christians
(and on one or two others)*

Rémi Brague, *Eccentric Culture: A Theory of Western Civilization*

Pierre Manent, *Seeing Things Politically*

Albert Camus, *Christian Metaphysics and Neoplatonism*

Christopher Bruell, *Aristotle as Teacher:
His Introduction to a Philosophic Science*

Barry Cooper, *Consciousness and Politics:
From Analysis to Meditation in the Late Work of Eric Voegelin*

Josef Pieper, *What Does "Academic" Mean?
Two Essays on the Chances of the University Today*

Emanuela Scribano, *A Reading Guide to Descartes'
Meditations on First Philosophy*

Roger Scruton, *The Meaning of Conservatism*

René Girard, *A Theater of Envy: William Shakespeare*

H.D. Gerdil, *The Anti-Emile: Reflections on the Theory and
Practice of Education against the Principles of Rousseau*

Joseph Cropsey, *On Humanity's Intensive Introspection*

Josef Kleutgen, S.J., *Pre-Modern Philosophy Defended*

Plato's Bedroom

Ancient Wisdom and Modern Love

DAVID K. O'CONNOR

ST. AUGUSTINE'S PRESS
South Bend, Indiana

Manufactured in the United States of America.

1 2 3 4 5 6   21 20 19 18 17 16 15

Library of Congress Cataloging in Publication Data
O'Connor, David Kevin, author.
Plato's bedroom: ancient wisdom and modern love /
David K. O'Connor.
pages cm
Includes index.
ISBN 978-1-58731-652-4 (hardback)
1. Love. 2. Plato. I. Title.
B398.L9O26 2015
155.3 – dc23   2015032130

∞ The paper used in this publication meets the minimum requirements of
the American National Standard for Information Sciences – Permanence of
Paper for Printed Materials, ANSI Z39.48-1984.

ST. AUGUSTINE'S PRESS
www.staugustine.net

For my students of thirty years:
If I didn't know you, I would have forgotten myself.

Contents

PROLOGUE

Diego Velazquez's wonderful painting "The Toilet of Venus" (painted around 1650, the so-called "Rokeby Venus") is an uncanny representation of Plato's erotic anxieties, and of ours. Displayed at the National Gallery in London, and reproduced on the cover, the image depicts a rear view of Aphrodite – her Roman name is Venus – goddess of sex and beauty, who reclines and gazes in a mirror held by a winged and beribboned Eros, whose Roman name is Cupid. Eros is represented as a child, indeed as the son of Aphrodite, as was common in post-classical art. We do not know who the model was, but her personal beauty and sexiness have been elevated into the realm of myth.

The strikingly original composition, especially the mirror reflecting Venus's face, provokes a complex response. The mirror implies both the narcissism of the subject, as if Venus is admiring her own beauty, and her seduction of the viewer or painter, since her eyes in fact are portrayed as looking at the space in front of the painting. But the viewer is also framed as a voyeur, since Venus is atypically depicted from the back, not as exhibiting herself in frontal view. Venus's eyes in the mirror could be read as her enjoyment at being seen, as if her own beauty became visible to her only through the doting eyes of the viewer; but her gaze could equally be disapproving, or coolly non-committal, unsettling to the viewer's gaze. In addition, the unusual rear view and the mirror emphasize the ways that beauty is mediated, only indirectly available, including in this very painting, but with the indirection intensifying what is flirtatious and seductive in the image. The model's gaze watches the painter as he – and it is inevitable, isn't it, that this painting hides a male painter? – fashions her into the ideal image of the goddess. But perhaps the fashioning eye always re-makes, improves, idealizes its object? The indistinct face in the mirror is both less personal and less idealized, or at least less youthful, than the monumental body, white as alabaster. Did Velazquez see the model at all, or did he efface her, cover her in paint, and have designs only on the goddess beyond? Who is praised by this work of art, woman, goddess, or painter?

Velazquez has also done something unusual with the conventional figure of Eros as a boy, simply by making his posture and attitude more truly childlike than the rambunctious and leering cupids in so many paintings. The god of love appears a bit unsure of his place here, his body somewhat in retreat and his face with a quizzical tilt, admiring his beautiful mother without quite understanding her, entangled in her gaudy ribbons. Velazquez seems to draw our attention to a tension between eroticism and childhood innocence that is not usually conveyed with the figure of Cupid.

The elements and themes of this painting – Aphrodite and her service by Eros, the mirror and the wings and the ribbons, the eroticism of reclining, the elevation of earthy sexiness into mythic eroticism, the intense mediation of desire, the uncertain terms of erotic praise, the innocence of Eros – suffuse Plato's two great erotic dialogues, the *Symposium* and *Phaedrus*. The artist has drawn model and viewer into Plato's bedroom.

Chapter One
PHILOSOPHY AS LOVE POTION

The ancient Greeks called love by the name of a god. What name do you call it?

Modern English has lost its belief in romantic magic. We speak about love in a disenchanted language, a language that seems suspicious and cynical about falling in love and being in love. We need to replace suspicion and cynicism with wonder and gratitude.

Sometimes it seems as if modern English came to bury love rather than to praise it. To refuse to praise something that deserves praise, to reduce what's great to something smaller, so we can control and judge it, makes us smaller, too. But praising love is the central project of the speakers in Plato's great dialogue about love, the *Symposium*, which is why that old book is such a powerful potion against disenchantment. Plato's speakers, reclining on couches in a sort of intoxicated bedroom, mostly fail, of course – just like we do. But they listen to each other and appreciate each other's words, returning with interest to what they've heard, finding their own words: a model for us. Plato lets us follow their attempts to find the right words, or to accept the full consequences of the words they already use. The *Symposium* is the story of men who aren't quite ready to mean what they say about love, who look for ways to escape or control what their speech seems to demand from them or commit them to. Because when they talk about love, they mostly talk about themselves.

But who else would they talk about? We are no better, and no worse, than these men were. It would be a false modesty to insist we can talk about love while avoiding the first person point of view, as if an abstract and impersonal theory of love were within philosophy's reach. To others scrambling up love's craggy ascent, we can suggest no holds more secure than the motley of stories, experiences, and desires we used on our own climb. "In these provinces of inquiry," I say with John Henry Newman, "egotism is true modesty," because "each of us can speak only for himself, and for himself he has a right to speak." Whether we want it or not, when we talk about love, we are fated to be self-reliant, even if what we say runs the risk of sounding idiosyncratic or whimsical. I hope it is somewhat better than whim at last (I quote Ralph Waldo Emerson), but we cannot spend the day in explanation. But this right to speak for ourselves brings with it the responsibility to listen to others, and we'll be trying to keep our ears as open as our mouths. We'll start the listening in this chapter with two contemporary artists, the filmmaker Atom Egoyan and the writer Andre Dubus, who have tapped into the same sources of joy and anxiety that Plato is exploring. Their story-telling helps us to appreciate Plato's insights for our own lives here and now.

The wonderful names of love

The Greeks called love by the name of a god. The name is Eros, the root of the English word "erotic." Because I like the way we modern English speakers inherit something precious from the Greeks, I prefer the phrase "erotic love" to "romantic love" as the name of that special energy we get from falling in love and being in love. But I've found people often take the word "erotic" in a narrow sexual sense, reducing the realm of the Greek god to something little better than lust and pornography, as if Eros lived in a brothel, not a bedroom. So I tend to speak of romance rather than eros. The words "romance" and "romantic," though, have quite a different root and represent a different inheritance. A "romance" was originally a particular kind of story, especially popular five hundred years ago or so, full of fantastic journeys and adventures. The use of "romantic" in modern English to mean "characteristic of falling in love or being in love" is quite recent, only about two hundred years old. Now, the notion that love is an adventure story is a good one, so I'm happy to use the phrase "romantic love"; but even the best story isn't quite as good as a god.

I would love to rescue the word "erotic" from this vulgar reduction, but once a word falls into a culture's gutter, it's hard to
set it back on the high road. We see the same problem with other
words the Greeks used to talk about love. The Greek name for the
goddess of beauty and sexual love was Aphrodite. There was a
common Greek word based on Aphrodite's name, *aphrodisia*,
which means "the things of Aphrodite." This is the typical Greek
word for sexual pleasure, especially that most intense and complete
of sexual pleasures, what in polite English is called "sexual intercourse," or in more emotional language, "making love." Now
think of the difference between inhabiting a language where the
sexual vocabulary comes from the goddess of beauty, and inhabiting one where it comes from the same part of your language as
words like "appendectomy" or "influenza." After all, "sexual intercourse" is a medical phrase, too. It isn't a phrase that makes an
activity sound like something anyone would particularly want to
do: "Would you like to have sexual intercourse this afternoon?"
"No, I think I'll go to the dentist instead." The phrase "sexual intercourse" is supposed to sound neutral and objective, not interesting and, well, sexy, like Aphrodite.

This flat phrase "sexual intercourse" entered the English language in 1798. Its first appearance is in a famous treatise on population by Thomas Malthus, the first person who used the phrase
to refer to "the things of Aphrodite." Malthus argued that population will typically increase more quickly than the production of
food, and he speculated about what public policies might prevent
the misery that results when too many people have too little to eat.
He used the phrase "sexual intercourse" to refer to the actions between men and women that caused population to increase. In other
words, "sexual intercourse" entered modern English as a way to
refer impersonally to a very personal act, in an effort to bring
human sexuality under control by public health authorities. "Sexual intercourse" is the way that we describe human sexuality when
we're thinking about public health policies, such as, say, purifying
water supplies, or quarantining carriers of a dangerous infectious
disease. At the same historical moment a lot of human ingenuity

was being devoted to those kinds of public health questions, human ingenuity started to invent a medicalized vocabulary to think about human sexuality.

Much of the sexual vocabulary that we think of as completely natural is in fact a very recent addition to English. The word "sex" itself, used to refer to what we now call sexual activity, is barely a century old. The English language had the word "sex," of course, for a long time. It referred to the distinction between male and female. But the use of "sex" to refer to sexual activity, to sexual intercourse, to the wonderful "things of Aphrodite," only emerged around 1880 or so. The more emotional and literary phrase "making love" is even more recent in its specifically sexual meaning. This phrase used to refer to the special attention and private conversation that two people would devote to each other during courtship. A modern reader of a nineteenth-century novel, expecting the sexualized meaning rather than the older meaning, might be shocked to read that a young man and woman were "making love" in full view of dozens of other visitors at a party. But this older meaning, focused on attention and conversation, was still common until perhaps seventy years or so ago. "Making love" has been reduced and narrowed, declining from an art of conversation to little more than a physical fact.

I want Plato to help us escape this dilapidated linguistic neighborhood. But in modern English, the Greek name of the goddess of beauty and sexuality, Aphrodite, has been pretty much ruined. Even the goddess herself has been medicalized, made into a drug, in the word "aphrodisiac," a word that can't be retrieved for romance, I think. It sounds more like a poison than a magic potion. Perhaps you will suggest we use the attractive Latin version of Aphrodite's name, Venus, and see what resources it may offer. Alas, Venus has suffered a worse fate than Aphrodite. The only current English phrase that makes use of her divine name is "venereal disease." The adjective "venereal" is hardly ever used to say anything else, and the very fact that it derives from the name of the goddess of love comes as a surprise to many. In previous centuries, a poet or a spouse might have said, "Come my love, let us enjoy our venereal delights," and not meant it as a joke. But no more. Imagine a store advertising the holiday cards lovers buy for each other for St. Valentine's Day, with the heading "Venereal Greetings." Those cards won't be big sellers, except with the most ironic or antiquarian couples.

The steady pressure on the English language is a steady pressure on our erotic world. One of the great philosophers of the twentieth century was an Austrian, Ludwig Wittgenstein (1889–1951), who was as brilliant and funny as he was morose and anxious – a combination of darkness and light not unusual in the personalities of geniuses. Wittgenstein was obsessed with ways we are enchanted and bewitched by language. A memorable and pithy aphorism of Wittgenstein's captures this magical embrace in which language holds us: "The limits of my language are the limits of my world." Now, it is only young children, or people no longer young but still childish, who think every limit is a loss, a loss of freedom. More mature and thoughtful people understand how limits are also powers. The "no hands" rule of soccer or the boundaries on a basketball court do not so much constrain us as empower us; they give us a place to play. A child might complain, "Let me catch the ball with my hands! It's not fair I have to kick it"; or demand to shoot a basket from the bleachers. There's something comical about seeing a child frustrated like this, but we all feel that way sometimes, and we rebel against the very limits that make something possible. We are like the man who wakes one morning, puts his feet on the floor, and says, "Damn! Held down by gravity again!" He fancies that without gravity's limit, he could fly like a bird, not realizing it is as hard for a bird to fly as for a man to walk. His feet on the floor give him the power to walk, and without gravity's limit he would merely float into the nothing. He may even learn to dance. – However much we may have fantasies of escaping to the wild and making up all the rules for ourselves, our real lives are in the city limits. We need limits to find expression, and to have any game to play at all. No language is more enchanting and bewitching than the language of love. What romantic games does this language let us play? What constraints does our language put on us, and what mistakes does it tempt us into?

The language that we have to describe our lives has a lot to do with what we think is possible or likely in our lives. Plato in the *Symposium* has every speaker deploy a mythological language about love and erotic life, a language full of heroes and gods and goddesses. The speakers disagree with each other about all sorts of things, but they do agree on one most important thing: romantic love, and the desire that is a part of it, have about them the scent of the sacred, some kind of breaking open of the everyday human world into something more divine. Plato's men would have been puzzled and dispirited by the language of love that immediately comes to a modern English speaker, a language about controlling a danger to public health, or about a merely bodily act. First to Plato's mind is a language primarily designed to express the praise and celebration of something sacred.

But we shouldn't think the Greeks had no anxieties or fears about this sacred realm of love. The Greeks didn't expect their gods to make them comfortable, or to be nice. (Being nice seems to be the most popular virtue these days, as when students complain a teacher isn't "being nice" if the teacher holds the students to high standards. Maybe more teachers should be like Greek gods.) The Greeks often found the divine baffling, and sometimes terrifying. They didn't expect to be comforted by the aphrodisiac, by the things of Aphrodite. They expected to find the experience of love exhilarating, but this romantic exhilaration was a sharp mixture of pleasure and pain. Sappho, the finest of all Greek love poets, knew what she was talking about when she coined the word "bittersweet" to describe erotic love. Sappho presented herself as Aphrodite's special favorite, but when the poet prays to Aphrodite for help in her love affairs, the smiling goddess grants the prayer always with laughter, teasing Sappho for her fears and infatuations. We still tease our friends about their love affairs, even when we sympathize with their bittersweet romances.

Aphrodite is the lead divinity of love, but Dionysus is a close second in Plato's language world. As Aphrodite presides over erotic exhilaration, Dionysus, the god of wine and of theater, presides over ecstatic experience and intoxication. Since Plato's *Symposium* is a drinking party – the Greek word *symposium* just means "drinking together" – the dialogue invokes images of Dionysus and ecstasy; and since this symposium is dedicated to speeches about love, it also invokes Aphrodite and the exhilaration of falling in love and being in love. Dionysus was usually represented as a young man of exotic and rather feminine beauty, adorned with ivy and violets, often with a company of female revelers and enchanted wild animals, especially panthers. "Ecstasy" comes from two Greek words that together mean "to stand outside, to break out of"; and the exemplary Dionysian experience is to be broken open and swept away, abducted by the god. And as exciting as that experience may be, it's not *nice*, and sometimes it feels like a terrible threat to one's identity. The most tragic of all Greek stories of Dionysus and his ecstasies is Euripides's tragedy *The Women of Dionysus* (often called by its Greek title *Bacchae*). The key moment in the tragedy comes when the central character, a new ruler named Pentheus, loses his grip on his identity under the influence of the god. This young man, repulsed by the undignified revels of the elders of his city, has been resisting Dionysus and putting on a tough manly exterior. But Pentheus is unmanned by the god and dressed in the tires and mantles of Dionysus's female revelers, and in his women's clothes he wanders from the city to be destroyed in the wild. Perhaps the most beautiful story of Dionysian ecstasy is more ambivalent about the identities lost and gained under the god's influence. In the ancient *Homeric Hymn to Dionysus*, pirates spy Dionysus, sitting on the beach with his wind-blown hair, and they bind and kidnap him, thinking he is merely a young man they can sell for ransom. But once they are back on the sea, their ship sprouts vines and flows with wine, and wild animals roam the deck, as Dionysus sits silent and smiling while around him all turns to chaos. Finally the terrified crew are transformed into dolphins and leap into the sea. Is this an evil fate for the pirates? Well, from a merely human view, perhaps it is. It isn't nice, at least, to lose one's humanity. But is it not a wonder, to become a dolphin, and to be at home in the boundless and mysterious ocean?

This pagan experience of the gods, and especially of love, might well unsettle the language many people use about God, and especially about Jesus. From the way we take up the deep truth that "God is love," you might think Jesus was about the nicest guy who ever lived. Our encounter with such a nice guy god would hardly be unsettling at all, because there would be no challenge in it. Of course, that comfortable view of what God might be won't survive a moment's reading of the Gospels. Jesus was a lot of things, but the first thing that sprang to people's lips who had actually met him wasn't, Oh, what a sweetheart. There was something too edgy, too striking, too challenging about Jesus for that sort of reaction. The much-loved Christian author C.S. Lewis had a fine way of making this point, and unsettling comfortable Christians. Lewis's *The Lion, the Witch, and the Wardrobe* is organized around a central Christ figure, a lion named Aslan. When the heroes of the story, the Pevensie children, first learn about Aslan, they are anxious about meeting a lion, and they ask whether Aslan is really safe, and wonder whether he is wild or tame. Their mentor, a talking beaver helpfully named Mr. Beaver, does not give them comfort, though he does give them hope, when he says Aslan is neither safe nor tame, though he certainly is good.

The way of love is wonderful: it is by abandonment. We abandon a safer and tamer self, the more to abandon ourselves to the good of love's exhilarating ecstasy. We leave the limits of a more comfortable world to accept the demands of a new one. Plato's *Symposium*, and his *Phaedrus* too, try to find ways philosophy can promote this reception of the new love. But before we can be open enough to receive, we must diagnose the anxieties and fears that keep us closed, that make us want to control love like a tame cat rather than riding the lion. The men we meet in the *Symposium* try to use philosophy to protect themselves from love, to avoid its demands and ecstasies, even while they praise love and long for it.

This anxious combination of resistance and longing is our romantic fate, too. It is as if love slips through our fingers at the very moment we clutch at it the hardest. We clutch at comfort and control only to find ourselves swimming in vulnerability. I found myself confronted powerfully with my fantasies of control by one of the most erotic movies I've ever seen: Atom Egoyan's *Exotica*. It is a work for our time fit to stand comparison to Sappho's discovery of Aphrodite's bitter sweetness, and to send us leaping from the safe ship of our theater chair into a Dionysian ocean.

Unsettling erotic needs in Atom Egoyan's Exotica

The movie *Exotica* (1994, written and directed by the distinguished Canadian filmmaker Atom Egoyan) unsettled me, and I think it will unsettle you, too. Some movies merely shock, and no philosophy comes from it. But not this movie; watching this movie is like having Socrates himself come upon you in the street. He starts up what you think is a pleasant conversation, but it ends up forcing you to examine what you have always thought was settled. This is a movie that challenges the superficial view of sexual desire and romantic love typical of so many movies, whether they are comedies or dramas. *Exotica* sees the exhilaration and ecstasy of love to be intimately bound up with pain and need, not just with lust and pleasure. What pain and which needs? Recognizing the answers to these questions is a test of the viewer, of us. We viewers are brought into a deeper understanding and sympathy for the characters and their sufferings, but we are also tempted many times to jump to conclusions about the characters, before we really understand them. We are tempted, I would say, to take ourselves to be superior to the characters, because we can be cool observers of their crazy lives. Aren't you ever tempted to congratulate yourself when you notice the crazy love lives of your friends? "I don't let Aphrodite and Dionysus get so out of hand!" *Exotica* showed me how false I was when I felt this way, and the discovery was chastening. Not only was I being unfair to their complexities; I was avoiding my own.

Exotica is tightly organized, with all the pieces connected, every moment and detail seeming to offer a commentary on every other moment. The movie's thoughtfulness is in these details. We'll have to simplify this detailed thinking to discuss some general themes and to connect the movie to Plato and to Shakespeare. So I'll focus on only one or two of its parallel plots.

Atom Egoyan is the sort of filmmaker who wants you to think about how you experience his movies. The opening scene of

Exotica has a brilliant way of revealing an unsettling truth about viewers: we are people who enjoy observing other people's intimate moments. We share the view of a customs inspector at the Toronto airport, training a younger man to spot smugglers. They stand in a room with a one-way mirror, observing the passengers. One awkward-looking man, Thomas (Don McKellar), seems nervous, and he stands gazing into the mirror, not seeing the two customs officers studying his face. "You have to ask yourself," the older officer tells the younger, "what brought the person to this point. You have to convince yourself that this person has something hidden that you have to find." But for the customs officer, as for us viewers, this telling of secrets is all one way: we enjoy seeing what we don't want to show. The director invites us to have this unsettling thought: when I enjoy this movie, I am enjoying spying on its characters. I put myself into a position of power and superiority over them. We may watch dangerous gods play with them, but we'll be sitting safely on the other side of the mirror, like God's spies.

The movie immediately intensifies the viewer's anxiety about being a spy by suggesting we are also voyeurs, gazing with surreptitious pleasure on other people's erotic lives. We are now in a "gentlemen's club," called Club Exotica, where an almost all male audience pays to gaze on women's bodies. There is a DJ named Eric (Elias Koteas), playing music and improvising introductions for each dancer to help along the fantasies of the customers. The words Eric uses to conclude his fantasy introductions are shockingly close to the advice of the customs officer: "You too can have one of these girls come over to your table and show you the mysteries of her world. Trust me, gentlemen, trust me." Later in the movie, we discover that the club also has one-way mirrors, for customers who like to watch in secret. The next dancer, Christina (Mia Kirschner), is dressed in the plaid skirt and white blouse common as school uniforms for teenagers, and Eric plays on this costume as he says over the microphone, "What is it that gives a schoolgirl her special innocence? Her sweet fragrance, of fresh flowers, of late spring rain? Or is it her firm young flesh inviting your every caress, inviting you to explore her deepest and most private secrets?" A natural bower, an innocent romp; a mystery, a secret, a hidden precious treasure: and you can know it, without exposing yourself to being known. The men in the audience sit with their drinks and watch the show, most of them stone-faced and intent. They do not look like men attracted to a woman, but like potential buyers giving a cool and neutral appraisal of a used car, or a side of beef. They want the pleasures of seeing without the vulnerability of connecting.

When her dance is over, we see Christina at a table, talking with a customer, a man we later learn is named Francis (Bruce Greenwood). We can't hear what they say, but what do we expect a man who pays women to dance naked for him to say? Francis pays Christina, then gets up suddenly and leaves. We next see him in his car, with a teenage blond, Tracey (Sarah Polley), in the passenger seat, parked in a seedy neighborhood. Francis gives money to the girl, and asks if she's available next Thursday. The strip club, the unsavory neighborhood, the money, the empty expression on the blond girl's face: what does the viewer think is going on? Well, I find that most viewers are like me, and we think the girl is a prostitute, one with whom Francis has a regular "appointment." So what Francis says when she gets out of the car is shocking and disgusting: "Say hi to your dad." It is bad enough that Francis is paying a teenage prostitute – remember that the dancer Christina, the one Francis seems to like most, was also dressed like a schoolgirl – but is her father also her pimp? My mind takes the evidence and makes of it a dirty story, of lust and seedy pleasure.

Part of the genius of Egoyan's movie is to show me that the dirt is in my own mind, not in the characters. The movie finally reveals every one of these characters to us, and each lives a different story from the one we imagine. We can only follow Francis, but the movie loves all the characters; there isn't a bad guy in the whole story.

The next time we see Francis, he is working at his job, as an auditor for Revenue Canada, the Canadian tax collection agency. Francis has been assigned to investigate a store that specializes in exotic pets – and the store owner is Thomas, whom we saw at the airport in the opening scene. Thomas, it turns out, really *is* a smuggler. Even from behind the one-way mirror, the customs officers didn't discover his secret: Taped to his stomach to incubate them, Thomas has the eggs of a hyacinth macaw, a rare type of parrot that can't be legally imported. (In a nice visual joke, macaws show up as pets at both Club Exotica and at the apartment blond Tracey shares with her father. Perhaps they are customers of Thomas?)

As Francis sits down to examine the store's disorganized records, he makes small talk with nervous Thomas. "I suppose you have to be pretty careful with the temperature, with the animals," he says. "Well, they're a lot hardier than you might think," says Thomas, and Francis responds with some irritation, "I wouldn't think they're not hardy. Just because they're exotic doesn't mean they can't endure extremes. It is after all a jungle out there." The pet store and Club Exotica, it turns out, have some interesting parallels. Both are full of interesting creatures we might be tempted to treat as pets, to be bought and sold, as if we were superior to them, their oddities and eccentricities nothing more than curiosities for our viewing pleasure. But these "exotic" animals, human or not, in fact are enduring, are capable of living through suffering and trauma. The movie will show us that Francis and schoolgirl Christina are just such exotic animals, surviving as best they can in a jungle of pain and need.

The movie begins to give us troubling clues that we haven't understood Francis's connections to the two young women, Tracey and Christina. Scenes cut back and forth between the two. Francis picks up Tracey at her apartment, where Francis talks with her father, who, we now learn, is Francis's brother. Our first reaction is yet more disgust; it is bad for a man to buy a young prostitute, it is worse if she is pimped by her father, but it exceeds all limits if the poor girl is also the man's niece! But Tracey is no prostitute, though we aren't yet sure what she is. Francis drops her off at his house, where she practices piano and flute. A large photograph of Francis's wife and daughter hangs over the mantle, and Francis tells Tracey he'll be back before it gets late. The photograph is a frame from a home video, and as the scene fades out, the video starts to fill the screen: we are watching a home movie made by Francis. The scene shifts to Francis at the club, watching Christina dance. She comes to his table, and this time we find out what they talk about. "What are you thinking?" Christina asks, but we can tell this conversation is being repeated, is a sort of ritual between them. "I was just thinking," Francis says in a tight voice, "what would happen if someone would hurt you?" "How could anyone hurt me?" Christina asks. "If I'm not there to protect you." Christina sounds like she is trying to reassure Francis. "You'll always be there to protect me." But Francis looks at Christina, though he seems to be speaking about someone else. "An angel. Why would someone want to do something like that? How could someone even think of doing something like that?" "You mustn't worry," she says, but she sounds worried. As before, Francis leaves suddenly. Are we seeing a twisted sexual fantasy, Francis imagining Christina being attacked – by whom? himself? – and then rescued, as he becomes Christina's protector? Is this what Francis pays for at Club Exotica? Francis leaves the club and takes Tracey home to her apartment, and they talk about the strained relationship Francis has with her father, his brother. He pays her as she leaves the car. But why did he bring Tracey to his house when he went out to the club? Does he just want someone to enjoy his piano? And why would he pay for that? The exchange of money must mean something to Francis we haven't yet understood.

The next time we see Christina and Francis at the club, their odd relationship reaches a crisis. "How could anyone hurt you, take you away from me?" he says again, and leaves. But this time Eric, the DJ, follows Francis and speaks to him without being seen. Eric is jealous of Francis's intense connection with Christina, and he and Christina were once a romantic couple. Flashbacks earlier in the movie have shown us how they met when they were a few years younger, as teenagers. We have seen them in a few quick scenes, out of the city, walking in an open field, alone together even though other people are walking nearby. They are part of a large group searching for a lost girl, and Christina tells Eric she babysat for her a few times. Now their relationship is over, but Eric is still upset to see Christina so intimate with Francis. He tempts Francis to take a dangerous step. "She seems to have a bit of a thing for you," he says to Francis, "why don't you give her a little touch?" Francis knows the club has a strict rule against customers touching the dancers. "What happens when I touch her?" he asks, and an image flashes through his mind, of the video of his wife and daughter. There is a boundary, a limit; and he decides to test that limit and do what Eric suggests. He goes back to a table, and when Christina comes to dance, Francis reaches out his hand and touches her stomach. Eric sees his chance, and throws Francis out of the club into the street, and Club Exotica bans Francis from coming back.

Francis, bleeding and bruised, drives Tracey home. She doesn't understand what's happened to him. "You think this is normal? What we do? We don't speak about it." Francis thanks her for worrying about him, and gives her money as she leaves. The next day, Tracey decides "to talk about it." She tells her father she no longer wants, as she says, to "babysit" for Francis. "There's no baby to sit," Tracey says. Her father says she is "housesitting," not babysitting, but Tracey refuses to play this game any longer. We viewers finally start to fathom the ocean of pain beneath the surface of Francis's odd behavior. "He has me come to his house," Tracey says, revealing the secret, "so he can pretend Lisa is still alive." Lisa, we now learn, was Francis's daughter. He pays his niece to come to his house to hold on to a routine that made sense when his daughter was alive, a routine now repeated as a ritual he can't give up, not yet. He can't stop hiring a babysitter because he can't yet accept the death of his daughter.

Every daughter is precious to her father. But why does Francis feel such an extremity of grief, why does he mourn so interminably? How did his daughter die? The answers are bound up with the ritual conversations Francis has with schoolgirl Christina. Francis is forbidden to return to the club, but he can't give up his connection with Christina, however eccentric it may be. In his audit of the pet store, Francis has discovered that Thomas is running a large and lucrative smuggling operation. He uses this incriminating information to blackmail Thomas into helping him get back in touch with Christina. He gives Thomas a hidden transmitter, and listens in his car outside the club. We viewers are once again put into the same position as the characters in the movie, spying and hiding, as Thomas strikes up a conversation with Christina about a man who was thrown out the other night. "He is a very particular case," says Christina about Francis. And now she reveals to Thomas, and to us, the key fact about Francis's daughter we did not know before: she was murdered, and before the murderer was caught, the police had suspected Francis himself. But Thomas, like us, still doesn't see why his daughter's murder should make Francis so attached to Christina. "Francis and I have a very special relationship," she says, "then he chose to violate it." Thomas keeps questioning her, and Christina starts to cry. "I need him for certain things and he needs me for certain things," she says, "he violated that in his role, in what he's supposed to do for me." Thomas doesn't understand. "What is he supposed to do for you? He comes to this club and he pays you. What has he done for you?" It's just money for sex, isn't it? What kind of emotional connection do you think you have with Francis? Christina can only repeat, "He was always paying me to do him this favor," and she is called away before she can explain what the favor is, what needs they served in each other. Eric speaks to Thomas, and reveals that he is the one who provoked Francis to the dangerous touch.

Francis has heard all this in his car. He comes to the door and begs the owner of Club Exotica to allow him back. Why did you touch Christina, the owner wants to know. Francis offers a puzzling response: "I needed to make sure." But what would you have done if she had let you touch her? "I'd have been disappointed," Francis says, because "that's not the way she was raised." Francis's talk of "disappointment" makes no more sense to the owner than Christina's talk of "violation" did to Thomas. After all, she takes off her clothes, for pay, in a club, for him. Their relationship looks purely mercenary, sex for money. But Francis talks about her as if he had raised her himself, and she talks about him as if he were taking care of her. They share some need and some connection we can't understand and they can't express. It's like trying to interpret an oracle.

The next day, Francis meets Thomas at the pet store again. "Did you know," Thomas asks him, "that they" – he means the people at Club Exotica – "knew about your daughter?" Francis tells the story about being suspected by the police. The police told him, Francis says, that his wife was having an affair with his brother, Tracey's father. They suggested to him that his daughter was not fathered by him; and so – his voice breaks when he says this – "They thought I could harm her." A month after they caught the murderer, his wife was killed in a car being driven by his brother. So we finally understand what Francis had been saying to Christina. He has been repeating over and over again the same sentence – Who could harm her? Who could harm her? – because he is still trying to answer the police and to save his daughter, and perhaps his wife, too. His mourning is interminable. Francis now focuses all his pain and anger on Eric: "He took something very special from me, and I've had too many special things taken from me." He gives Thomas instructions to go into the club and touch Christina, just as he did, so that Eric will throw him out too; and when Eric does, Francis has brought a gun to kill him. We viewers are ready, I think, to accept this revenge fantasy.

But Atom Egoyan was not. As Francis waits outside with his gun, he is startled to see Eric appear across the parking lot, walking toward him. And then Eric says something to unsettle our revenge fantasy: "Don't be afraid. I know everything about you. I found her. Your little girl." The scene flashes back to Eric and Christina in the field with the search party. Together, they see a crumpled figure lying in the grass: a body, dressed in the plaid skirt and white blouse of a schoolgirl. Christina hides her eyes on Eric's shoulder; they've found Lisa, Francis's precious daughter. Eric and Christina form a bond in this shared horror, a bond that explains Eric's jealousy. Eric weeps as he puts his head on the shoulder of Francis, still holding the gun as he embraces this man who shares his pain. Inside the club, Thomas reaches out his hand and touches Christina's thigh. She removes it gently; no need to see a violation. No one is shot, no one is thrown in the street; all is understood, all is forgiven. Egoyan reads the oracle's riddle.

A final flashback: the video of Francis's daughter and wife, but now we see the scene as real life, I mean, of course, as part of the movie. Mother and daughter sit at a piano, playing together, while Francis holds the camera. There's a knock at the door, and when Francis answers, we recognize Christina, a younger, girlish version of the sexy woman we've seen. She has come, a bit early, a bit lonely, because she is the daughter's babysitter. We could have inferred this revelation from an earlier flashback to the search party, when Christina told Eric she had babysat for the lost girl; but at that point we didn't know the lost girl would turn out to be the dead daughter of Francis, and I think most viewers are like me, and only feel the revelation now. Later, as Francis drives Christina home, he praises Lisa's talent for the piano, and he says, "We're thinking about buying her a better piano, an exotic baby grand." Now we understand better why Tracey was brought to the house to keep that piano alive. Young Christina doubts her parents get excited when they talk about her. Francis tries to cheer her, and tells her his daughter says she's a good listener. "If there's ever anything you want to talk about, about what might be going on at home, or whatever, you know I'm here," he says, as he drops her at home and pays her for babysitting. This is the final piece of the puzzle, the key clicking in the lock. Francis and Christina were not trading sex for money. "He was always paying me to do him this favor," she had said to Thomas, and now we know the favor: listening, and babysitting. No one who sees *Exotica* will doubt that these are deeper needs than lust and pleasure.

Let me conclude with an aspect of the movie I can't discuss more fully here, on a theme that will return in later chapters. *Exotica* is unusual in uncovering how complex our sexual, erotic, romantic response can be to pain and trauma. But it is even more unusual, I think, in uncovering the secret need of its characters for procreation. This secret need is indicated by a striking parallel between Thomas the pet store owner and the owner of Club Exotica, a woman named Zoe (the name means "life" in Greek). Thomas inherited the store with the exotic pets from his father, and Zoe inherited Club Exotica from her mother. The macaw eggs taped to Thomas's belly, smuggled through customs, are an image of, I want to say, a mercenary pregnancy. In a subplot I haven't discussed, Zoe is really pregnant, but her pregnancy is mercenary, too. She has made a contract with the DJ, Eric, to give her a child. A couple's wild adventure, through sexual love toward new life, has been tamed by Zoe and Eric, made into an economic transaction. As the customers at the club turn sex into money, so do Zoe and Eric turn begetting a child into money, sanitizing it and taking their emotions out of the bargain. These two mercenary pregnancies, which use money to manipulate or control the desire for offspring, are the opposite of Francis's use of money with Christina, his desperate attempt to recover his lost child. Money for Francis is not control, but mourning, mourning for his lost wife, too, but especially for his lost daughter. The need at the erotic heart of *Exotica*, then, is for procreation. The gentlemen's club is a hidden maternity ward, if only its denizens could be unsettled enough to acknowledge their true needs.

Drinking with the gods in Plato's *Symposium*

In Greek, "symposium" simply means "drinking together"; why did Plato think a drinking party would be an ideal place to learn about love? Because this type of party was a festival of the gods Aphrodite and Dionysus. This doesn't mean a Greek symposium was a pious and decorous affair; far from it! It was a revel, full of the boozy boasting and embarrassing candor you might expect from intoxication and the loss of inhibitions. But isn't all this revelry and sensuality the exact opposite of the sort of judicious rationality we expect out of philosophy? Was this famous philosopher a bit out of his senses when he wrote such a thing? Plato is playing with these expectations, showing us how philosophy's public face of sober reason can be a mask for an underlying passion philosophers are fearful of owning. The *Symposium* starts off making us think we will get to play the cool voyeur, but by the end it does what *Exotica* does, and throws us into the Dionysian dance.

The story of this drinking party is told to us by a silly man named Apollodorus, who is asked, for the second time in a couple of days, to tell a story he happens to know, the story of a drinking party celebrating the success of the tragic poet Agathon, a party that happened some seventeen years earlier, when Apollodorus was still just a boy. This party was at the house of Agathon, and Socrates and Alcibiades were both there. Agathon, poet and dramatist, was still a young man then, barely thirty years old, a hot new talent, edgy and innovative, and at the time of the party he had just won first prize in one of Athens' religious festivals, a remarkable and prestigious achievement. Tragic poets presented a set of four plays, and a jury voted on the best set. Each set had three tragedies and a fourth play, called a "satyr play," because the chorus was a troupe of unruly and bawdy satyrs, mythical creatures half human and half goat. (Satyrs were often depicted in the company of Dionysus.) A satyr play presented a comic parody of a tragic story, and lightened the mood of the audience after the usually dark themes of the tragedies. (These bawdy satyr plays are the origin of the English word "satire.") Plato makes use in the structure of the *Symposium* of the fact that the three serious tragedies in a set were followed by the satirical comedy of the last play: the last speech, given by a drunken and very funny Alcibiades, is described by Socrates as a satyr play.

What revived so much interest in this long-ago party that Apollodorus was asked about it twice in two days? Without saying so directly, Plato gives us enough clues to answer this question: people remembered this party when Socrates was indicted for corrupting the young (in 399 BC). Socrates's relationship with the notoriously brilliant and licentious Alcibiades, the most charismatic and controversial politician of his day, was the star example of such corruption, at least in the minds of Socrates's enemies. The rest of the *Symposium* is the recollection by Apollodorus of the speeches on love given at this famous party.

Like Shakespeare's plays, Plato's dialogues often begin with an opening scene that suggests important themes for the rest of the work. This little scene with Apollodorus being asked about

Agathon's long-ago party accomplishes two things. First, it focuses the reader on Socrates's influence on men like Alcibiades. Was the influence of Socrates, and more generally the influence of philosophy, on such ambitious and attractive men good or bad? This question is the focus of Alcibiades's own speech at the end of the dialogue. Second, through the personality of Apollodorus, the scene raises the question of how philosophy, with its emphasis on self-control, can be consistent with love, with its emphasis on abandonment. Apollodorus fancied himself a true and dedicated philosopher, imitating Socrates's extraordinary talent for close logical analysis, not to say for verbal combat. But where Socrates was a great conversationalist, engaging and good-humored even when his criticisms cut deep, Apollodorus was merely blunt and hectoring. His speech was only a superficial imitation of Socrates, too hard and harsh to be an accurate image. But while in words Apollodorus put on a "tough guy" show, in deeds he was emotional and rather effeminate, traits that earned him the nickname "Softy." In Plato's dialogue *Phaedo*, which takes place on the day Socrates was executed, Apollodorus weeps and wails, until Socrates chastises him for acting like an uncontrolled woman. Near the beginning of the *Symposium*, one of his friends laughs at Apollodorus's tough talk, and points out the incongruity of someone who fancies himself such a hard-nosed talker being called Softy. So in action, Apollodorus is too soft to really be like Socrates. We might say Apollodorus is a distorting mirror of Socrates, too manly in speech, too womanly in deed. Does true philosophy, as represented by Socrates, unite the masculine and the feminine? This tension between the hard and the soft in the life of true love runs through the entire dialogue.

So Apollodorus begins telling the story of Socrates and Alcibiades at the house of Agathon, seventeen years ago. It turns out Apollodorus has learned the story from one of Socrates's admirers from seventeen years earlier, a little man, Aristodemus, known as "Shorty." (The social circle around Socrates seems to have enjoyed nicknames. Another of Socrates's closest friends, Chaerephon, was known as "The Bat," for his squeaky voice and his tendency to get in an emotional flutter.) Aristodemus is the reverse of Apollodorus as an imitator of Socrates: whereas Apollodorus was too soft to be like the real Socrates, Aristodemus was too hard and crude. Apollodorus was attracted by Socrates's power in speech, but Aristodemus is attracted more by the example of Socrates's way of life. One day seventeen years earlier, Apollodorus tells us, Aristodemus came to visit Socrates. He was surprised to find Socrates getting all dressed up, something he rarely did. In particular, Socrates was putting on a pair of fancy shoes, something completely out of character for Socrates, at least as Aristodemus understood Socrates's character. Socrates was well known for his simple way of life, dressed in simple clothes verging toward the shabby, and habitually barefoot, summer and winter (which also comes up in Alcibiades's speech at the end of the *Symposium*). Socrates, we might say, stayed close to nature, and Aristodemus admired and imitated this simple natural life, but in a rather superficial and mechanical way. He imitated the outward features of simplicity – the old clothes and the bare feet – without much understanding of the inner principle behind it. To go to a dinner party at the house of the beautiful young man Agathon, Socrates makes himself more beautiful. Beauty draws even Socrates out of his everyday self, which is the only Socrates that Shorty ever sees.

Like Apollodorus seventeen years later, Aristodemus wanted to imitate Socrates. But Shorty falls short of Socrates; he is too small, not of physical stature, but too small of soul. There is a side of Socrates that he is too short to see. It is consistent with Socrates's simple life to go to a fancy drinking party with the celebrities of Athens, and to take his place among them. Socrates, unlike his imperfect imitator, doesn't mind putting on a show now and then. Drawn to the simplicity and self-control of Socrates, Aristodemus doesn't know how to dress up. We could say that just as Apollodorus makes Socrates harder than he really is, Aristodemus makes the man he admires simpler than he really is. They both see something that is true about Socrates, but they make imitation easier by reducing the original. Plato is challenging the reader to see Socrates whole, without cutting him down to our size, or making him fit some version of the self we are already comfortable with. And by showing these two men trying to make Socrates more comforting, Plato holds up a mirror to us, so we can see our own tendency to do the same thing.

Socrates was delighted by the unexpected visit from Aristodemus, and he immediately says to him, "Come along with me; I'm going to a party at Agathon's house, to celebrate his victory at the tragic competition." Aristodemus, barefoot as usual and in his simple and rather shabby clothes, is reluctant; he isn't dressed up, and he wasn't invited. But Socrates tells him not to worry, and promises to say he has invited Aristodemus himself when they get to Agathon's house. Being Socrates's friend will be enough, it seems, to dress up shabby Shorty and guarantee he'll be welcomed. But just before they arrive, something pops into Socrates's mind, and he stops right by the side of the street to think about it! Socrates will get dressed up for a party, but he won't let that get in the way of thinking. This is just the first, rather comic instance in the *Symposium* of how nothing can distract Socrates from his core identity as a philosopher: not being late for dinner, not the rigors of summer heat or winter cold, not drinking a pitcher of wine, not being seduced by a young beauty, and not even facing death in battle, all of which we will hear about later on in the evening. By the way, Plato never tells us what Socrates stopped to think about; perhaps he was planning a speech about love?

Socrates stops and thinks, and he sends poor Shorty on to Agathon's house, so that he arrives not only uninvited, but without Socrates, who had made him come along. Aristodemus tries to wait outside, but one of the servants sees him and brings him in. So here he is, brought before Agathon and the celebrities of Athens, in his shabby clothes and uninvited, without Socrates to introduce him: an embarrassing situation. Lucky for Aristodemus, Agathon is a very cultivated man. "Aristodemus, you're just in time for dinner," he says, "I was looking to invite you yesterday and couldn't find you anywhere. I'm glad you showed up." Now it's always possible Agathon really had been looking for him, but it seems more likely that we have here the elegance and quick thinking of Agathon. He's the sort of man who knows what to do when an unexpected person is embarrassed to show up on your step when you're about to have dinner. The thing you do is to say, "Ah! I wanted to have you here all along." He finds a spare seat for Aristodemus and makes him feel welcome; but he also asks him where Socrates is, since Agathon knows Aristodemus is always following Socrates around. We readers are a bit like Aristodemus, welcomed into this famous party, allowed to overhear the magnificent speeches, even if we don't quite measure up to the standards of beauty of the invited guests. Our love for Socrates is enough to get us in the door.

Agathon is a very clever host in other ways, too. When Socrates does finally finish his thinking and come in, after dinner has already started, Agathon has arranged things so that there's only one place for Socrates to sit down, on Agathon's couch. At a Greek symposium, the guests were seated two men to a couch (only men were guests), with the couches arranged in a large circle. They would recline on their left side and eat food from small tables they could reach with their right hand. After dinner, the guests would spend the evening drinking wine from a large bowl passed around the circle, telling stories and singing songs. So there's a certain amount of elegant artifice in Agathon's arrangement of the seats: he sees to it that he's the person who's closest to Socrates. Agathon clearly wants to show off, to all the celebrities at the party, but especially to Socrates. To be admired by Socrates: that is a prize he would love to win. Everyone knows Socrates has a reputation for being a "lover of wisdom," which is just what the Greek word "philosopher" means. And so to be admired by Socrates seems to be a celebration and a proof of one's own wisdom.

Just how much Agathon desires to be praised and admired by Socrates becomes clear shortly after Socrates enters and is assigned to the couch with Agathon. When Socrates comes in and sits down, there's some playful banter comparing the claims to wisdom of Agathon and Socrates. Agathon says, "Socrates, come lie down on my couch, because I hear that by being close to somebody who's wise, I can have his wisdom rub off on me." There's clearly a sexual undertone to what Agathon is saying, and Socrates plays along.

"Agathon," he replies, "it would be splendid if we could get wisdom just by physical contact; it would be like making water run from a full cup into an empty one by putting a wool thread between them." (This actually works, though it's slow. But I wish Socrates had used wine instead of water in his image; dare I say it would have fit the context of a drinking party even better than Plato's own words?) Plato develops this playful image – wisdom flowing from something full into something empty, as if through physical contact, indeed through sexual contact – in deeply serious ways throughout the dialogue. We will see the model of emptiness and fullness developed in the speeches of Aristophanes and Agathon, and in the speeches of Socrates and Alcibiades. At this early moment of the dialogue, we readers don't yet see just how deeply serious this playful image will turn out to be. Plato's art, like Shakespeare's, often shows us how much more significance there is in what we say than what we first acknowledge; we need to grow into our own words. In the writing of these masters, every word is a drop that contains an ocean.

Agathon cuts short the banter comparing their wisdom by saying to Socrates, "Enough of this for now! But later on, the god Dionysus will judge between us." This, too, is a playful remark whose serious consequences we understand more fully later. Dionysus, we noted earlier, is the god of both wine and theater. Agathon, of course, is a man of the theater, and so to set up Dionysus as the judge of wisdom is already to favor Agathon over Socrates. The sort of wisdom that can appeal to a popular audience in a prize-winning performance is quite different from the wisdom of Socrates, usually revealed only in private conversations, in words that are not dressed up and adorned for the public eye. Agathon's Dionysian wisdom loves display, but Socrates's philosophical wisdom loves to hide. Can Socratic discretion and privacy compete with the appeal of theater? What will happen when Socrates's private life is exposed to public view? Alcibiades will put this question to the test, when his speech reveals the hidden secrets of his own relationship with Socrates. And Dionysus as the god of wine plays a part in this revelation as well. As this drinking party proceeds into the night, the wine loosens the tongues and the inhibitions of the speakers. Love may have truths that require ecstasy and intoxication to do them justice. Perhaps there is something shameless and wild in love that this god's sponsorship alone makes possible. Agathon's playful remark, then, prepares us readers for a judgment about love's wisdom that will depend on the resources of wine and theater.

Agathon, then, has all but promised to bring the god Dionysus into the party later in the evening, as the judge between himself and Socrates. Of course, this is a playful promise, not a serious one. Agathon and Socrates are playing about wisdom, and Agathon promises to play more later. But as the guests are finishing dinner and deciding how to enjoy themselves for the rest of the evening, the conversation takes a sudden turn, away from Dionysus, and away from Aphrodite, too. Because this turning away is playful and comic, we readers might underestimate its importance. But playful seriousness is Plato's favorite way of telling a story, where the full significance of something that starts small is revealed only later in the dialogue. Plato also uses this moment to introduce the speakers we haven't yet met.

As it happens, the symposium this night is really the *second* victory party celebrated by Agathon. (It was an important victory, after all! Why not have two parties?) He had put on an even bigger party the night before. And as would be natural in ancient Greece, and is just as natural today, the people at that big party tended to drink too much. All the guests at the party this evening, except for Socrates and Aristodemus, were also at the bigger party yesterday. So everyone is still feeling the effects of last night's heavy drinking, and they all have a bit of a hangover. You might say that Dionysus has given them all a bit of a beating, and they're still recovering themselves. At any rate, the oldest man from the previous night's party, Pausanias, makes a confession and a suggestion. "I'm simply too weak from last night's drinking to have another big evening," he says, "and so I suggest that tonight we don't expect everyone to get drunk again. How shall we manage the drinking most comfortably?" Pausanias is in his mid-forties at the time of the *Symposium*, and he has been in love with the beautiful Agathon for many years, long past the point where ancient Greeks would have expected a pair of men to have gotten over any romantic feelings for each other.

Pausanias knows he's not the only guest in this condition; and Aristophanes, the greatest writer of comedies in Athens, immediately agrees: "I don't want to drink too much, either; last night I was really drenched." (Aristophanes uses a Greek word that is the root of the English word "baptized.") Hearing that comment, another guest, a man named Eryximachus who happens to be a doctor, decides to poll the rest of the guests, except for Socrates, for their opinion. – Socrates, he says, won't care whether they indulge in heavy drinking or not, since he alone of all the party is hardly affected by intoxication, a point made again much later by the drunken Alcibiades. The philosopher seems exempt from the weakening effects of Dionysus, and he can remain calmly undisturbed when all around him is a drunken chaos. – So Doctor Eryximachus turns to Agathon and says, "Excellent news for light drinkers like me and my friend Phaedrus here, and for Aristodemus. But how about you, Agathon? You and Aristophanes are the big drinkers in the crowd." Agathon confesses that he, too, is too weak to drink, and so all the participants reach an agreement: just drink as much as you find pleasant, and let's enjoy some sober conversation. Doctor Erixymachus can't stop himself from giving a bit of medical advice: it's never good to be intoxicated, but especially not after the excesses of a previous night. He is clearly known for giving rather too much of this sort of advice, and for having a very high opinion of the authority of medical science. His friend Phaedrus jokes, "Well, I would always listen to your advice, Eryximachus, but this time probably everyone else will, too."

So in this scene, a number of striking things happen. All the guests, with the important exception of Socrates, agree to exclude wine and its intoxication. This exclusion is particularly surprising, because the two great men of the theater, Aristophanes for comedy and Agathon for tragedy, are naturally also the biggest drinkers. After all, Dionysus is their patron deity. Yet they agree to the exclusion. They all justify this exclusion with the sober advice of a doctor, and with the promise that they will have a rational conversation, undisturbed by Dionysian intoxication. But this philosophical justification, as we may well call it, doesn't seem entirely honest. It isn't because they all have such a strong desire for rational discussion that they are being so sober. It is because they are too weak for more drinking, too weak for Dionysus. But of course it is more flattering to oneself to say, "I want to be sober and rational, and so I will avoid drinking," than it is to say, "I tried drinking last night, and I'm just not strong enough for it tonight." So somehow the god Dionysus is being controlled or put to the side. The speeches about romantic love that are going to be given this night are taking place under a kind of shadow, a shadow of weakness, or at least a shadow of unreadiness for intoxication. The sort of ecstasy, the stepping out of one's self, that goes along with Dionysus is something that these speakers are not ready for. Philosophy likes to praise itself is for its sobriety, for being cold-blooded and tough-minded. Plato gives us the suspicion, in this comic scene of the group's hangover, that sobriety can become a mask for weakness. Only Socrates's sobriety avoids this suspicion. We must watch to see if Plato finds a way to reinstate Agathon's original generous invitation to the god, when he invited Dionysus as a figure of wisdom and judgment.

Immediately after these men make the decision to exclude the Dionysian, they make a second fateful decision to exclude something divine. The doctor Eryximachus again takes the lead in proposing the exclusion. "Since then it is decided that no one shall be compelled to drink more than he pleases," he says, "I think that we may as well also send away the flute girl who's just arrived. Let us devote the present occasion to conversation between ourselves." A Greek symposium, at least a fancy and expensive one like Agathon's, would hire a female flute player to provide musical entertainment. The instrument she played was a reeded woodwind, less like a modern flute than like an oboe or clarinet. Its sound was enchanting and hypnotic. Such music was often thought of as especially soft, making the soul more tender and receptive. It was not uncommon at a symposium that such a hired woman, in an all-male party awash in wine, was expected to provide sexual as well as musical entertainment. The musician was debased to the prostitute, a corruption made more convenient by the fact that the men were reclining on couches, a bedroom awash in wine. Perhaps Eryximachus was as interested in throwing out this corrupted sexuality as he was in excluding music for the sake of rational conversation.

But the threatened corruption comes from a false masculinity, not from the flute girl. These men claim that they're going to replace the pleasures of feminine music with the pleasures of manly conversation. Rational, reasoned conversation requires them to exclude something that in their minds is too feminine. There's something softening about music that they don't want a part of. It's going to be a man's night, pure and simple. The atmosphere is going to be very "macho," to use the excellent Spanish word for this attitude of assertive masculinity. But a man who sees nothing in women to admire or desire for himself, will either reduce the feminine to a contemptible toy, or be forced to reject it as a softening temptation. One of the guiding themes of the *Symposium* is how to save both the masculine and the feminine from these two hopeless alternatives. A more complex masculinity must integrate aspects of the feminine, and a more complete woman would not find alien to herself what's best in men. Apollodorus's softness masked with false hardness, and Aristodemus's rejection of beauty masked as an embrace of simplicity, are personal versions of the same exclusions enacted by the whole party of men, with Eryximachus, the spokesman of medical authority, in the lead. Just as we watch for Plato to invite Dionysus back to the party, so we watch to see if he can find a way for the flute girl to play for us after all.

Dionysus and Aphrodite in Andre Dubus's America

Wine, theater, and love are an old story, but a story that can be made ever new. I've been grateful to the writer Andre Dubus for helping me experience this renewal.

Andre Dubus (1936–1999) was a "writer's writer," successful but not especially famous, well-known and much loved among other writers. (His son, Andre Dubus III, is also a successful writer, and sometimes confused with his father.) He was a master of the short story, and in his own way a distinctively Roman Catholic voice in contemporary literary America. I discovered Dubus through my wife, who admired his stories and thought they did especially fine work in their descriptions of the thoughts and lives of women. She still treasures the response Dubus sent to her note thanking him for his stories. A little later I discovered over lunch that a friend at my university, not a faculty member but a writer himself, was also a big admirer of Dubus. The two of us decided to nominate Dubus for an honorary degree at Notre Dame, thinking that so distinguished a writer with such a distinctive Catholic voice deserved our university's recognition and gratitude. We made a plan to meet two weeks later to write up the nomination. But just one week later, on February 24, 1999, Andre Dubus died. – For working writers, purchase is the sincerest form of flattery, following the advice of John Ruskin, "A book worth reading is worth buying." But they still appreciate the note. When you read something that makes you grateful to the author, don't wait to say "Thank you."

Two successful movies were made from Dubus's earlier stories shortly after he died, *In the Bedroom* (Todd Fields, 2001, nominated for five Academy Awards) and *We Don't Live Here Anymore* (John Curran, 2004). The four Dubus stories I'll be thinking along with at various times in this book all come from the last collection he published before he died, *Dancing After Hours* (1996), and I'm still hoping a director will take them up. These four stories are connected to each other, in effect a novella, focusing on the romantic story of a particular couple, Ted Briggs and LuAnn Arceneaux. Thinking about what I call "the Ted-and-LuAnn novella" has helped Plato's old book come alive for me and my students, and the *Symposium* has cast a bright light on Dubus's accomplishment. Ted and LuAnn seem to live a romantic life Plato had already foreseen and analyzed two thousand four hundred years ago. The best old books are still modern, indeed are more contemporary than all but a very few contemporary books. As Ezra Pound said, literature is news that stays news; and Plato is both literature and philosophy. Dubus was not a philosopher, but his themes and his observations about how we live now have an astonishing intimacy with the *Symposium*.

The first of these Ted-and-LuAnn stories, "Falling in Love," introduces us to Ted, before he meets LuAnn. Ted is a large, strong man, a man's man, with a limp and a bad knee left over from being injured in an explosion during his service as a medical orderly in the Vietnam War. He is a bit, then, like the men at the *Symposium*, with a "macho" exterior that masks a softness within. For Ted, his softness comes from his woundedness. He works as a lawyer in Boston, and when he's not working, he looks for women and thinks he falls in love with them. He meets an attractive young actress, Susan, and they fall in love, or at least into bed, over drinks at the party after her brilliant performance in a play. (So Dubus imagines love being nurtured by theater and strong drink, a love potion, as much as Plato did in the *Symposium*, or Shakespeare in *A Midsummer Night's Dream*.) Ted Briggs is not a theater person. He was a soldier, and the terrible experiences of war have not let go of him. His limp is the physical sign of a psychological wound that has never healed. Susan enjoys giving Ted a place to forget his wound. "When they made love," Dubus says, "she could feel the war in him, feel him ascending from what he had seen." He pursues women who will understand this lingering wound and guilt, and who will pity him for it. But, like Shakespeare's Othello, the literary exemplar of the man's man, he is embarrassed by how much he seeks pity and comfort, and so lives a constant tension between clutching at a woman's softness and pushing it away.

The exhilaration and ecstasy Ted has with Susan lead to terrible pain. Their affair comes to a sad end when Susan accidentally becomes pregnant. Susan announces to Ted that she will abort the child, and rejects Ted's fervent proposal of marriage. Neither Susan nor even Ted had given the slightest thought to marriage before the moment Susan tells Ted she's getting an abortion. Ted is just as surprised to be making a marriage proposal as Susan is surprised, and irritated, to receive one. No wonder that Susan is irritated by Ted's unexpected proposal; if the condition of their lovemaking had been to accept a child should pregnancy result, she would not have made love with Ted at all. It is only at the terrible moment when he hears Susan say she must end the pregnancy, that Ted is ripped open to what falling in love means to him: that rejecting the child of their sexual union is to deny their love altogether. Until that moment, he had not understood what he had been saying when he said "I love you" to Susan, or to any other woman. He is not the first man, nor the last, to discover what love means to him only when his heart breaks. Dubus has emphasized this sad fact by punning on the title of the story. "Falling in Love" usually means, of course, the story of the beginnings of love. But Dubus has Ted suddenly perceive, when Susan tells him she is getting an abortion, that "something inside him was falling, and it would not stop until it broke."

"Falling in Love" is the story of how Ted comes to realize that the easy romantic life he's been living, drinking with women on weekends and making love with them when they're willing, isn't true to his heart's desire. Ted's manliness has been incomplete and distorted, motivated by a fear of letting himself go, of accepting the commitments that real love requires. To put Ted's case in mythological terms: He has been pushing away Dionysus and Aphrodite every bit as much as the weak men at the beginning of Plato's *Symposium*. Drinking too much doesn't make a man a Dionysian, and having sex without commitment doesn't make him a follower of Aphrodite. To follow the gods, to experience what's sacred in erotic life, a man must accept the transfigured identity these sacred experiences invite us into. And so must a woman: women can distort romantic life, can refuse it as much as men, fearing to abandon themselves to everything that love should mean. We are only partial men and partial women when we cling so desperately to a fantasy of erotic control.

How does Dubus think his way down into the predicaments of romantic love that his characters face in the modern world? The modern world of this story is the 1970s in America, which by now can seem a long time ago to younger people. Another of the Ted-and-LuAnn stories, set perhaps twenty years later, mentions a difference about that earlier romantic or sexual world, something Dubus must have thought important: it was a world before AIDS, before anyone had heard of or been frightened by this new and deadly venereal disease. There was something carefree or careless about the romantic world Ted and LuAnn inhabited, in those days before the AIDS plague arrived in America in the early 1980s, first among men who had sex with other men, but then becoming a part of the lives and imaginations of everyone. The story requires Ted (and LuAnn in the later stories) to start from an attitude toward love and sex that today feels more irresponsible or thoughtless, or at any rate naively untroubled, than it did before AIDS. I don't know if this new venereal disease has made people any more sexually virtuous, but it has made them more self-conscious.

But if the romantic attitudes in "Falling in Love" are in this respect different from the more somber mood of contemporary America, in another respect contemporary attitudes are still like the ones at the heart of Dubus's story. The story thinks through some human possibilities invented or discovered only with the invention or discovery of certain kinds of contraception. Toward the story's end, the question of contraception and true love is made explicit in the rather crude comments of Ted's drinking buddy and frequent companion in romantic pursuit, a dark-skinned Greek with the significant name Nick Kakonis. Nick is a bit older than Ted, and more superficial, both less manly and with less of an interior self. Nick's last name suggests the Greek version of one of the devil's name's, "The Evil One." Nick's first name, in the form "Old Nick," is also an old name for the devil. This name comes from the notorious Renaissance political philosopher Niccolò Machiavelli, whose cynical views – his admirers would call them "realistic" views – of politics and human virtue seem shocking and diabolical even now, five hundred years after he put them into print. Ted's friend Nick, it turns out, tempts Ted to live a rather cynical romantic life, one that seems easy and pleasure-filled, but that cannot satisfy Ted's true desires.

A particular temptation to control romantic love, made possible or at least much more seductive by modern contraceptives, lurks in Ted's heart, and also in LuAnn's in the story that introduces her, "All the Time in the World." Dubus clearly found it lurking in his imagination, too, and he tells these stories about love in part to understand himself and his own temptations and imperfections. This temptation, where conception and procreation would be unhappy accidents rather than ecstatic consummations, becomes most clear when Nick is trying to comfort Ted after the affair with Susan has collapsed, and Ted is grieving both for Susan and for the loss of their child. As men often do when they comfort a friend, Nick offers Ted some advice. (In the last Ted-and-LuAnn story, "Out of the Snow," Ted has matured past the typical male tendency to offer advice as comfort, and he responds to a troubling moment in LuAnn's life by listening, silently and lovingly, as she describes her pain. Good advice for men, and for many women, too.) Nick tells Ted, with the jocular roughness of male friendship, that next time, he should "get one on the Pill." Ted just as roughly rejects the advice, and says he can't go back out into the romantic world with nothing but his heart and his – well, let's say his "virile member," to use a precise but much more proper term than Ted actually uses. He has been living a thoughtless romantic life, and his grief has taught him not to do that anymore. "The Pill isn't a philosophy," he says, and philosophy is what he needs. (I love that line, of course.) And he tells Nick, much to Nick's surprise, that maybe he wants a wife. It is a pity he had to lose a child to realize he wants a wife, but better late than never.

Ted is not yet sure what he really wants, but his grief has already taught him he no longer wants what Nick is offering him. He tells Nick he will go on a vacation, a kind of silent retreat, since he will go to Mexico, where he doesn't know the language. He'll bring some books – I would recommend Plato's *Symposium* – and have a few beers, but not do any heavy drinking. (So like Plato's men, he still has a hangover, after taking a beating from Dionysus.) And he will, he says, "look the demon in the eye." Nick, that friendly demon, tries one last temptation, and tells Ted not to blame himself, to believe that everything with Susan and the abortion was "just something that happened." He tempts Ted, in other words, to let himself off the hook, to refuse responsibility for the life he's been living. It is exactly the attitude – of keeping at a distance the consequences of one's romantic choices, of treating love as something that happens to you rather than something you invite and accept, as if love is like falling rather than flying – the very attitude Susan took to getting pregnant. She felt unlucky, Dubus tells us, and says the abortion is "something I have to do," rather than seeing it as what she chooses. Those who love us often play the devil, and comfort us by offering to let us off the hook, to diminish our responsibility for what we have chosen.

But the story ends with Ted at last resisting the temptation. (This is a conclusion Dubus must have liked, because the last Ted-and-LuAnn story, "Out of the Snow," ends with LuAnn resisting Ted's attempt to let her off the hook for a moment of ecstatic violence.) Ted does not want his anger at Susan to be the last word. He wants to transform anger into reflection, and indeed to repent of the life he shared with Susan that led them both to such a mournful end. For his grief has revealed to Ted an awful fact about this relationship with Susan and all his previous relationships. In all of his romantic, sexual relationships, there was a hypothesis, their secret, never-spoken, but very real condition, that any child conceived from the lovemaking in the relationship would be killed. Ted no longer wants so unsettling a starting-point to go unremarked in his love life. Nick tells Ted he's looked at the demon enough; time to get over it and get back in the romantic game. But Ted says, "I haven't looked at it, I've fucked it." Why does Dubus end the story with such a crude statement? Well, this crude four-letter word for lovemaking appears a number of times in the story, and it is never a happy or cheerful word, oddly enough. When Susan says to Ted after rejecting his marriage proposal and deciding on the abortion, "I wish I'd never fucked you," the word is angry and ugly, and she uses it to strip away all the tenderness of their past, to toughen herself for their severed future. In modern English, the word is much more often used to express anger than desire, detached from its sexual meaning, and used as nothing more than a "meaningless intensifier" (as the *Oxford English Dictionary* says). Ted uses the word here because the "demon" in his romantic life has reduced all his lovemaking, no matter how tender and sincere it seemed, to something with a hidden withholding, a resistance to the very intimacy the lovemaking was supposed to express. He now feels he has never made love with anyone; all he has done is fuck people. And he is angry with himself for living this way.

The main line of this story, then, is Ted Briggs's growth in self-knowledge. He discovers his true romantic self requires being part of a male-female couple, open to new life. He recognizes he has been a false man when he has sent away the female that completes a fertile couple. (And he has conspired in the false femininity of the women he has loved when he makes their infertility as a couple a condition of their relationship.) He comes to realize he has been hiding from himself what he really wants from love, and now wants to acknowledge this desire for an open future of begetting and giving birth. He has been so intent on using romance for comfort from the sterile pain of the war, he had overlooked the fruitful pain of an open future with a lover. The labor of growth is painful and mournful, but by the end of the story we see Ted ready for a new and more honest way of life, as he escapes the evasions and temptations that his friend Nick represents, and that Nick is still captured by. We never hear of Nick again in the Ted-and-LuAnn stories, and one suspects that to build a relationship with LuAnn, Ted needed to leave his old Nick behind. Every advance of self-knowledge can also feel like an abandonment of a dear old self; every heaven of growth can seem like a hell of a loss.

I have been emphasizing the mournful side of Ted Brigg's romantic growth, but of course there is more to any love story than mourning. "Falling in Love" shows us how Ted and Susan experience the joys of Dionysus and Aphrodite, too, even if in the end they try to kick these unsettling gods out again, when their love leads them to places they aren't willing to go. Dubus enjoys telling the story of why Ted and Susan are so attractive to each other, and of how they meet each other's needs. Their attraction is surely not merely physical, not mere lust. They are impatient and not fully honest in bringing their relationship so quickly to sexual expression, it's true, but it would be a cynical and reductive view of their attraction to think sex is all there is to it, as if falling in love were no more than a twitching of nerves and a secretion of hormones. What is it, then, that makes each see the other as a lover?

The story begins with Ted and Nick planning to go to a play directed by Nick's sister, but they drink too much and arrive only for the party afterwards. Susan stars in the play, as a character breaking out of a confined life and finding her own freedom, and her own chance for love. The play's title is "The Rehearsal," by the French dramatist Jean Anouilh, and Dubus lets the word "rehearsal" occur a number of times in the story, to remind us that theater and playing a part belong in a love story. Dubus's imagination here follows the path of the masters, of Plato setting the *Symposium* at a theater party, and of Shakespeare making *A Midsummer Night's Dream* a story about love as playacting.

The two men go less for the play than because they expect to find interesting and "easy" women, ready to have sex with a handsome enough man. (Doesn't every man think he's handsome enough to get lucky? No wonder Dubus makes Ted a smoker of Lucky Strike cigarettes.) Theater people seem always to have a reputation for easy morals and sexiness, as much in our time as in Plato's, when theater and eros went together so naturally at Agathon's house. Dubus introduces the reader to beautiful 22-year old Susan. She has been "acting with passion," Dubus tells us, "for seven years." This is exactly how long Ted Briggs has been home from the war, a fact Dubus puts into the story to let us discover one of those delicious little private facts that make one person the perfect match for another. Susan has been playing a succession of roles on stage with passion for seven years, the same seven years Ted has been pretending to fall in love with a succession of women.

Susan is introduced to us with this rich description: "After the play, how did she feel? She felt larger than the room. She did not show this to anyone. She acted small, modest. . . . And she knew that she could show her elation only to someone with whom she was intimate. To anyone else it would look like bravado. Her work was a frightening risk, and during the run of the play she had become her character as fully as she could. And she knew that what she felt now was less pride than gratitude." Why does this talented young woman need a lover, then? She doesn't need approval, nor does she need praise. She knows in her heart how well she acts, and how well she abandons herself to the character she plays. What she seeks is a lover who gives her space, for her own fullness, for her own gratitude. Susan isn't looking for someone to listen to her boast about what a great actress she is, or to flatter her. She feels that being such a fine actress, so able to step outside her ordinary self into new lives, is a gift, and she needs someone with whom she can say "Thank you," with whom she can express her gratitude without sounding like she's boasting. But of course with most people, even with people who are our good friends, it's very difficult to express gratitude for our gifts without sounding like we're boasting. And so Susan makes herself small, to contain the fact she is so full, the room can hardly hold her fullness. I remember a student of mine telling me that when something good happened to her – a good grade on an exam, a new idea for a paper – she didn't feel like it was real until she told someone about it. She wasn't looking for praise or approval; she just needed expression. The act of telling our story is part of what it means to live inside that story. For Susan, her gratitude becomes real when she shares it with a lover. Your parents may take pride in your accomplishments, your brother or sister can share your happiness, and your friends may celebrate your successes. But only a lover, Susan thinks, can give you the space to see your own accomplishments as wonderful, and to feel grateful for them. She can see herself only in the mirror of someone who is in love with her.

After she has inhabited a character so fully over the run of the play, Susan will, after a few days, feel all the more empty. Dubus describes her as feeling "arid," that is, dry and parched, seeking spiritual rain, like the dormant plants in a desert. She needs a new play, to water her soul again and make it fertile, to feel the new growth. So her grateful fullness after her performance is followed by a longing emptiness. Susan's life as an actress, this interplay of fullness and emptiness, mirrors her romantic life. She becomes filled with Ted's love, but when later in the story she has an abortion – to remove the physical child that fills her – she is, Dubus says, filled by a "desert," and it will take new love and new work to flood her soul again with life and happiness. Susan is living with the painful reality presented so playfully by Agathon's image of the full cup and the empty one. Acting and loving are aspects of one and the same life.

Susan seeks a lover because only the secure intimacy of falling in love and being in love lets her express her ecstatic gratitude. The exhilaration of romantic love lets her open up. Susan can find this intimacy only through physical intimacy; she doesn't know how to be in love without making love. She knows in her heart that something is too quick, too "easy," as she says, about this way of living. But her need for intimacy gets the better of her knowledge that a bedroom isn't the best place to start to find it. Susan's relationships follow a sad pattern, of early hopes for real love, impatient sexual expression, and painful break-ups. Her desire for a lover is perfectly sincere and even noble, but her impatience defeats the growth that would be her desire's true satisfaction. She grasps at sex the way a child grasps for dessert before a meal begins. We will get to that lovely cake as the consummating celebration of the feast, and enjoy it all the more because we have not started with it. But if we eat the cake first, we flatten our appetite for the nourishing food that patience puts first. Susan wanders in an arid emptiness, the desert of her aborted love.

When Susan and Ted leave the party to spend the night together at her apartment, Ted asks her, "Were you good in the play?" The answer "Yes" filled her, Dubus tells us, but she does not answer right away. First she takes a long drag on the Lucky Strike cigarette Ted has given her, and enjoys the smoke filling her lungs from bottom to top, delicious and dangerous. "I was great in the play," she says, exhaling one great cloud of nicotine and gratitude. In Dubus's stories, cigarettes and alcohol are always good things, because the physical pleasures they give are also psychic and spiritual pleasures.

In the last Ted-and-LuAnn story, LuAnn, having a cigarette after a moment of violent crisis, calls smoking "this strange sacrament of the earth." Here, the smoke that fills Susan comes from the cigarette offered by Ted: she is lucky he has given her what she needs to feel gratitude. Dubus gives this a comic but perceptive touch when the lovers talk after they make love. "Let's have dinner tonight," says Ted, "French, for the play." "That you didn't see," comes Susan's tart reply. "I wish you had seen me," she says, and he promises, "I'll see the next one every night." But they are fooling themselves. It does not even matter that Ted and Nick were drinking and too late for Ted to see Susan's performance. Her exhilaration in this lover's presence does not depend on him being an insightful theater critic, after all. Ted seeing *her* is not what's important. She needs to see *herself*, her own wonderful goodness, and Ted's love lets her do that. Her goodness doesn't satisfy her until it is reflected back to her by a lover, and her success is not real until she can express the words of gratitude and hear them echo back in the strange and tender tones of romantic intimacy.

How finely Dubus has observed lovers in this scene. If you think someone who falls in love with you will share all your passions and want to watch all your performances – well, you're really hoping for a lucky strike! A lover's joy comes from seeing you exhilarated, not from being exhilarated by the same things you are. To take an example from another excellent Dubus story, "Adultery," suppose you are writing a book. Perhaps you require your spouse to read all your pages and say, "How finely expressed and insightful, great writing." Or is it enough, really, for your spouse to say these words for you, even if the pages are skimmed or forgotten altogether? That might be all you needed. When Susan, now sharing her risky and exhilarating plan with this new lover, tells Ted she wants to go to New York City and pursue an acting career, Ted replies, "Good, that's where you should be." Remember: TED DID NOT SEE THE PLAY! But Susan is still pleased by his comment, even though Ted has never seen her do anything but drink at the party and make love in her bedroom. The conversation is laughable. You can imagine a scene like this that portrays the man as an insincere trickster, and the woman as a gullible dupe. But that isn't how Dubus makes us feel about Ted and about Susan. They may be fooling themselves, but they are not lying to each other. Ted is the mirror Susan needs to see her own grateful reflection. So, at any rate, is Dubus's picture of what a theater person like Susan seeks from a lover.

The divine names Dionysus and Aphrodite are ancient, but the experiences they sponsor are as real in Dubus's America as in Plato's Athens. It is our own lives that Plato describes. It may seem the opening scenes of the *Symposium* take their time getting to the theme of romance, but Ted and Susan's story shows Plato knew what he was doing. He introduces Dionysus and Aphrodite first, because they make the challenges of love real, not just an academic topic. Only after all of these opening moments, these drops full of oceans, does Plato have the theme of romantic love emerge. Doctor Eryximachus, for the third time taking the lead, proposes that they spend the evening responding to a complaint he has often heard from Phaedrus, that the god Love, Eros himself, has not been praised as he should be. Let each of us, he suggests, take a turn praising love, starting with Phaedrus, since his complaint is the father of the speeches. What a winding path Plato seems to have taken to announce this theme! And yet every step was well chosen. Why would Plato frame these speeches about love with these two exclusions, an exclusion of Dionysus and Aphrodite? The *Symposium* begins from the view that these two governing deities of human romantic life somehow have to be controlled, suppressed, restrained to open up a space for a real man to speak and live. Philosophy forces its entry into Agathon's house by throwing out the gods. Philosophy acts like a rude bully, and the rudeness casts the shadow of weakness and of wariness over the philosophical speeches the men will give. Part of Plato's literary accomplishment in the dialogue will be to show us how these attempted suppressions and exclusions of Dionysus and Aphrodite, of intoxication and of the enchantments of feminine music, gradually are overcome. The first three speakers, Phaedrus, Pausanias, and Eryximachus, start with the goal of making romantic life into a simply manly life. But even while they try to play this simple manly tune in their own speeches, Dionysian and Aphrodisiac themes insinuate themselves into the music. You can throw nature out of the front door, but it always sneaks in through the back.

Chapter Two

AVOIDING LOVE

The *Symposium* sets out to praise love because one beautiful young man, Phaedrus, has been complaining. The god Love, alone of all the gods, claims Phaedrus, has never been praised enough. It's no wonder that Phaedrus thought love deserved more praise than it had received: when he praises Love, he also praises himself. And who among us doesn't think we deserve more praise? When we talk about love, we mostly talk about ourselves, especially if we can discreetly praise ourselves in the process.

Just as Phaedrus sets the theme of love for all the following speakers, so too he sets the tone of veiled self-praise. Every speaker makes himself a hero or a god, a figure of myth. When we fall in love, we become a character in a story, more interesting to ourselves – not necessarily to our friends, who may get tired of hearing about us as romantic heroes long before we tire of telling them our story.

Plato makes his first three speakers all likable men who want to fall in love and be in love, but who are also anxious that their interest in love not look unmanly or soft. So they praise love, but they also try to keep Dionysus and Aphrodite outside the door. They don't want to abandon themselves fully to love, and they try three different ways to control love. I want to describe this situation by saying that all three *avoid* love, even when they think they are praising it. They substitute some other human experience for love, and praise the substitute to avoid what is awkward, embarrassing, and challenging about the real thing. This tendency to avoid love by embracing a safer substitute is a common enough experience in our lives, too. One of my favorite movies, *Hannah and Her Sisters* (1986, directed by Woody Allen), is a finely observed account of the avoidance of love, and we'll close the chapter with some thoughts about it.

The soldier, the professor, and love's substitutes

The first two speakers, Phaedrus and Pausanias, make an interesting pair. Phaedrus was a very handsome young man who had attracted many romantic admirers. No doubt he enjoyed being attractive, but he also was a bit worried that he might look somewhat soft and effeminate to other men. Phaedrus didn't want to come off as a pretty boy, and so he overstates the alternative of being a man's man, I would say. Pausanias had a different anxiety. He was worried about appearing to have too much interest in the mere physical attraction of his romantic partner, and so he overstates the purely spiritual or psychological benefits of being in love. Both speakers have true things to say about love, but they distort love to answer to their own anxieties.

To understand these anxieties better, I need to say a little bit about the social situation of romantic attraction between men in ancient Athens. The *Symposium* presupposes that older men, say in their thirties, will enjoy the physical attractiveness of young men in their late teens and early twenties. Romantic relationships between a younger and an older man could develop from this attraction, and these relationships are a main focus of the romantic experience praised by most of the speakers in the *Symposium*. Indeed, the celebration of exclusively male relationships over relationships involving women is a part of the "macho" atmosphere of the drinking party. As the dialogue proceeds, Plato undermines this exclusive male emphasis, but it is still an important part of the speeches.

These relationships between a younger and an older man were known as "pederasty," a Greek word formed from the words for "boy" (*ped*) and "love" (*erasty*). Pederasty is sometimes thought of on the model of homosexuality in the modern world, but this is quite inaccurate. In the first place, Plato and his audience did not expect that men who found other men physically attractive would have a "sexual orientation" toward men rather than toward women. The older men in these relationships typically were married to wives, and they loved their wives and had children with them. Second, these relationships were expected to be asymmetrical, befitting the different roles of the older and the younger man, making them different from romantic relationships where the two partners have the same mutual regard. So while we in our time and place might refer to both partners in a romantic relationship simply as "lovers" (whether the relationship is heterosexual or homosexual), in pederasty, the older man was called the "lover" and the younger man the "beloved." The roles of lover and beloved were distinct, and Phaedrus will praise primarily the beloved, while Pausanias praises the lover. In general, the beloved was expected to be younger and more beautiful, while the lover was expected to be older and wiser.

Our historical knowledge of these relationships – How widespread were they? To what extent was sexual behavior socially accepted within them? Were they confined to the social elite? What did women think about their husbands being involved in them? – is less secure than we might like it to be. In fact, Plato's two great dialogues on love, the *Symposium* and the *Phaedrus*, are our most important sources for reconstructing this social world. But at least it seems that in certain aristocratic circles in Athens, pederasty was not unusual, even though these relationships provoked a lot of social anxiety. Typically, once the young men themselves were considered to be fully mature adults, by their early twenties, they were expected to cease being erotically attractive to other adult men. Pausanias and Agathon were a notorious and well-known exception to this typical social process, because Agathon, who in the dialogue is in his early thirties, remained the beloved of Pausanias all the way into adulthood. But typically that's not the way the Greeks expected these homosexual, or more precisely pederastic, relationships to work. So we're in a context where there's a lot of anxiety about a kind of erotic attraction that it seems everybody at this drinking party has experienced. The problem is how to think of the erotic interest of an older man in a young man without somehow undermining your picture of the manliness, of the masculinity, both of the lover and of the beloved.

So both Phaedrus and Pausanias are addressing the anxieties that this social practice of pederasty clearly created in a lot of Athenians. (Plato and Aristotle are both credited with saying, "Philosophy begins in wonder." True enough; but I find philosophy usually begins in anxiety, too.) Phaedrus, then, is giving a speech that is primarily a defense of the manliness of the beloved, of the younger party. Pausanias is giving a speech that is primarily a defense of the self-control of the lover, of the older party. It's perfectly clear that Phaedrus was a very good-looking young man, and he may have had many lovers, at least potential lovers, whether they became actual lovers or not. And Pausanias was especially notorious, certainly famous, for being the lover of Agathon even into Agathon's adulthood. So Phaedrus is somebody who, when he's defending beloveds in general, is also defending himself. And Pausanias is somebody who, when he's defending lovers in general, is defending himself. When they talk about love, they're mostly talking about themselves.

Phaedrus wants to claim that the beloved, the younger party in a pederastic relationship, is like a mythological hero, indeed, like the very best hero of them all, Achilles, the hero of Homer's *Iliad*. Phaedrus starts off with a bizarre and quite funny praise of erotic love, though he seems to give his speech in a serious mood. For Phaedrus claims, the greatest thing about erotic love is that it makes you the best soldier anyone could be. Now, falling in love no doubt has all kinds of effects on us. Some people it makes into poets, or hard workers, or cry-babies, or opera fans; but how often do we think of love as making us into soldiers? Whatever erotic life might do for your bravery, it hardly seems like that's the central way love connects to human life. But you can see why Phaedrus, whose anxieties are about the effeminacy, the softness of the beloved, might choose this apparently odd focus for his praise of love. Like Apollodorus at the beginning of the *Symposium*, Phaedrus is anxious to show he's no softy, that he's a real man. That Phaedrus's emphasis on military virtue is a response to this anxiety is clearer in Greek, because the Greek word for bravery or courage, *andreia*, is built on the root *andro-*, which just means "man." In other words, the courage of the soldier just is the paradigm of manliness.

}47{

Phaedrus wants to give his praise of love and its manliness the prestige and authority of myth. To present your own life as following the example of a mythical hero is a way of making your own life more attractive, more elevated, more wonderful. But myth is a slippery thing. Myths have a way of meaning more than we say, of overflowing the containers we want to confine them within. Phaedrus wants to use myth to say what he wants to say, but the myth will also threaten to use him to say what it wants. Phaedrus and philosophers would like to master their words and make their myths behave, like Humpty Dumpty, but the words have a way of scrambling our eggs and knocking us from our perch. This is what happens to Phaedrus, as his myths threaten to escape from his control and to say something different from what he wants them to mean. As examples of famous lovers come into his imagination, we see Phaedrus trying to make them fit his desire to protect the manliness of love, but there are more things in his imagination than are dreamed of by his philosophy.

Phaedrus organizes his speech around the insight that being in love makes us more motivated to live up to an ideal than any other human relationship. He puts this by saying that we have a more acute sense of shame when we are with someone who is in love with us than we do with anyone else, even more than with a father or a close friend. Think of the pride we feel when our lover recognizes our accomplishments, or the embarrassment when we fail before their eyes. There is a special energy that this heightened romantic self-consciousness gives to us; we become better than our usual selves when we are trying to live up to the picture our lover has of us, and we feel a deeper pain when we fall short. The new, better self we strive to be under the gaze of love, and the extremity of pleasure and pain this striving gives us: this is Phaedrus's version of the ecstasy and exhilaration of love. Phaedrus suggests a thought-experiment to reveal the power of erotic shame. Imagine an army, he says, made up of lover-beloved couples. They could never be defeated, he says, because they would be so ready to die for each other. Under threat of death in battle, a man would sooner abandon his father or his comrade than his lover or his beloved.

Who would die for you? asks Phaedrus. The shame and aspiration we feel when we're in love will give you the answer: someone you are in love with. The death test reveals the unparalleled power of romantic love to make us into something new, something wonderful and strange.

Plato will consider various versions of the death test throughout the *Symposium*. The speeches of Aristophanes, Socrates, and Alcibiades all look back to Phaedrus's potent insight into love, shame, idealism, and death. But the first mythical exemplar of passing the death test that pops into Phaedrus's imagination complicates his strategy of showing that love befits manliness. He thinks of the famous case of a woman named Alcestis, whose name is the title of a tragedy by Euripides, which is probably the version of her story that Phaedrus (and Plato) had in mind. Her husband could be saved from dying and going to the underworld, to Hades, if he could find somebody who loved him enough to take his place. (Phaedrus doesn't name Alcestis's husband, Admetus, but he is named later, in the speech of Socrates. In fact, all three mythological examples Phaedrus uses will be taken up again later in the speeches of Socrates and Alcibiades.) So first Alcestis's husband went to his parents. He thought, what the hell, they're older, they're going to die soon anyway! But his parents wouldn't go. They wouldn't substitute for their son in the underworld. None of his friends were willing to die for him, either. The only person who is willing to substitute for him is his wife Alcestis. The gods are so astonished by her willingness to die so her husband can live that they restore her to life, and shower her with great honors and rewards.

We can see why this heroic death test came into Phaedrus's mind. But sometimes the first story that comes to mind has some awkward features, and Alcestis's story has at least two. First, Phaedrus wants a story in which the romantic hero is the *beloved*, like he sees himself, rather than a lover. But from the pederastic point of view of Phaedrus, the husband is the more lovable partner in a marriage, because, as Phaedrus sees things, a man is more beautiful and noble than a woman. So, on this view, Admetus was the beloved, the more beautiful one, the more noble one in the relationship. Alcestis is like the lover, less characterized by beauty. (This notion that men are more beautiful than women is probably the opposite of what most people would think now, but it is embedded in the dialogue.) But Alcestis is an example of the way that a lover will die for his or her beloved, even when the beloved's parents wouldn't. So her death test, dying for someone more attractive than herself, is not quite the right model for Phaedrus. Second, Phaedrus wants a story that emphasizes the *manliness* of the romantic hero. Phaedrus's imagination has backed him into a little bit of a corner here, because it turns out that one of the great examples of the power of love over death is a woman. He doesn't really want to project himself onto a feminine exemplar, does he? The myth doesn't mean quite what he wants to say. What happens to Phaedrus's defense of the manly beloved if it turns out a woman can be manly, or that the dichotomy between the feminine and the masculine isn't as clear as he wants it? We have to picture him realizing even as he tells this story that it won't quite do. This woman's story is the wrong story. Plato shows us something about the power of myth with the awkward fit between Phaedrus's "official" claims about love and the unofficial implications of this myth that overflows the vessel in which he tries to contain it. Myths leak.

So Phaedrus tries the next story of a heroic death test that pops into his imagination: the story about how Orpheus went down into the underworld to get back his wife Eurydice (Phaedrus doesn't name her, either). At least in this story the one who goes willingly into the underworld is both male and (as Phaedrus would see things) the beloved in the relationship. But other features of the Orpheus myth are just as problematic as Alcestis's story, if Phaedrus wants to project himself onto this mythical exemplar. The central difficulty is that Orpheus is too soft and musical to represent Phaedrus's manliness. In fact, he's the mythical founder of music. Orpheus went down into the underworld by using his musical enchantments to get past the underworld guards, but without really risking death. In the *Symposium*'s terms, bringing in Orpheus is like inviting Dionysus and the flute girl back. In the version of the myth Phaedrus tells (there are many other versions), Orpheus simply wasn't brave enough to get his wife back up from the underworld. He failed, as Phaedrus realizes, because of his softness and effeminacy.

These two mythical stories, of Alcestis and Orpheus, don't really support the view of the manly beloved that Phaedrus is trying to buttress with some mythical prestige and authority. But now he turns to a third hero, one who fits his view much better, the star of all Greek heroes, Achilles, main character of Homer's *Iliad*. As the story goes, Achilles's very close friend, a somewhat older man named Patroclus, is killed by the Trojan champion Hector, and Achilles kills Hector to avenge Patroclus. The gods have ordained that Achilles can live a long life in obscurity or a short life of fame; by avenging Patroclus, he chooses fame and early death. Phaedrus insists Achilles is better than both Alcestis and Orpheus, and so is more honored than they are. Orpheus, of course, wasn't even really ready to die for his wife, and tried to use musical trickery to get her back without sacrificing himself. But Achilles is better than Alcestis, claims Phaedrus, because Achilles is the beloved, Patroclus the lover, and it is more impressive for the beloved to die for the less attractive and older lover than it is for a lover, like Alcestis, to die for the more attractive and younger beloved. (Homer doesn't present Achilles and Patroclus as a pederastic couple, but they were presented that way in the Greek literature of Plato's time.) And, says Phaedrus, Achilles accepts death even though he can't get Patroclus back, where Alcestis and Orpheus both go down to the underworld only because they can save their spouse. It is more impressive, Phaedrus thinks, to die for a lover one can't save. Notice, too, that Alcestis and Orpheus both die for a spouse, and so point to marriage as the paradigm case of love, something else Phaedrus doesn't want. Finally Phaedrus has found a mythical exemplar for the manly beloved, and as he thinks about Achilles he can breathe a sigh of relief and say, "Now there's a man's man"; and though he doesn't say it out loud, his audience knows he is also thinking, "and I'm like Achilles, the beloved who would die for his lover. That's how noble I am." When we think about love, we are usually thinking about ourselves.

So Phaedrus has gone through these three mythical exemplars of erotic heroism. The first two don't really work so well for him, but the last one, Achilles, really hits the nail on the head. When Phaedrus turned to myth to give elevation and prestige to his praise of being a beloved, he ran into a problem. Myth has crossed the wires a bit in Phaedrus's imagination. The first example he thinks of where a hero goes down into the underworld to save someone else, passing the death test, is a woman and a lover! Then his mind moves to another example, but this one reveals someone who actually failed the death test, and who was a man and a beloved! Phaedrus is finding out that myth is full of power, but difficult to tame. Phaedrus is like a lecturer who says, "There are three examples you should remember of love and the death test." The lecturer first writes "Alcestis" on the chalkboard, begins to lecture, but starts to feel uncomfortable with her as an example. So next the lecturer writes "Orpheus" and starts again to lecture, but again stops because the example doesn't seem quite right. At this point, lecturer Phaedrus erases the chalkboard and says, "Don't think about those two anymore." And now he writes "Achilles," and wants us to see nothing but the soldier. But while lecturer Phaedrus may want to erase the feminine and the musical from his student's mind, writer Plato has left the traces behind of a more complex view of the integration of the male and the female.

Plato extends this interrogation of the avoidance of the feminine and the soft into the second speech, by Pausanias. Phaedrus was defending the manliness of the beloved, but Pausanias's anxieties are focused on the lover. He wants an account of the lover that makes him into a paragon of rational self-control. Why is this picture of the reasonable lover so important to Pausanias, as the picture of the manly beloved was important to Phaedrus? Because such a model of the lover would justify his own life: he talks about himself when he talks about love. Pausanias is still in love with Agathon, long after that love would have been socially acceptable in ancient Athens. Close and warm friendship between two adult men who had once been in a pederastic relationship: that would have been acceptable, even laudable. But Pausanias still feels that old flame for Agathon, a good ten years after Agathon has reached his erotic expiration date, by the standards of the day.

Pausanias also looks to myth for support. To understand what Pausanias is doing here, we need to keep in mind some basic facts about the Greek gods. The oldest gods are Uranus, the male god of heaven, and Gaia, the female god of earth. Heaven and Earth unite to produce children, and in the second divine generation, a son of Uranus, Kronos, overthrows his father. Kronos then mates with his sister Rhea, and their children are the third generation of divine beings, including the Olympian gods, led by Zeus, who in turn overthrows Kronos. This is the basic outline of the story told by the epic poet Hesiod in his *Theogony*, a title which means "the generation of the gods." After he comes to power, Zeus mates with many goddesses, producing a fourth generation of gods and goddesses.

Pausanias criticizes Phaedrus's account of love as too simple. There are, claims Pausanias, two completely different types of romantic love, one safe and worthy of praise, one that is dangerous and something to guard against. To explain this difference, Pausanias turns to Greek myths about the goddess of love and sexuality, Aphrodite. Pausanias reminds his audience that there are two different myths about the birth of Aphrodite, and Pausanias takes this to mean there are actually two different goddesses with the same name. One myth places her birth between the second and third generation of gods, the other not until the fourth generation. In the myth told by Hesiod, Aphrodite is older than the Olympian gods. She was generated purely from her father Uranus, the original god of heaven, without a mother, and so this Aphrodite is honored under the title "Heavenly Aphrodite." But in the story told by Homer, Aphrodite is the child of Zeus and a minor goddess named Dione, so she has both a father and a mother. This goddess, known under the title "Popular Aphrodite," is a fairly young goddess, since she is born in the fourth generation of gods, long after Heavenly Aphrodite. Heavenly Aphrodite is, so to speak, the serious big sister of a playful and wayward younger sister, giving sensible advice that is always ignored.

Heavenly Aphrodite, Pausanias claims, is the paradigm of safe, /
sensible love. In the first place, she is the elder goddess, and so is
more respectable and thoughtful than the younger goddess. In the
second place, she is all male in her origins, and anything that is
purely masculine, thinks Pausanias, must be better than something
that mixes the masculine and the feminine together. Heavenly
Aphrodite is the patron of the higher type of romantic love, the type
experienced in the right kind of pederasty, which is an all male love.
Third, this heavenly type of love, Pausanias says, is focused on the
soul and mind of the beloved, not at all on the body; and because
young men have better minds than young women – Pausanias is
playing to the prejudices of the macho audience – any man who is
"heavenly" himself will prefer men to women. The heavenly lover
prefers men – young, good-looking men, of course – because such
young men are more teachable, can have their minds improved by
a more mature and thoughtful lover. Popular Aphrodite is earthy
and associated with youth, with the passions and desires of common
people – not the self-control and rationality of aristocratic men like
Pausanias and his friends! This earthy Aphrodite is also not purely
male, but is a mix of her male father and female mother. And finally,
says Pausanias, someone devoted to Popular Aphrodite is more interested in the body than in the soul, and doesn't care whether a
good-looking body happens to be male or female. So Heavenly
Aphrodite sponsors a life of all male romantic love that focuses exclusively on the soul of the beloved, while Popular Aphrodite sponsors romantic desire for merely bodily and sexual pleasures,
pleasures that can be had from either men or women. Notice how
striking this last point is. Given his masculine prejudices, we aren't
surprised that Pausanias values men over women as objects of love.
But he ranks popular love below heavenly because popular love includes both men and women, not because it includes women as
such. His main contrast is between a love that is exclusively male
and a love that is, to use a word that becomes the focus of Aristophanes's later speech, *androgynous*, that is, both male and female.

Now, it's obvious this rigid dichotomy between the heavenly,
soul-centered love, and the earthy, sensual, body-centered love, is

covering up Pausanias's own anxieties about whether he can be a respectable adult man and still be in love with his boyfriend Agathon. Phaedrus defended his own respectability as a beloved by hiding behind the identity of the soldier. Pausanias will hide behind the claim that all he and other "heavenly" lovers really care about is the soul and mind of their beloved: he hides behind the identity of the professor or the mentor. Pausanias's description of pederasty makes it sound like there is no spark of romance, and no desire or temptation for sex, built into the experience. He has removed the anxieties of the lover by substituting the satisfactions of the teacher, as if he fell in love with Agathon and stays in love with him just to be able to make Agathon's mind more knowledgeable and his soul more virtuous. Pausanias flattens out the ecstasies and exhilarations of romance. A good teacher surely will love his students and want to see their minds and virtues flourish, but this is not the same as falling in love with them. Pausanias is right to look for some connection at the level of the soul, not just the body, when he analyzes romantic love. But he is comically one-sided when he denies any bodily, earthy aspect at all to romance. He exposes his anxiety by hiding his desire, making his desire more tame, both more rational and more masculine.

Phaedrus found that myths are slippery, and can say more than we mean them to. For Pausanias, the very myth of Aphrodite's heavenly origin slips through his hands just as he clutches at it the hardest. He wants this myth to give him a philosopher's Aphrodite, we might say, male, pure, and safe. But he reaches this safety only because he forgets to mention some very relevant details from Hesiod's account of how this all-male birth could occur. Aphrodite was generated without a mother, from her father Uranus alone, because Uranus was a tyrant to his consort Gaia. Uranus impregnated her, but he would not allow her to give birth, because he did not want any children who could be rivals for his power. Uranus's son Kronos attacked his father from Gaia's womb, and severed Uranus's male organ, casting it into the sea, and Aphrodite arose from the seafoam. In other words, Hesiod has written a story about the dangers of male tyranny over the female, and Aphrodite is the constant reminder that male tyranny cannot repress the female successfully. In Hesiod's story, Aphrodite is not "all male," as Pausanias pretends. Quite the opposite: she shows the female is always necessary and present, even when male power doesn't want it to be. As Phaedrus's story of Alcestis challenged what Phaedrus tried to make it say, so too does the story of Aphrodite's origin challenge the use Pausanias would make of it. Pausanias has sent the flute girl out of the front door, only to have her sneaking in through the back.

The love doctor and erotic management

The third speaker who takes the stage in the *Symposium* is Eryximachus, a medical man, full of advice, usually ignored by his friends, about healthy living, and particularly about moderate drinking. Every group of friends should have one person whose good advice they can laugh at and ignore. His speech will, of course, offer a veiled praise of himself along with its explicit praise of love. In one way, Eryximachus is the most modern of all the speakers in the *Symposium*, because he is the only one who bases his authority on being a man of science, particularly medical science. In our time, medicine makes even greater claims over love than in Plato's time, so Plato's implicit critique of Eryximachus's rather pompous, rather arrogant scientism is as important as ever. At the core of Eryximachus's speech is the notion of balance or equilibrium. The art of love, he suggests, is to find the right balance of elements, both in the soul and in the body. The moderate life of balance, whether in drinking or in love, is the one he recommends. It is the medical version of the equilibrium of fullness and emptiness in Agathon's joke to Socrates about lying next to him to receive the flow of his wisdom, now made into a kind of medical technology.

Eryximachus has an interesting name, a name that fated the man who bore it to become a doctor. The second syllable -*machus* comes from the Greek word "to fight," and the first syllable, *eryx-*, is the Greek word for a hiccup. So Eryximachus is "Doctor Hiccup Fighter," and as a writer, Plato couldn't resist the opportunity to use this name to comic effect. Because of the way the speakers are arranged on the couches, it really should be Aristophanes's turn to give the third speech after Pausanias. But Aristophanes, it turns out, has the hiccups and so he's not ready. Aristophanes says to the doctor, the hiccup-fighter Eryximachus, "You should either cure my hiccups or take my spot." The doctor, always ready to show off his medical skills, responds, "I'll do both," and he suggests some cures for hiccups for Aristophanes to try while he gives his own praise of love. These cures are things people still might try these days, ascending from gentle to violent: first try holding your breath, and if that doesn't work, try gargling; and if you still have a really stubborn hiccup, tickle your nose so that you sneeze, which should cure even the most violent case. This means that throughout Eryximachus's rather pompous speech about the power of the medical art to make erotic life calm and moderate, next to him is Aristophanes, the comic poet, turning red and gargling and sneezing, trying out Eryximachus's cures. Throughout the Love Doctor's elevated and serious speech about how the medical art is the true way to impose a moderate and healthy order on erotic love, Aristophanes produces a soundtrack of bodily explosions, hiccupping and gargling and sneezing. His disordered body is probably still suffering the effects of a hangover from the party the previous night, and its explosions hint at some experiences not dreamt of in Eryximachus's erotic philosophy.

No doubt Eryximachus's friends found this hilarious, but Eryximachus is the kind of lecturer who, even if everybody's laughing at him and carrying on, plunges right ahead. Finally he looks over at Aristophanes and says with a touch of irritation, "Well, I've come to the end of my speech, which is a good thing because I see that your hiccups are at an end, too." "Yes they are!" says Aristophanes, "and I have you to thank for the cure, my dear doctor." But the comic poet can't resist pointing out the discord between the speech and its soundtrack. "Surprising," he deadpans, "that this orderly body your medicine produces for us" – the order Eryximachus said medicine can bring to our love life – "only comes about through the disorder and violence of garglings and ticklings and sneezings." Plato uses Aristophanes to make fun of the prestigious scientific rhetoric of Doctor Love's speech, and in his own speech, Aristophanes will give a very different account of what love "cures" in human nature.

The action of the dialogue, then, provides a kind of commentary on the content of the actual speeches. Eryximachus praises himself and doctors like him for the scientific or technological control he thinks they have over causes of disorder like strong wine and sweet *aphrodisia*. As Phaedrus made fun of Eryximachus's sober advice about drinking, Aristophanes makes fun of his unromantic advice about love.

But there is more to Eryximachus than just a parody of a medical professional's view of erotic life. Eryximachus's speech introduces into the dialogue some new themes that will prove important in later speeches. First, Eryximachus's musical model of human life, even if rather flat and mechanical, is an important addition to the dialogue's themes. For the Greeks, the science of music's mathematical and geometrical structure was a recent and great accomplishment, with a lot of scientific prestige. Eryximachus applies this prestigious music theory to the control of erotic love. So Eryximachus sees love as a matter of proportion, like a musical harmony that has notes neither too high nor too low. Throughout this medical, musical speech of Eryximachus, we have the rather unmusical accompaniment of Aristophanes's garglings, ticklings, and sneezings. But at least Eryximachus does introduce the idea that love is connected to the musical aspect of human life, something the macho speeches of Phaedrus and Pausanias do little to recognize. Phaedrus's speech and Pausanias's speech both make some use out of poets, but they don't make much use of the very common notion that music broadly conceived, including literature and poetry, has a particularly intimate connection to erotic life and erotic experience. It may be that many people nowadays learn quite a bit about their erotic lives from doctors, but it's still true that most people get their ideas about what erotic life would be, about what a romance is, about how to kiss somebody, from watching movies or reading works of literature. So there's still a central role for poetry, again broadly conceived, within our sense of romance, of falling in love and being in love. It's true Eryximachus wants to control music by making it scientific, to bring it all under the control of the medical art. But even by doing that he introduces the question of music into the discussion of love in the *Symposium* in a way that wasn't really a prominent theme in Phaedrus's speech and in Pausanias's speech. Though Phaedrus's speech is built around a reflection on literary examples, most importantly Achilles, Phaedrus's own anxieties about how to keep love masculine tend to suppress the fact that how he thinks about love really is coming from a poetic background. Phaedrus presents himself as if he learned all about love in boot camp, as if being a military man really showed him the way to true love. But in fact, Phaedrus's speech could only be given by a lover of poetry. The same is true of Pausanias's speech. You might go so far as to say that before Eryximachus's speech, poetry and music were latent in the dialogue, as an anxiety or problem about the softness of poetry and music, compared to a certain ideology of being a real man. The problem was there, the anxiety was there, but now it's gotten on the table ready for conversation in Eryximachus's speech.

A second theme that Eryximachus's speech puts on the table is love as a vehicle of human access to something sacred or divine. Now, here again you might say this was latent in Pausanias's speech. After all, Pausanias introduces his own analysis of love by saying there are two types of romantic love, corresponding to the two goddesses, an elder and all-male Aphrodite and a younger, androgynous Aphrodite. So clearly Pausanias thinks of love as having a divine aspect. But Eryximachus is much more explicit about love as connecting us to the divine world. Indeed, consistent with his confidence that medical science can control love and make it safe and tame, Eryximachus thinks science can give humans control even over their communication with the gods, because medicine is the true art of divination. Divination was an established part of Greek religious practices, but it was always thought of as something mysterious and obscure, befitting the difficulty of tracing divine purpose from oracles, bird interpretation, or reading the entrails of sacrificial animals. We see the prejudices, the bias of Eryximachus in claiming scientific control in this realm, because he seems to treat divination as a matter of secure scientific knowledge. The Greek readers of Plato's own time would have thought that the need for divination shows human limitation, not human power. Divination shows that we have to be open to something, receptive of something from the gods, rather than showing that we have some technique that allows us to get what we want from the gods. Later speakers, especially Aristophanes and Socrates, take up this theme about divination, about love as a vehicle toward something divine or sacred. But when they take it up, they're much less aggressively optimistic than Doctor Love about the human ability to control that access to the divine, to get what we want out of it.

There is one more theme that Eryximachus's speech gets us closer to. Here it's not that Eryximachus makes wholly explicit something that's only latent in the other speeches. I think even with him, this theme is only latent. It will become fully explicit only in the next speech, in Aristophanes's speech. This theme is how to understand human erotic powers in a way that respects and integrates male and female experience, the problem of androgyny. And given the participants in this particular drinking party, it's not surprising to discover a romantic anxiety that somehow maleness is going to be infected by, infiltrated by something effeminate. We saw how powerfully this anxiety worked itself out in Phaedrus's speech and in Pausanias's speech. Eryximachus's speech, I think, without knowing it, starts to put pressure on a sharp distinction between male and female, and pushes us toward an image of love where our richest experiences of falling in love will be things in which we combine male and female elements, in which the way that a specific culture codes what's male and what's female starts to break down. The boundaries culture sets up between the masculine and the feminine don't hold up very well.

Eryximachus unwittingly introduces androgyny into the discussion because medicine leads him to take the body more seriously than the first two speakers did. Pausanias introduced a distinction between the earthy Aphrodite and the heavenly Aphrodite, and Eryximachus wants to use that distinction, too. But when Doctor Love appropriates Pausanias's terms, he also makes a fundamental change in what they mean. Pausanias had claimed that heavenly love is concerned only with the soul, earthy love only with the body. Because males have better minds than females, he went on, and the soul is primarily mind, heavenly love turned out to be exclusively directed toward males. Earthy love, on the other hand, cares only about the body; a female body can be as attractive as a male body; so an earthy lover will be sexually interested in males and females indiscriminately; in a word, earthy erotic desire is androgynous. In Pausanias's view, then, the orderly and heavenly love is all about the soul, the disorderly and earthy love is all about the body. Pausanias's strict soul/body dichotomy protects the lover and the beloved from any suspicion against their manliness. And when Pausanias talks about the concrete experience of love, it's all about the lover educating the beloved. It's almost as if love would be more convenient and have a kind of conceptual clarity for Pausanias if only we didn't have bodies at all. Eryximachus, though, is a medical man and so his authority rests on claims not just about the soul but also about the body, about the natural world, not just about a heavenly world. So when Eryximachus constructs his own version of Pausanias's distinction between heavenly love and earthy love, the doctor insists both soul and body can be either well-ordered and heavenly or disordered and earthy. For Eryximachus, the body in itself is not essentially mixed up, impure, as it was for Pausanias; nor is the soul in itself necessarily the principle of order, since soul can be either earthy or heavenly, orderly or disordered. In other words, Eryximachus reinterprets Pausanias's heaven/earth dichotomy so that it no longer supports Pausanias's male/female ideology.

Now, Eryximachus doesn't do much with this idea, and he doesn't seem to be aware that what he has done with Pausanias's words challenges the sort of masculine ideology that's in Pausanias's speech, and Phaedrus's speech, too. But still the use that Eryximachus makes of Pausanias's own distinction between the heavenly and the earthy turns out to undermine one of the main claims that Pausanias made. We saw that the myths Phaedrus and Pausanias wanted to say supported their macho pretensions in fact were rather slippery, and more meaning leaked out of them than these men intended. Now, Doctor Love shows that a theory can elude a clutching hand as easily as a story. The next speaker, Aristophanes, who has a very good ear and is very observant, is going to exploit this latent tension, and he will make androgyny one of the central themes of the story he tells about the origin and nature of romantic love.

Plato intended Eryximachus's speech, I take it, to be rather comical. There's an aspect of parody in his speech. But that doesn't mean it doesn't have a serious point. The first three speeches form a set together, and the dialogue then makes a new start when it gets to Aristophanes's speech. I think that most readers of the *Symposium* would acknowledge that the first three speeches are all somehow less interesting, less thoughtful, than the speeches that follow. But the imperfections of these three speeches are important, because they pose a whole series of questions about the nature of erotic love that the later speeches will address more adequately. None of the speeches is a very satisfying account of erotic love, but yet they're very perceptive as views of the anxieties that might be provoked in us by coming to terms with erotic love. And I use "coming to terms with" here quite literally. They're seeking a vocabulary, looking for the right words, so that the structures of their language will correspond to the structures of their erotic world. It's part of Plato's special genius as a writer to be able to take specific words, or small bundles of related words, a vocabulary, and to explore the resources of that vocabulary. What can you think about love if you sound like Phaedrus? What can you think about love if you sound like Pausanias? And what can you think about love if you sound like Eryximachus? The thought experiment of the *Symposium* requires us to explore the limits of the romantic worlds we would inhabit in these vocabularies, with the hope of finding a language that lets us escape.

Avoiding love in Woody Allen's *Hannah and Her Sisters*

I've suggested that the three first speakers in the *Symposium* all present themselves as figures of authority and self-control: the soldier, the professor, and the doctor. In each case, the speaker tries to avoid or suppress Dionysus and Aphrodite, because these unruly gods are a threat to the manly self-image each wants to defend. But this avoidance and suppression is not successful; in every case, the suppressed still peeks through. Especially interesting is the way Plato makes the feminine intrude into the man's romantic world each speaker wants to inhabit. Phaedrus couldn't avoid Alcestis, Pausanias couldn't make Aphrodite all male, and Eryximachus couldn't maintain a rigid distinction between the body as mixed with the female and the soul as purely male. The next speaker, Aristophanes, will explode this strategy of suppression, and bring androgyny to center stage, after which the question of how to integrate the male and the female is an explicit concern of every speaker. This integration is impossible, as Plato saw it, without giving up a certain ideal of control and self-sufficiency.

One of the best explorations of the ways that false images of self-control can destroy romantic love focuses on women rather on men. *Hannah and Her Sisters* (1986) was written and directed by Woody Allen, one of the most distinguished American filmmakers of the last fifty years. He won an Academy Award for best original screenplay for the movie, and two of the actors, Michael Caine and Dianne Wiest, won awards for Best Supporting Actor and Actress. (Woody Allen, by the way, studied philosophy when he was in college. It shows in his movies.) The plot focuses on Hannah (Mia Farrow), a woman in her later thirties who is an accomplished actress, and her complicated family.

The three key scenes, one year apart, all happen at the family's annual celebrations of Thanksgiving, expensive and magnificent parties organized by the big sister Hannah. At the first party, we hear a voiceover from Hannah's husband Elliot (Michael Caine) describing how beautiful Hannah's little sister Lee (Barbara Hershey) is. Lee lives with a much older man, her former college professor. She clearly admires Hannah, but she also enjoys the flirting of Elliot. Middle sister Holly (Dianne Wiest) is the rebel among the sisters, constantly borrowing money from Hannah, never paying it back, and resenting her own dependence on her big sister. We also

meet the sisters' parents, once moderately successful actors themselves, now entertaining everyone with tales of how beautiful and
handsome they used to be. The mother is drinking too much, and
the father is playing a Broadway standard on the piano (from the
musical *Pal Joey*, 1940, by Rodgers and Hart), "Bewitched, Bothered, and Bewildered." This song becomes the musical signature of
the movie, and pops up several times. Its lyrics tell of the ecstasies
and exhilarations of falling in love, with an emphasis on love's dan-
gerousness. This sets a mood for the romantic complications that
follow.

In addition to this song, Woody Allen gives us two other clues
to the mood of the movie. At the first of the three Thanksgiving celebrations, Hannah's father mentions her acting success in the role
of Nora in Henrik Ibsen's classic 1879 play *A Doll's House*. Nora
is a famously strong female character who frees herself from an oppressive marriage in which, she comes to think, she is treated as a
doll rather than an adult. At the third Thanksgiving, at the movie's
end, Hannah's mother congratulates her for being cast in the role
of Desdemona in Shakespeare's *Othello*. Desdemona, of course, is
almost the opposite of Nora, and she is murdered by her jealous
husband. Woody Allen wants the viewer to think about Hannah's
story with these two great predecessors in mind. We will think about
Othello at length in the next chapter, but I want to mention this
much here: Othello kills Desdemona in part because he cannot bear
to be dependent on her. No one kills Hannah in Woody Allen's
movie, but her self-sufficiency comes close to destroying her life.

This movie, like many of Woody Allen's movies, could be criticized for being formulaic, that is, for having characters who are
representative of a point of view or of a type, rather than becoming
real human beings. The movie *Crimes and Misdemeanors*, which
many people think may be Woody Allen's best, was made just after
Hannah and Her Sisters, and it seems to me to be a much inferior
movie exactly because the characters represent abstract types or
ideas rather than real people. In *Hannah*, too, the people certainly
are types in a way, but at least to my eye this movie is successful in
making these types utterly human beings. I can focus only on the

two characters who bring the issues of control and self-sufficiency into the sharpest focus, the oldest and the youngest sisters. Hannah is the big sister in her family. We see her as the product of a certain kind of childhood. (The idea that as adults we are still what our childhood made of us is crucial to the movie *The Hairdresser's Husband*, which we will consider in a later chapter.) She's the product of being the person in her family who made everybody else whole, who fixed things, and especially the person who fixed things between her alcoholic parents. As the littlest sister, Lee has been able to avoid responsibility, to be the one taken care of, rather than the one taking care of someone else. If Hannah is an exemplar of independence, Lee is an exemplar of dependence: on her sister, on men, and on alcohol.

To all appearances, Hannah and Elliot are happily married. This is a second marriage for both of them, and Elliot is grateful to Hannah for bringing order into what had been a chaotic life. He also seems to enjoy the children from her first marriage, who live with them. But Elliot's gratitude for Hannah's help is beginning to turn into impatience at her control. He starts to imagine an alternative relationship, where he would be the one inspiring gratitude rather than the one giving it. It is this desire to do rather than to be done to that leads Elliot to act on his attraction to Lee. She is the opposite of Hannah, always falling in love with older men she sees as mentors; Pausanias would have loved her. Elliot is always giving Lee suggestions about books and music, and he hatches a plan to gauge her interest in him. He arranges an apparently chance meeting near a bookstore, near where Lee goes to meetings of Alcoholics Anonymous, which has kept her sober after many years of drunkenness. Elliot gives her a book of poems, directing her to read a particular page that, he says, reminds him of her. ("Bewitched, Bothered, and Bewildered" plays in the background.) Later, Lee reads the key line from e.e. cummings "somewhere I have never travelled,gladly beyond":

"nobody,not even the rain,has such small hands."

Before long, Elliot and Lee arrange an afternoon tryst in a hotel bedroom. "That was just perfect," she purrs, "you've ruined me for anyone else." Lee wants to be the one done to, and Elliot is happy for the chance. "I want to do things for you," he says, "Hannah doesn't need me as much." That night Elliot gets into bed with Hannah, and he weighs the dreamy passion with Lee against the cozy reality with Hannah. He feels guilty, but he doesn't break off the affair. He wants to be needed, and so he likes Lee to be needy. We next see Elliot and Lee in another hotel room, dancing while Elliot gives Lee more wine. In choosing between the sisters, it seems Elliot prefers needy intoxication to controlling sobriety; but both sisters have inherited their roles from their childhood with their alcoholic parents. You can interpret this scene as Elliott giving Lee wine to make her more pliable, so you can put the blame on the wayward husband. But a different reading seems to be more consistent with the character of Lee in the movie. Lee drinks the wine in order to give herself more deniability about what she's doing. Then she has a way that she can slough off the responsibility onto something else, and onto someone else, which is one of her most defining character traits. She avoids love because she avoids responsibility.

Lee is a gorgeous, attractive woman. Her neediness – "You've ruined me for anyone else" – is sexy and flattering, and plays to the fantasies of the older lover as mentor. Part of the aesthetic power and of the moral dubiousness of this movie is that it makes you fall in love with such a horrible person. (I am assuming you agree it is horrible to sleep with your sister's husband.) This movie walks a very tight line. It's on a high wire, because in the end it wants to be a comedy. People do not suffer for their moral depravity in this movie. They are always redeemed from it.

While Lee, the little sister, constantly puts herself in the position of dependence, Mia Farrow's character, the oldest sister, constantly avoids a situation of dependence. Lee achieves her freedom by turning herself over to others. Her freedom comes at the cost of responsibility. Hannah's freedom is the opposite. Hannah achieves freedom by being completely responsible for everyone, even for her parents. Woody Allen uses the movie, you might say, systematically to explore some human options, some temptations that we have. All of these temptations are ways of avoiding something that love might demand.

Hannah never discovers that her husband is having an affair with her youngest sister. But she feels his distance and coldness. Hannah's first husband had been sterile, and so the children she has were conceived artificially or were adopted. She and Elliot had talked in the past about having a child together. But now when she mentions this, Elliot is rude to her. He berates her for the very things that had always before made him grateful, for her energy and willingness to organize their family life and to plan for their future. "It's all very pre-conceived," he snaps at the confused Hannah, who has no idea why her husband suddenly sees her as controlling. But children are a commitment to a future he is no longer sure he wants. Everything that was once a gift and a plan is now a chain and a threat to his freedom.

All of these problems about Hannah's self-sufficiency come to a head on the second Thanksgiving. Holly, the rebellious middle sister, has written a script for a movie and passed it around to family members. She has been helped by Hannah's first husband, Mickey, played by Woody Allen himself, and the two of them have struck up a romance. (Woody Allen seems to have really liked the "sleeping with sisters" theme.) Everyone thinks it's a great story, except Hannah, who is very angry. It's clear the script has drawn on their family experiences, and Hannah doesn't like the picture of herself. "Can I not accept gestures and feelings from people?" she complains to Holly. "You make it sound like I have no needs or something. You think I'm too self-sufficient?" Holly tries to soothe Hannah's anger. "You're so giving, and we're all grateful," she says, but Hannah isn't soothed. "You're grateful, but resentful." Holly responds that Hannah never seems to have any problems, and that such perfection can be hard to be around. I do have problems, says Hannah, but "I don't want to bother anyone." Holly gives a simple answer: "I want to be bothered." We remember that being "bothered" is the musical signature of love in this movie, and the point is driven home when we see Hannah questioning Elliot later that evening, as in the background, "Bewitched, Bothered, and Bewildered" plays. "Do you find me too giving, too competent, too disgustingly perfect?" she asks. "I need someone I can matter to," he responds, and we remember his words to Lee. "It's hard to be around someone who gives so much and needs so little in return." Heartbroken and desperate, Hannah doesn't know what to say. "I have enormous needs," are the words she finds.

Hannah, as that scene shows us, is someone who never wants to reveal herself to others as needy. She says to her sister Holly, "I don't want to bother anyone." The word "bother" in this movie has been loaded up with significance through the music of the movie. Perhaps we have to abandon ourselves to being "all hot and bothered," a favorite phrase of Eric the DJ in the movie *Exotica*, to experience a certain kind of romantic love. So when Hannah says in that scene, "I don't want to bother anybody," what other people hear is that "I don't want to be loved by anybody." I want to love, but I don't want to BE loved. I want to give, but I don't want to be given. So the particular kind of big-sister syndrome from which Hannah suffers is that of trying to take on too much of the role of being the director of everybody else's life. A benevolent director, to be sure, but taking on that director role makes her feel controlling to others.

So Hannah's self-sufficiency, her unwillingness to reveal need to others, to give anybody else anything to do in loving her, comes under question in the movie. Now, it was exactly Hannah's directorial skills that attracted Elliot to her in the first place. Elliot mentions that his life was a mess before he knew Hannah. The very thing that attracted him to Hannah is now the thing that he's finding suffocating. So he looks for somebody whose life he can direct. The Lee that we see in this movie has a whole series of relationships to older men, older men who can teach her things, who can be her mentors. Hannah wants to be the mentor. She's the one who makes other people's lives better. Whose side are we supposed to be on when it comes to Hannah's self-sufficiency? Hannah, of course, does not interpret herself as a person with no needs. In what I think is the most horrifying line in the whole movie, a deeply disturbing line because it's so very sad, she says to Elliot, "I have enormous needs!" Imagine being in a position where you have to convince your lover that you have any need of him. It's a terrible situation for her. All of the things she thought she was giving to others as a gift, all of the help, all of the avoidance of bothering them, are now being thrown back into her face as if they were exercises of her selfishness rather than of her selflessness. People can't feel gratitude toward her because there's nothing they've been able to give back.

This aspect of Hannah of course has something comic about it. I know that when I was a kid, every Christmas my dad would give my brothers and sisters and me some money and then we'd go to a shopping center and he'd tell us to buy something for my mom. He would never have told us, "Buy something for me." And he would have felt really weird if that's what we did with the money. He was a much better gift giver than he was a gift receiver. He did get better about it when he got older – not greedy, but better about accepting gifts. But it took him a long time, I think, to learn to be able to accept a gift from one of his children. In effect, that's the way, it seems to me, that Hannah treats her sisters and her parents, and also her husband.

What kind of accomplishment then, overall, is this movie as an exploration of some of the challenges of marriage? In a way, the movie is extremely optimistic, because despite their marital disasters, despite growing up in a marriage that itself was a disaster, these characters find a way to love. They don't, it's true, have much success with their first spouse. It seems the view of marriage behind this movie is something like this: practice makes perfect. So that people get better by working out some things with one spouse and then grow up enough to make a real marriage with another spouse. I don't think we're to understand Hannah as ever discovering that her husband Elliott has been sleeping with her sister Lee. So we're not forced to confront Hannah's ability to work through that very specific form of infidelity. But we do see in the movie that all of the couples end happily. They all find a way toward love. But that bright comic side of the movie is counterbalanced by a very dark undertow, an undertow that makes fidelity in marriage look like something not only difficult, but perhaps impossible, and not only impossible, but perhaps not worth having even if it were possible. The infidelities in this movie turn out not to go very deep into these characters. They overcome them much more easily than, say, Othello was able to overcome even his mere fantasy of Desdemona's infidelity. Does this lightening of marital infidelity, as I think of it in this movie, make for a more optimistic or a more pessimistic view of what marriage is, of what marriage would call us to become? It seems to me a very live question, a question that the movie deserves us to ask. To find this movie merely entertaining is not really to enter into it. The movie is calling for a judgment. My own judgment on the movie is quite negative. As successful and as entertaining as I think the movie is, I think it's immoral. I think the movie is trying to make us take up a comic view toward our own temptations, toward infidelity. Perhaps that's not fair, but then I didn't say I was going to be fair.

At the third and final Thanksgiving at the end of movie, Woody Allen showers us with happy couples. Lee has broken off her affair with Elliot, and married a professor. Elliot and Hannah seem content with each other again. But it's the middle sister Holly who gets the last word. She has now married Mickey, and she has a surprising announcement for him: "I'm pregnant." I have known some viewers so cynical that they refuse to accept the wonder of this happy ending. Some take Holly's pregnancy as a final bitter dig at Hannah, proof that she is so unable to be receptive of another's love that she made Mickey infertile; others take it as proof of Holly's infidelity to Mickey, with minds as suspicious as Othello's. The miracle of comedy cures Mickey's infertility, just as watching the Marx Brothers earlier in the movie cured his suicidal depression. And so the movie ends with one of the oldest happy endings of all, the conception of a child. The procreation of a child with another human being is the most extreme integration of the male and the female one can imagine, and the least self-sufficient act as well. *Hannah and Her Sisters* ends as Phaedrus, Pausanias, and Eryximachus end: by gesturing, wittingly or not, toward an escape from a false self-sufficiency that seemed to be their main topic.

Three men, three ways of avoiding love, making it simpler, easier, and more manageable than an abandonment to love's true exhilarations and ecstasies could ever be. Plato makes these ways of avoidance vivid and palpable by showing us men – attractive, funny, likable men – who are so much like us, and who hold up to us a clarifying mirror. These three men still believe in love's magic, even though their fears make them try to tame love's wildness. In the next chapter, we will consider a more radical experiment of Plato's: a man so cynical he stops believing in love, and rejects it altogether. Perhaps the greatest literary exploration of this radical rejection of love is Shakespeare's *Othello*, a play that gives a horrible twist to Phaedrus's death test for lovers. Phaedrus had introduced the connection between love and death as something positive, because it gives an answer – "someone in love with you" – to the question, Who would die for you? Shakespeare explores the dark possibility that the same answer fits the question, Who would kill you?

Chapter Three
KILLING LOVE

Where do we find ourselves, so far in our thinking about falling in love and being in love? We started out by making romantic love, erotic love, love where sexuality is an important aspect of that love – we started out by making that kind of love more problematic than we might usually expect it to be. That's why we started off with Dionysus and Aphrodite, unsettling gods that the Greeks used to think about things that still are alive for us. I shared with you some experience I had with the movie *Exotica*, for me an especially unsettling experience, for which I'm grateful to its director and writer Atom Egoyan. Egoyan leads us down a path whose end we can't predict, and whose beginnings are hidden from us. We are expecting something about lust or about sex, but what the movie gives us is something about need and about pain. Let me put it this way: when we watch *Exotica*, we're confronted with the notion that sexuality drives down into aspects of our lives and our personality that are quite different from what the rather superficial kind of popular romantic movie, comedy or drama, might have made us expect.

Having gotten unsettled enough to learn something new, we turned to Plato and saw how, in the *Symposium*, Plato's own philosophizing is built around a certain view of what romantic life is, and of what it can be. Indeed, it's central to the Platonic view that what romantic life *is* depends on what it *can be*, even if we never reach that "can be." As romantic and sexual human beings, we're open to becoming more than we start from. We don't "settle down," as people sometimes say, when we fall in love, but become restless and searching in a way we could scarcely imagine before. So that the romantic life is a life of aspiration, not simply a life of comfort or a life of achievement: it is abandonment. There's always something incomplete or imperfect that our romantic existence brings home to us, makes real to us.

Philosophy teaches a hard fact about reality, about making things real: we often fear and avoid reality. This fear is never more potent than when we are falling in love, losing ourselves and searching for that new self of lover and beloved. Andre Dubus tells stories about people like Ted Briggs and LuAnn Arceneaux, characters who break my heart when I watch their hearts being broken; but the heartbreak is also a breaking open to new and more real love. Woody Allen's movie *Hannah and Her Sisters* follows the same path, with characters who avoid love until they find a way to accept its demands at the end of the story. And so too Plato, like Atom Egoyan and Woody Allen, tries to uncover what we fear when we avoid love, or when we impede our pursuit of love with fantasies and strategies of control and management, trying to tame the lion or manipulate the experience. The *Symposium* starts out with a whole cast of would-be lion-tamers. They all want love, but they want to avoid something in its commitments and ecstasies, too. Plato expects we'll recognize a bit of ourselves in all of these timid lovers – and who isn't made timid by love? – and be in a better position to overcome our fears once we acknowledge them.

The timid lover is a comic figure, and we readers smile with sympathy at his or her stumbling pursuit of love. But the avoidance of love haunts Plato and Shakespeare in a more extreme and deadly form than this. We perform a comedy when we avoid love even as we pursue it; we create a tragedy when we reject love and destroy it even while we demand it. It is this more radical, more cynical, and more deadly rejection that will be the topic of this chapter. Shakespeare's tragedy *Othello* and Plato's dialogue *Phaedrus* will be our conversation partners, along with two movies, Jocelyn Moorhouse's *Proof* and Alan Rudolph's *The Secret Lives of Dentists*. These two movies seem to me to understand the issues raised by Plato and Shakespeare, and to illuminate those issues more vividly than any theoretical account could. How astonishing, how Plato and Shakespeare remain contemporary, and give us tools to understand the art and literature of our own time more richly. I want to mention my gratitude to the American philosopher Stanley Cavell, whose difficult insights into Shakespeare, and into *Othello* especially have informed everything I think about this play. (Cavell's Shakespeare essays are collected in *Disowning Knowledge*.)

Love in hell: the word world of Shakespeare's *Othello*

Let me start with the names of love – I mean, of the lovers – in this play, Othello and Desdemona. The main characters are Othello, a great naval captain, and Desdemona, the beautiful young woman with whom he falls in love. Othello leads the forces of Venice in their wars with the Turks, but he is himself a North African, a Moor. He is much valued for his military prowess, but he is racially an outsider to Venetian society. His racial differentness makes him rather exotic and curious to the Venetians, fascinating but also uncanny, as if an air of the magical hangs about him. One of Othello's subordinate officers, named Iago, tempts Othello and makes him suspect Desdemona has been unfaithful to him. Iago succeeds by presenting to Othello a series of accidents, especially Desdemona losing a handkerchief that had been a gift from Othello, as a coherent story of Desdemona having a sexual relationship with another officer, Cassio. Othello murders Desdemona in a fit of jealousy, then kills himself in a fit of despair. Of course, there are a thousand beautiful things in *Othello* that such a plot summary could never capture. But even if we focus just on this bare skeleton, Shakespeare has put plenty of flesh on the bones.

Every reader will notice that Desdemona's name confronts us with the word "demon" at its heart. This word will turn out to be central to the vocabulary Shakespeare uses in this play to create a certain kind of mood. One thing that makes Shakespeare such a genius is the way he creates the thought world and the word world of each of his plays so that every play is entirely distinct. Othello, for example, doesn't sound like any other character in Shakespeare, not even the other great tragic figures such as King Lear, Macbeth, or Hamlet – and none of them sounds like the others, either. This is something Shakespeare does over and over again. And it's not just that particular characters have their own distinctive way of thinking and feeling, and inhabit their own particular word world. It's that you might say the play as a whole has a permeating atmosphere that comes out through the vocabulary not of this or that character, but rather the entire vocabulary in general.

One central part of this mood-making vocabulary, the word world of *Othello*, is a set of words connected with unintelligible evil, with a category we can think of as diabolical. The most famous and most penetrating description of the character Iago in *Othello* comes from the Romantic poet Samuel Taylor Coleridge. Coleridge was a fine poet himself, but he also wrote the earliest literary criticism of Shakespeare, I believe, that starts to do justice to Shakespeare's distinctive genius, some two centuries after Shakespeare lived. (So don't complain too much when you think you haven't been appreciated or understood.) Coleridge noticed that at various points in the play, Iago suggests reasons he might dislike or even hate Othello, yet none of these alleged "reasons" really makes much sense of Iago's actions in destroying Othello. It looks more like Iago is trying to find a rationalization for his actions, not a real reason. Coleridge memorably described this as "the motive-hunting of a motiveless malignity." (I've always wished I had written that; and now I have.) In other words, we will try in vain to understand Iago's evil will toward Othello; his hatred exceeds any motive we might identify. This, Shakespeare is showing us, is what evil looks like when it has no object, when an evil or malicious purpose has no further goal. So one of the terrible puzzles about *Othello* is how love can survive in a world where there is empty malice.

Shakespeare captures this terrible world in the demon that stares out at us from the middle of Desdemona's name. But there is more than just the devil in Desdemona, which is a rather Christian idea, after all. The name "Desdemona" has a more pagan significance, something closer to the imagination of Plato. It comes from a Greek word whose closest English translation is probably "superstitious." The word describes people who are always worrying about making sacrifices to the gods, or about being attacked by black magic. This meaning of "Desdemona" as superstition, though, is derived from the two parts of the name, the first syllable "des" and the root word "daemon." A daemon is a divine spirit that supports, governs, or influences your life, and this life-daemon is closely connected with notions of fate, or doom. This pagan Greek conception of a life-daemon is something like the Christian popular belief in a guardian angel, but a life-daemon doesn't have to be good. The first syllable of Desdemona's name, "des", in Greek means that something is bad or unhealthy. Desdemona's name, then, could tell us she is a woman who's under an evil fate, or that she is living an infected life.

Perhaps somewhat less obvious than the demon in Desdemona is the HELL in the middle of Othello. Shakespeare based *Othello* on an older Italian story. In Shakespeare's own time it may well be that the name "Othello" would have been pronounced more in the Italian style, as "Otello" without the "th" sound in the middle. This would make the sound of the name, not just its spelling, closer to containing a hell. Part of our burden of reading, the task of interpretation of this play, will be to try to understand what creates that hell at the middle of Othello's life. More or less since commentary on *Othello* began, critics have complained that it doesn't make sense that Othello stops trusting Desdemona, that Othello listens to Iago's slanders against her. The explanation for why Othello so tragically turns against Desdemona cannot be simply that Othello misreads the evidence Iago presents against her. There must be something in Othello that predisposes him, even tempts him, to believe Desdemona to be unfaithful, or he would never be so easy for Iago to convince. I am tempted to go further and say, Desdemona's infidelity is something Othello longs for, something that would fulfill a dark wish he has. His jealous and murderous rage is not just the force of evidence misconstrued. It's rather the seeking for something he can call evidence of something he already wants. The charge of infidelity is the motive-hunting of a malignity hiding a secret motive. What then is Othello's secret, that attracts him to the hypothesis of Desdemona's infidelity?

Besides this diabolical word world, this creation of something like hell on earth, another aspect of the word world of this play comes out from the first scene: the reduction of human sexuality to a bestial vocabulary. Iago is characterized by his use of a vocabulary that reduces sexuality to something animal. Iago is one of the great masters in literature of making sex seem dirty, of making it seem that to express our sexuality is to debase ourselves. The romantic cynic may be right to deflate our pretension to be more than human, to be angels; but we must not let the cynic insinuate the despairing thought that because we are not gods, we are nothing but beasts.

We'll want to think about how "wording the world" (an excellent phrase of Stanley Cavell's) in this play has its effect on us as readers of this particular tragic romance. The reductiveness, the cynicism of Iago is not something that we readers of the play observe as cool outsiders. Part of Shakespeare's magic trick is to make not just Othello influenced by Iago, but to make us influenced by Iago. It seems to me that Atom Egoyan in *Exotica* accomplished something like what Shakespeare accomplishes in *Othello* through Iago. *Exotica* confronts us with the fact that we bring the dirty mind to the movie. We find the movie to have a dirty mind because we're prepared to find it, indeed are hoping to find it. So too, Iago brings out to the audience that we too are ready to accept Iago-like reductiveness, animality, as our picture of sexuality. Maybe we do not play at being Iago always all the time, and maybe never as applied to ourselves. But Shakespeare and Egoyan force us to consider whether we sometimes play Iago as a strategy to be a privileged observer, watching those fools who fall in love, laughing scornfully as they interpret their own sexual interest in each other with high-minded rhetoric. Our laughter shows we think we understand what it's *really* all about. So the figure of Iago, clearly a diabolical figure, is meant to confront us with the demon in Desdemona and with the hell in Othello, but is also meant to confront us with the Iago in ourselves, with the temptations that we feel, especially when we feel bitter or rejected, to reduce human sexuality to something that's merely animal, something that's bestial.

Iago will exploit Othello's tendency to think of his beloved Desdemona as an angel, something above mere human flesh and blood.

Othello's despair of this false Desdemona distorts the real and most human woman into nothing but a beast. The false standard is held too high for humanity to attain it, and then is easily used as a weapon against humanity.

We see Shakespeare and Iago creating this mood of the beast in the opening action of the play. (Throughout *Othello*, Iago is portrayed as a director of a play, staging actions, teaching other characters their lines, and improvising a role for himself. Shakespeare wants us to think about the man who wrote this play, and wonder how much of Iago's diabolical emptiness reflects the dark side of theater's ability to manipulate its characters and its audience. In other words, Shakespeare doesn't shrink from identifying himself with Iago.) Iago is stirring up a disturbance in the street outside the house of Desdemona's father, one of the leading men of Venice. Using vile images of bestial sexuality, Iago taunts the father that his young virgin fair-skinned daughter has eloped with the older and dark-skinned Othello: the lovers, Iago taunts, are "making the beast with two backs," and "an old black ram" is mounting "your white ewe."

The father raises a search party to find the couple, and Iago goes to Othello, to warn him, he claims, but really to make Othello look guilty by getting him to flee. Iago is urging Othello, "Look, you'd better run away, they're after you, they're really angry!" But Iago's trick doesn't work, because Othello is so self-assured he will not run away from the father's mob. "The excellent military service I have done for the Venetians," he says (I paraphrase Shakespeare), "will speak more loudly than the complaints of Desdemona's father. I am no boaster, but if anyone thinks Desdemona is too noble to be my bride, I can tell of accomplishments that prove my very great worth." My being loved (by Desdemona) and my loving (of Desdemona), Othello claims, are justified by my successes. I'm not going to boast right now, but if I have to, I can tell everybody how great I really am, and prove that I *deserve* Desdemona. And then Shakespeare has Othello say something very revealing about how he understands his own deservingness, a sentence I think is the center of this play. "For know, Iago, but that I love the gentle

Desdemona, I would not my unhoused free condition put into circumscription and confine for the sea's worth." Let's unpack this sentence a bit and linger over it. If it weren't for my love for Desdemona, Othello is saying, my "unhoused free condition" would never be domesticated. I cannot be confined in a house. – It's part of Othello's sense of his own nobility that he has not "settled down," that he remains a free spirit. This notion that a real man is undomesticated, wild and free, would be easy to find in songs and stories (and real-world attitudes of both men and women) from our time, too, though rarely so powerful in their expression. To put the point bluntly, Othello thinks there is a kind of threat in taking a wife. Othello, like one of the men LuAnn sleeps with in Dubus's "All the Time in the World," has problems with the C-word, commitment. His own sense of his nobility is so bound up with his sense of his freedom that it's difficult for Othello to translate his nobility into a noble love. Love looks like confinement, a home like a prison. The sentence also shows that for Othello, the opposite of the confinement of a house is the open unboundedness of the sea. His whole life, of course, has been spent on the sea, in wars and adventures; what will become of that life when he has a wife? Unless he can make of married life a war and an adventure, won't he be abandoning himself? He has made himself a man on the sea, and he suggests in the sentence that this manliness is something he is giving up for "love [of] the gentle Desdemona."

Othello goes on to say, "My parts, my title, and my perfect soul shall manifest me rightly." What an extraordinary phrase of self-description: "my perfect soul." Why, we must ask, would a man with a perfect soul, a complete and self-sufficient life, have any interest in a wife? What view do we have of what would count as our own perfection? How much of our self-image is an image that repels the notion that we depend on others, that we can be anchored by them? Because if they can be our anchor, we must admit that our ship could become unmoored, adrift, without them. How much of our self-image makes out of our house, out of domesticity, out of the notion that we would be married for better or worse until we die, how much of our self-image creates of that sort of house a prison? Something that we'll be chained into? So that we're giving up a picture of our own freedom, and in that respect our own perfection when we take on the burden of loving another person in a marriage. Othello calls it "circumscription." I think Shakespeare meant us to hear the "script" inside the circle of this word: married love, for Othello, threatens to put him into a role in someone else's play, where his life becomes scripted rather than free. It is only the director, not the actor, who gets to make up the parts.

I posed a question about this play. Is there a secret in Othello that would make him *prefer* to think that Desdemona is unfaithful to him, rather than to trust her? It seems obvious from the outside, to us, that the evidence that Othello takes mostly from Iago as proof of his wife's unfaithfulness, is insufficient to justify Othello's conclusion. Why is that not equally obvious to Othello? Is there something in Othello that makes him see these chance events, these innocent interactions, especially the accident of the lost handkerchief, in the way Iago the director wants him to see them? To fear being scripted by Desdemona, but to memorize all the lines from Iago's script, seems the choice of furious idiocy. Why does Othello suspend his disbelief to enter Iago's diabolical theater?

Iago realizes that the evidence he assembles into an infidelity plot is not convincing in itself, indeed is not even plausible. But, as Shakespeare has him say, "Trifles light as air are to the jealous confirmations strong as proofs of holy writ." It is the jealous mood that controls the appearance of truth, and the trifling bits of evidence are mere occasions of the passion. Othello's violent skepticism about Desdemona's fidelity is grounded in a groundless mood, a mood that makes Iago's play look true. Othello demands that Iago bring this horrid play to its horrifying conclusion, and show Desdemona in the very act of copulation with her illicit lover. "Prove my love a whore," he rages, "be sure of it." And then this perfect soul utters the words that I take as the emblem of all his demands: "Give me the ocular proof." Proof, proof, proof; kill, kill, kill. One word brings the other.

Think of the way that we, most of us not heroic military officers, tend to reach conclusions that outstrip the proof of the evidence when we're predisposed to accept a certain kind of view. It's not even that this is always a bad thing. After all, if we needed to wait around for sure proof about everything, we would mostly be paralyzed. How much of our lives really operate on the basis of secure evidence in that sense? We're forced to make do over and over again with some view of the world and with likelihood, and then fit the evidence into it. To expect the evidence of our lives, including our love lives, to amount to proof is to make an extraordinary and perhaps an inhuman demand. How indeed could Desdemona have proved herself, once Othello's entire way of understanding the world put himself at its center as a man who'd been betrayed? It is not just paranoids who interpret the world from within a point of view. It is all of us. We have neither the cognitive power nor simply the bare time to test everything. So that the way things count for us as evidence is always open to a kind of comic misinterpretation. And indeed, this particular tragedy runs very close to the line between tragedy and comedy. It's easy to imagine a few little changes – Iago exposed a few minutes earlier and Desdemona saved and Iago punished, with Othello laughing at how gullible he had been – so that the play had a happy ending, a kind of poetic justice, as we tend to call it. When Othello falls into a kind of epileptic trance because his anger and his grief become so potent, it would be easy enough to reformulate those scenes and play that as a comic loss of control, rather than a frightening loss of control.

So the human situation that Othello finds himself in is the one we find ourselves in, a world of facts that we call evidence that never quite amount to proof, never quite amount to justification. Othello's position in his marriage is not all that different from the position of every man and woman who, when they take their marriage vows, celebrate something they can't really see, something they cannot know the end of. A wedding is not a celebration of a love already accomplished. It's a promise into an unknown and open future, a future that may be for the better, but that may also be for the worse. We will never have the ocular proof, and if we abandon ourselves to the wish for the ocular proof, we will blind ourselves to what marriage is and must be.

So the tragedy of *Othello* is a way of thinking about the commitments of marriage. Of course, we hope that our own married lives don't come crashing down around us, with the structure of evidence we've built up over time, the proofs of love, suddenly susceptible to reversal, everything seen in a new and very bitter light. We hope that never happens to us. But is the reason we aren't exposed to that kind of tragedy, that we're so much smarter than Othello? That we're better men or better women than Othello or Desdemona? What would it take for us to rest secure in the honesty of our spouses and the honesty of those around us from whom we get evidence and information, ideas about what we are and what our spouses are?

Othello raises in an especially unsettling way an epistemological problem about the marriage commitment. The way this play understands human cognition and its weaknesses, focuses us on the difficulty that our life will be cast into, if we're constantly demanding something that counts as proof, because a reliance on proof might itself be a rejection of trust. Now, trust, too, exposes us. But it might be that a demand for a certain kind of security or a certain kind of evidence or certain kind of proof will expose us as well.

The blind eye of love in Jocelyn Moorhouse's *Proof*

The movie *Proof*, directed and written by Jocelyn Moorhouse in 1991, taught me a lot about Shakespeare's *Othello*, and about the human tendency to fear love so much we are willing to blind ourselves to it, and even to kill it. (Don't confuse this movie with the 2005 movie of the same title, starring Gwyneth Paltrow.) The audience can enjoy early performances by two actors, both in their first important movie, who later became very big stars indeed. Russell Crowe is here, before he went on to star in blockbusters such as *Gladiator* and *A Beautiful Mind*, and Hugo Weaving, who became famous as Agent Smith in *The Matrix* and the Elf-Lord Elrond in Peter Jackson's *The Lord of the Rings* movies. To my mind, the work of both actors in this early, small movie from Australia is as good as anything in their more famous movies.

This magical movie conjures the same dark spiritual territory as the idea behind *Othello*: the human tendency to make inhuman demands on knowledge, especially in love. The writer and director Jocelyn Moorhouse comes up with her own penetrating version of Othello's impossible demand for "the ocular proof" of Desdemona's infidelity. I don't know if she had Shakespeare in mind when she came up with her splendid idea, but whether intentionally or not, Moorhouse's thoughtful movie captures the heart of Othello's violent skepticism as well as anything I've read or seen.

Proof tells the story of a blind man, Martin (Hugo Weaving), who is fiercely committed to his own independence. Martin hates to rely on anyone, and he constantly tests everybody he lets into his life, watching for any sign anyone may try to take advantage of him. Like Othello, he refuses to be pitied, and he takes this refusal to such an extreme that he also in effect refuses to let anyone love him. He aspires to a freedom and self-sufficiency as absolute and inhuman – a "free unhoused condition," a "perfect soul" – as the freedom to which Othello clutches. Othello says he would give up this absolute self-sufficiency only for his beloved Desdemona; but the tragedy's bloody end reveals he will sacrifice even his precious wife on the altar of independence. Othello's demand for the ocular proof of infidelity, proof of Desdemona's breach of trust, is a mask of how Othello turns a blind eye to Desdemona's love, refusing any proof she could offer. Martin lives out Othello's hell in physical blindness.

The movie opens with still photographs of Martin's dog, Bill, outdoors, apparently in a park. A particular photograph of this dog will later play a crucial role in the plot. We have our first view of the central character, the blind man Martin, walking down the street with his white cane tapping the ground in front of him. The movie camera zooms in for a close-up of an odd detail: Martin is carrying a camera on his belt. The movie's camera emphasizes Martin's camera, and the close-up is a visual invitation from the director to put ourselves in Martin's position: we viewers are blind except for what we are shown by a camera.

We next see Martin leaving a restaurant through the back exit, into a cluttered alley. He stumbles, knocking over some trash cans, and inadvertently he injures a stray cat, named Ugly. Andy (Russell Crowe), a charming but rootless young man working at the restaurant, has been taking care of the cat, feeding it scraps. Andy happens to be outside, so he sees the accident and picks up the apparently dead cat while he watches Martin walk away.

Martin walks home, and it starts to rain. He gets inside his house and starts to change out of his wet clothes. We hear all the sounds in the house – a drip, the fire in the furnace – with heightened precision and vividness. Though we are viewing a movie with our seeing eyes, the scene forces us to mirror Martin's own experience of a world of sound – the director again invites us to put ourselves in Martin's position. Suddenly, as he starts to undress, he hears the sound of a cigarette ash being flicked into an ashtray. It is his housekeeper, a woman named Celia (Genevieve Picot), smoking on the couch. About Martin's age, Celia is slim and severe in appearance, and her voice is flat and rather cold, like a doctor giving a diagnosis or a boss a termination notice. Martin has brought home some of his photographs from the drugstore, where they've been developed. (This was before digital cameras, of course, so the film in a camera had to be taken to a store to be developed into photographs.) "Can I look at your photographs?" Celia says, and offers, "I could describe them for you." Martin declines rudely, and we get the sense that this conversation has occurred before, with Celia's offer and Martin's rejection a regular part of their tense relationship. Martin goes to a safe where he keeps his money (and, we learn later, the most important photograph he has ever taken), to get cash to pay Celia for her housekeeping. Martin covers her eyes as he opens the safe, keeping her blind to what's inside it. Celia offers to help him get dinner ready, but Martin again declines her help. Celia turns to leave, but to remind Martin of how much he depends on her, she moves an ashtray from its usual place so Martin will stumble into it. This woman is determined for Martin to acknowledge how much he needs her, and Martin is just as determined not to acknowledge any needs at all.

Why is Martin so wary of Celia? The movie takes us back in time, to Martin as a little boy, already blind, perhaps six or seven years old. Flashbacks throughout the movie to Martin's boyhood will show us why he has become a man who is so distrustful of any help or dependency. We see the boy Martin standing at his sleeping mother's bedside. He can't see her, but he gently runs his hand over her closed eyes and her cheek, down onto her chest. His mother is startled awake, a bit embarrassed by his innocent touching. "You can't touch people whenever you want," she scolds him, "fingers aren't the same as eyes." Young Martin interprets his mother's startled response to show that his way of knowing – touching not seeing – is too intimate to be acceptable. This blind boy will grow up thinking people don't want him to know them, just as his mother wanted to limit how he touches her. We understand that Martin's rude rejections of Celia are repetitions of his frustration when his mother didn't let him know her, as if she was keeping a secret from him.

We return to the restaurant. Andy is working, a day after the accident in the alley with Ugly. Martin is sitting at a table, but the busy waitress doesn't notice him when he tries to order. Not only is Martin blind, he feels as if other people are blind to him. Rather than continuing to ask for help, he takes control of the situation. He picks up a wine bottle and starts to pour it onto the table, pretending that he missed the glass. Now the waitress has to notice him. She thinks he needs help, and rushes to the table. Martin ignores the spilled wine and simply orders his dinner. He has pretended to need help pouring the wine to get what he wants. But the scene jumps to Martin leaving unnoticed through the cluttered alley behind the restaurant, because his food never arrived. Andy sees him again, and challenges him, telling Martin he has to pay just like anyone else – an important moment, because it shows Martin that Andy won't treat him differently just because he is blind. Andy tells Martin, "You killed Ugly," and shows him the injured cat, still lying in the alley from the day before. Andy thinks the cat looks dead, but Martin touches the cat and knows it is alive – Martin knows more by touch than Andy did by sight. We realize that Martin's life is in some ways more intense because of his blindness, a less superficial life perhaps, one that feels the interior life of things.

Martin takes the cat, and Andy drives them to the veterinarian's office where Martin usually takes his dog Bill. In the waiting area, filled with people and their pets, Martin unexpectedly takes out his camera and directs Andy to hold up Ugly the cat for a photograph. Andy is embarrassed, as all the people in the room wonder what he's doing with this odd blind man with a camera. But when they see Martin taking pictures, they all want to have pictures of themselves with their pets, and soon Martin has snapped dozens of photographs capturing every human and animal and every feature of the room. The movie doesn't show these pictures being taken, as moving. It shows us the still photographs, as if we are looking at them after the event was recorded. Why, we wonder, were the people waiting there with their pets so eager to have their pictures taken? After all, unlike Martin, they could see the room right then. What is it about a photograph that could be more interesting, more of a story, than the actual event? It's as if the photographic record of the event is more real than the event itself.

The movie deepens our puzzlement about the reality of photographs when Andy and Martin talk on the drive home. Andy laughs and says, "A blind photographer. Now that goes down as the weird sight of the week." Martin tells the story of how he came to have a camera. "My mother gave me a camera when I was a boy," he says, and Andy doesn't understand, and asks, "Sort of cruel, wasn't it?" But Martin explains, "I wanted a camera. I thought it would help me to see." We start to understand this odd comment – how could photographs that a blind man can't see be thought to help him to see? – the next day, when Martin visits Andy at the restaurant. Martin arrives with the photographs, and asks Andy to describe them to him, briefly and accurately. (So Andy will be allowed an intimacy that Celia was forbidden.) As Andy looks at the pictures, Martin takes out a small machine, and appears to be typing something. In fact, he is typing Andy's brief descriptions onto Braille labels, to put on the back of the photographs. Andy is embarrassed again, and asks Martin why he's doing this. And then, in the most important sentences in this movie *Proof*, Martin explains what he gets from this odd process, of blindly taking pictures that he then asks someone to describe while he labels them. What I get, he says, is "Proof – that what's in the photograph is what's there." Andy, a rather carefree and unreliable young man, is uncomfortable with being taken so seriously as a truth-teller when he describes the pictures. "That photograph," he says, "could be anywhere of anything." "Except it wasn't," Martin responds, and he reminds Andy that he had been more aware than Andy himself of many of the features of that waiting room, especially of the sounds and scents, both animal and human. "This," Martin says, holding up one of the photographs of the waiting room, "is proof that what I sensed is what you saw through your eyes – the truth." Martin says he likes Andy's simple and direct style of description, and he offers to hire Andy to describe photographs for him. Andy is happy to keep up the descriptions, but he scoffs at the idea he'd do it for money. This exchange shows us Martin wants to control Andy, as he controls Celia, paying them to help him rather than trusting in their concern and friendship, in their love. Moorhouse uses money as an instrument of erotic control in *Proof* rather as Egoyan used it in *Exotica*.

Once Andy has agreed to describe Martin's photographs, as a friend rather than an employee, Martin turns very serious, and says to Andy, "You must never lie to me." Andy responds simply, "Why would I do that?" But the scene now flashes back to a moment that has haunted Martin's ability to trust anyone's love. Martin's mother is looking out a window with the boy. She describes the sight and the sound of a man outside in a garden, raking leaves. But young Martin refuses her description. "I didn't hear him," he says, "he's not there. There's nobody there." Martin's mother, who must daily endure the boy's distrust, his angry attempts at independence, wearily responds, "Why would I lie to you?" It is the very question Andy has just asked. But young Martin spits out a savagely unfair response to his weary mother: "Because you can."

This is the central moment in the movie because it reveals Martin's unbounded skepticism of everyone who would love him. Martin wants proof, and so he rejects trust. Martin, man or boy, approaches everyone who would like his trust – his mother, Andy,

Celia – as if they may be an Iago, or Descartes's evil demon. Such wanton devils fool us for their sport, and their motiveless malignity has no explanation. Martin is afraid people will take advantage of his blindness, and this fear creates a world inhabited by more devils than hell can hold. To protect himself from unproven beliefs, Martin excludes himself from trusting love. No love can ever prove itself enough to withstand Martin's groundless suspicions. And so by protecting himself from imagined Iagos, Martin makes himself an Iago, a monster of motiveless doubt, incapable of falling in love or being in love. He is as impregnable and as closed as a grave.

From this defining center, the movie exposes the impossible, inhuman demand that Martin makes for the ocular proof. Celia will be the instrument of this exposure. Andy has seen Celia in some of Martin's pictures. He describes her as plain, but not unattractive, and asks Martin about her. "Celia has no heart; I hate her," Martin responds savagely. "She wants me," he goes on, but "I know that if I continue to deny her what she wants, she can never feel pity for me. Instead I can pity her." Martin experiences Celia's love as pity, and he interprets pity as demeaning, as something that challenges his self-sufficiency and his manliness. He would rather be cruel to Celia than be pitied by her. At least this is what Martin says. We suspect, of course, that he both wants her pity and fears it, as Othello both loves Desdemona for pitying his sufferings, yet is unmanned by accepting this pity as the basis of her love.

This interplay between pity and desire enters the movie when Celia is making a cake at Martin's house. When Martin smells it baking, he uses money again to reject any help or free gift from her. "What's that going to cost me?" he says meanly. But Celia is baking the cake because it's her thirtieth birthday, and she hopes Martin will celebrate with her. Indeed, she wants Martin to accept her housekeeping as love, not as paid service, and to give up some independence for her love. She says to him seductively, "You know what they say: once you're over thirty you can't call yourself a girl anymore; you have to admit to being a woman. But you wouldn't know about that, Martin, the difference between a girl and a woman, would you, Martin?" Celia puts Martin's hand on her blouse, feeling her breast. Martin pulls away, and says, "You won't get a birthday present from me, Celia." What an extraordinary thing to say! When she offers him a gift – the cake, and her body, too – he speaks as if by receiving these gifts, he would be the one giving the gifts. For Martin, every reception is an expenditure. Celia can put ashtrays in his way, or offer him cake and sex, but Martin will not acknowledge any need for this woman. In particular, he won't let her do what Andy does: be his eyes. Celia is jealous of this trust, and she sets out to destroy it.

In a laugh-out-loud sequence worthy of the best madcap comedies, the movie shows us the growing friendship between Martin and Andy. As in many a love story and every buddy movie, the friends bond through an adventure. Andy decides to become Martin's eyes more thoroughly than by describing still photographs, and takes the blind man to a drive-in movie. As in the opening close-up of Martin's camera hanging on his belt, the director invites us to put ourselves in Martin's place, with charming but unreliable Andy in the place of the director. We – I mean, Martin and we viewers of *Proof* – trust ourselves to someone who controls what we see in a movie. The movie Andy chooses is a cheap slasher flick, with topless teen-age girls threatened by a knife-wielding killer, no doubt more suited to Andy than to Martin's refined tastes. Andy leaves to get some food at the concession stand, and Martin starts touching things to explore the car. He unknowingly holds up a package of condoms Andy has stashed in the car, and the people in the car next to him think he is making an obscene offer to them. The misunderstanding escalates into a fight, and when Andy returns, the two drive off in a panic, with Martin somehow ending up in the driver's seat. Martin drives under Andy's direction, but they are soon in a minor accident – no surprise with a blind driver! When the police arrive, in a moment of inspiration, Martin calls out, "I can't see!" as if the accident has blinded him. The sympathetic policeman – he thinks Andy and Martin are lovers – tells Andy at the hospital, "It looks like your friend Martin has been blinded." But of course the doctor examining Martin knows better, and she says to Martin, "You've been blind all your life. What were you doing driving a car?" Martin gives a reply that he and Andy laugh about on the drive back to Martin's house: "I forgot." Like many playful words, this comment of Martin's also reveals a serious truth. By accepting Andy's friendship, Martin has indeed forgotten to be blind. He has stopped redoubling his physical blindness with a spiritual blindness to love and trust. Martin sees Andy and is seen by him. Their relationship heightens the cruel contrast with Martin's rejection of giving and receiving with Celia.

Back at Martin's house, Andy notices a photograph on the mantel. It turns out to be of Martin's mother, and Andy describes it for him. Martin says, "I never went out with my mother at all. She was embarrassed by me. She always wanted an ordinary child she could do ordinary things with." We remember the earlier scene, with the boy Martin's groundless skepticism toward his mother. He has twisted his own embarrassment about depending on her, into a memory of her embarrassment. "One day," he goes on, "I might show you a photograph, just a garden that was visible through one of the windows of our flat. But it's the most important photograph I've ever taken. I was always trying to catch her in a lie." "Why would your mother lie to you?" Andy asks, repeating the earlier question about motive at the heart of the movie, and Martin gives another version of his savage answer: "To punish me, for being blind." Of course, not the mother but the son is doing the punishing, a spasm of rage against not seeing, against not having proof, and interpreting the lack of proof as lack of love. Andy can't understand the absoluteness of Martin's demand, and asks, "Does it really matter if she lied to you about some garden?" "Yes. It was my world," replies Martin. Now we understand: Martin turns his demand for an impossible knowledge into a life of world-destroying rage. Andy is sure to fall short of Martin's impossible standard of truth, and Celia makes sure that he does.

Martin regularly takes his dog Bill to run in the park. Martin takes pictures there, and later he has Andy describe them. Martin is puzzled that sometimes when he calls Bill, the dog doesn't come right away. The solution to this puzzle leads Andy to lie to Martin about what's in a photograph. Andy happens to stop by the house when Martin has gone to the park, so he goes to see him. But as Andy approaches, he sees Bill, walking toward Celia, who holds the dog when Martin calls him. Martin points the camera this way and that, snapping pictures, trying to capture whatever might be preventing Bill from coming when Martin calls him. Andy tries to get out of the camera's view, and Celia silently lets Bill go and leaves the park without Martin knowing she has been there. Later, Martin asks Andy to describe the photographs, as Celia stands quietly in the back of the room. Andy sees the pictures of Celia holding back Bill, with himself in the background, trying to jump out of the frame. He glances at Celia as she smiles at him, and he lies to Martin about the picture, and says Bill is with another dog. Martin is surprised, but he accepts this as the solution to the puzzle of why Bill doesn't always come when he calls. Celia is pleased to have forced Andy to choose to protect her rather than to tell Martin the truth, and gives her own suggestive comment about who this other "dog" may be: "Probably a bitch, on heat."

Celia now tries one last desperate plan to get Martin to accept her love. She takes a photograph of Martin on the toilet, and threatens to pin it to his clothes unless he spends an evening with her on a date. She has a much better sense than Andy of Martin's tastes, and takes him to the concert hall, without telling him where they are. They listen to Beethoven's Fifth Symphony, music he loves, and Martin is deeply moved; it is the first time he has heard and felt this music in a live performance. Martin thanks Celia, and thinks the evening is over, but Celia insists they go back to her apartment. "I'm a bit of a photographer myself, Martin," she says, and Martin asks, "What do you photograph?" "Things I love," she replies, and the camera pulls back, revealing to us in a shock that the walls are covered with photographs – of Martin. "Tonight's been all I've hoped for," she says, as she starts to unbutton her blouse, "and more." She tries to seduce him, but Martin runs from the apartment, wandering panicked along the street, looking for a taxi, until Celia drives by and picks him up. "I do everything for you Martin," she says, "I'm like a wife to you, but you don't trust me. I want your trust, I want your respect." She wishes for his love, but she asks at least to keep her job as his housekeeper. "I was right, you enjoy it," he spits at her, meaning that she enjoys his savage cruelty, when of course she endures it out of love and infatuation. Celia takes him home in silence.

Martin lies on his bed crying. A flashback shows us the memory behind the tears. The boy Martin's mother is telling him she is dying, and that he must go to live with his grandmother. To be vulnerable to his mother's death is as impossible for the boy Martin as to be dependent on her love, and he responds with his typical denial. "You don't want to see me anymore," he says, "you're just saying you're dying to get away from me. You're not telling the truth, I'll never believe you." And the camera then gives us a moment of terrible and revelatory sadness, as the boy Martin, alone with his mother's casket, raps on it with his hand and says, "It's hollow." Not even death can bring him the touch of the real. Martin would rather think his mother abandoned him, than think he was vulnerable to her death.

In her bitterness, Celia seduces Andy, unwilling to have Martin accept anyone else's love if he won't accept hers. "You lied for me, in case," she says to Andy, and we know she means, in case you wanted to betray Martin to be with me. Celia arranges to meet Andy at Martin's house – she is still Martin's housekeeper – when she knows Martin will walk in and discover their affair. Martin has taken Bill to the veterinarian, and Celia has pinned to Bill's collar the photograph from the park, of herself holding Bill with Andy in the background. The doctor notices the photograph and describes it to Martin, who comes home and confronts Andy and Celia. "Celia and I are in love," Andy says, and Andy and Celia leave for Celia's apartment. When Andy sees the walls covered with pictures of Martin, he realizes she has manipulated him. "He won't forgive you, not now," she says, and with Andy we realize that was her goal, to destroy their trust and friendship.

If this movie were satisfied to follow *Othello* on the path of tragedy, it would end on this view of Andy's betrayal and Martin's refusal of trust. But instead it presents a more hopeful vision of Martin's reconciliation with his mother, with Celia, and with Andy.

First Martin visits the cemetery where his mother is buried. Martin asks the caretaker, who has shown him to the grave, a question the caretaker finds very odd, but that we viewers understand: "Do you ever get cases of an empty coffin being buried?" But now Martin accepts that his mother truly died, that her casket was not hollow, that she loved him all along, and that he was denying her love. We then return to Martin's house, where he finally tells Celia the truth and ends their relationship. "I'm sorry I tormented you for so long," he says. "I knew how you felt about me, and it was wrong of me to exploit your feelings. You're fired." Celia can't resist giving Martin one more reminder of how much she has done for him and how much he has needed her, and she puts a coatrack in the doorway as she leaves Martin's house for the last time.

The reconciliation between Martin and Andy comes when Andy returns to apologize. Martin says to him, "You should have taken care, Andy. I'm a blind man, I'm not like other people. You can't know how important truth is to me." Andy realizes he has fallen short of the standard by which Martin lives his life, but Andy also thinks Martin's standard is impossible, pitiless and inhuman. "Everybody lies," he says, "but not all the time." Martin replies, "How can I believe you?" holding on to an absolute demand, all or nothing, truth or demonic illusion. Andy replies, "You can't," that is, you can't believe me, if by "believe" you mean, know that what I say is true with absolute certainty, without risk or any possibility for doubt. "You tell the truth, Martin, your whole life's the truth," Andy goes on, "have some pity on the rest of us." It is a beautiful moment, and Andy's request for pity is also a reflection on what truth is for human beings, less a matter of knowing with certainty than of acknowledging with trust. Martin's life is no human life, because he has made truth pitiless. And at last, Andy's friendship and love make Martin capable of giving and receiving pity. Martin takes an old photograph from his safe, and trusts Andy to describe it. "It's a man in a garden," Andy says. "Keep it," Martin replies, and we see a last picture of Martin as boy, in front of a window. He doesn't need the photograph anymore. Martin no longer expects proof, because he accepts love.

And the viewer realizes that Martin is no more blind than we are, and no less.

Pity and the killing man

Let me go back to the question, why is Othello so susceptible to the insinuations that Iago makes about Desdemona? What I'm going to propose as an answer to this question, my account of Othello's murderous secret, is certainly a controversial way of reading this play, and you shouldn't accept it on my say-so, any more than Othello should have believed Iago. Here I am also pushing farther an insight of Stanley Cavell's, so you should test him, too. But one of the facts about the action in this play that's quite striking, so it seems to me, when we really think about this as an acted-out narrative of how things happen, is how the conjugal embrace, the consummation of their marriage, of this newlywed couple, Othello and Desdemona, is interrupted. I believe Shakespeare intended us to realize that the marriage is never consummated, and to take this as the clue to Othello's secret.

In the opening scene, Othello and Desdemona are closeted in their honeymoon bedroom at an inn. (The name of the inn is the "Sagittary," named after the constellation Sagittarius. Sagittarius is a mythical centaur, part human, part beast, that is, horse. In astrology, the constellation governs a tension between the human and the animal. Even in this little detail, Shakespeare has focused us on the problem of reconciling the heavenly, the human, and the animal in sexuality; Iago has just taunted Desdemona's father that "you'll have your daughter covered with a Barbary horse.") They hear the mob with Desdemona's father outside. And Othello needs to leave the bedroom and come downstairs and address the mob, after telling Iago he will depend upon his perfect soul. A bit later, it turns out that there's a sudden emergency, a military emergency in Cyprus, and Othello must immediately sail away there to take care of it. Desdemona pleads that she be allowed to go along to Cyprus, or at least to follow after.

Desdemona's request to live with her husband follows upon quite a different request the Moor had just made of the Venetians.

Othello tells the assembled Venetian authorities that he is ready to go off to this new crisis with the Turks, and even says that he recognizes in himself a taste for the rigors of war, so that "the flinty and the steel couch of war" is more attractive to him than "a thrice-driven bed of down." This rhetoric of hardness and manliness is not so surprising in itself, but the context gives it a very sharp point indeed. For Othello has just been pulled from his marriage bed on his wedding night. At that moment to say one prefers a couch of stone and metal to a tender bed with one's wife – well, it is no idle rhetorical boast. Othello requests for Desdemona only that she be taken care of back in Venice in a way that's befitting of her status both as a member of a Venetian noble family and as his wife. It is suggested that Desdemona stay in her father's house, but neither the father nor the new husband want that, and Desdemona herself rejects it, too. "Nor would I there reside to put my father in impatient thoughts," she says – and what thoughts do you suppose those are? The thoughts of bestial sexuality that Iago planted in her father's mind from the street, with his taunts about black rams and white ewes, and the beast with two backs. Desdemona knows her father would be disturbed by thinking about her sexual relationship with Othello, even though he is now her husband.

So Desdemona makes her own request, different from Othello's. She begins by stating, politely but clearly, the erotic nature of her love for Othello. "That I did love the Moor to live with him, my downright violence and storm of fortunes may trumpet to the world." I am passionately in love with the Moor, she says, and my passion compels me already to violence and risk with him, as my break with my father shows. I want, she says simply, "to live with him." In Shakespeare's time, as in ours, there's something of a euphemism in this kind of context when we talk about two people "living together." The phrase clearly implies that the couple's shared life includes a sexual relationship. Desdemona may be as brave in her way as Othello is in his, but she is not willing to wait in a lonely bed, stone or not, while her man is away. "If I be left behind, a moth of peace, and he go to the war," she says, "the rites for why I love him are bereft me. Let me go with him." The rites are bereft me. What are these "rites for why I love him" of which Desdemona will not be bereft? Well, they're the very rites that Othello and Desdemona have just been interrupted from enacting, the rite of making love, which would have consummated their marriage. Shakespeare is assuming here the old Christian tradition that the sacrament of marriage is completed, not by the wedding vows alone, but only when those vows are celebrated and ratified by the first act of marital intercourse. The lovemaking itself is the sacrament, and Desdemona's word "rite" is perfectly clear and precise in this context. She will not be married if she cannot "live with" Othello. Alas, the young bride has no better luck after she has chased her husband to Cyprus. The night Desdemona arrives there, Othello is again called from bed by a street disturbance orchestrated by Iago. Othello apologizes to Desdemona, "It is the soldier's life, to have their balmy slumbers waked by strife." Othello is not likely to be apologizing for literally being awakened from sleep here. The couple's "balmy slumbers" are another way of referring to their lovemaking, just as in modern English we do not mean a couple is tired if we say they want to sleep together.

Othello supports Desdemona's request to join him in Cyprus, but he lessens its passion, and indeed rather makes it sound as if he isn't too interested in making love with his new wife. "I beg it not to please the palate of my appetite, nor to comply with heat," he says, since "the young affects" are "in me defunct." He means to assure the Venetians he won't be distracted from the business of the war by the presence of his sexy young wife. But does it not go a bit overboard to say that his sexual passions – the "young affects" – are "defunct," that is, extinguished? This would make any marriage bed, stone, steel, or down, a cold one. This is not the only passage where Othello or other characters comment that the heat of erotic passion is cooled in him because of his age. There are also many passages where a question is raised, even by Othello himself, about how this older man, with his dark skin and foreign origins, can be sexually attractive to such a beautiful young woman.

I think all of these nuptial interruptions plant in the reader's mind this question: have Othello and Desdemona consummated their marriage? Indeed, can they, given Othello's passionless condition, his "weak function," as it is once called? At least, one might wonder if there's not a part of Othello – I'm not sure I want to specify which part – that is not so very eager to consummate the marriage. I suggest Othello is confronted by a loss of his own potency, or at least a diminution of it, by this very beautiful and, as we've just seen, very passionate young woman whom he's just taken as his wife. This loss of potency is sexual, but not only sexual; it is a threat to Othello's sense of the perfection of his soul, of his freedom and self-sufficiency. In Venice, when Othello must come down to the mob from his wedding night; when they're separated by the crisis in Cyprus; and finally in Cyprus when their reunion "slumber" is disturbed: in all of these episodes, it turns out that the marital *coitus* is always *interruptus*. On all of these occasions, their marriage is disturbed from being consummated, and their marital vows do not come to full perfection in the marital act. Shakespeare assumes throughout the orthodox Christian understanding of the rites of marriage, where the consummating sexual act is the *private* completion of the sacrament of which the vows are the *public* completion.

This interruption of the rites of the nuptial bed, then, continues throughout the play, and reaches its horrible climax in the final scenes, and gives them a very particular awfulness, as a kind of Black Mass of marriage. Othello is coming to Desdemona's bed, and she knows he intends to kill her. Desdemona says to her serving woman, Iago's wife, "Put my wedding sheets on the bed." Now, that simple gesture holds within it an awful significance. Going all the way back to the Old Testament, there was a tradition that the wedding sheets start out pure and white, but in the first act of marital intercourse they will be stained by blood, a blood that's understood as the sacrifice of the woman's virginity. What does Desdemona's request for wedding sheets mean? Surely we're not to understand Desdemona to be asking that bloodstained sheets be put on her bed. She's asking that pure white sheets be put on her bed, sheets that show her willingness to be sacrificed, to become the bride of Othello. But Othello refuses to spill her blood – sexually yes, by not consummating the marriage, but he also refuses to kill her in a way that would spill her blood. He wants to kill Desdemona, but he also wants to preserve her. He imagines her as "monumental alabaster." Think of that extraordinary image. On the one hand, to make of Desdemona an alabaster monument is almost literally to put her on a pedestal. Othello makes of her something like a statue, not a perishable woman of flesh and blood, but a permanent emblem of a perfect beauty. That's one aspect of alabaster, or marble. But of course, the other aspect of alabaster is that it's used for funeral monuments. So to make something alabaster out of her, is at one and the same time to treat her as an impenetrable beauty, not a flesh and blood woman, and to treat her as something dead to you, something that deserves to be dead. Desdemona is sacrificed on her wedding sheets, but instead of the sacrifice of the completion of the wedding vow through sexual consummation, Othello sacrifices her by strangling her. Even in murdering her, he refuses to accept what she offers. (In the law of the Old Testament, the meat of a strangled animal is taboo, untouchable. In Homer's *Odyssey*, Odysseus tells his son Telemachus to put the unfaithful and lascivious serving women to the sword; but the sexually unformed young man instead hangs them. The substitution of strangling for stabbing, as an act of perverted sexual purity cast as a sacrilegious sacrifice: Homer and Shakespeare have plunged into the same awful depths.)

On this reading of the play, what's at issue for Othello is his own ability to accept his wife's sexuality as a sacrifice, and to accept his own initiation into a domesticated life. The constant interruption or avoidance of that consummation then becomes the central theme in this play. A man of Othello's particular type of greatness faces a terrible obstacle making a marriage, making of himself a spouse. To make of himself a spouse, Othello would have to accept something from Desdemona. To make of her a corpse, he need accept nothing at all. Desdemona's death preserve's Othello's unhoused free condition.

Othello's secret, then, is that he can't accept the gift of Desdemona's love without feeling unmanned. Think here of the scene, perhaps the most gorgeous speech of all in an unusually gorgeous play even by Shakespeare's standards, where Othello defends himself against the charge that he must have used witchcraft to get this beautiful white woman to fall in love with him. How could a middle-aged, dark-skinned, thick-lipped, big-nosed guy like Othello have gotten this beautiful, fair-skinned Venetian noblewoman to fall in love with him? Desdemona's father and some of the other Venetians think it had to be magic, black magic. Othello defends himself by relating the true magic behind their love. "Her father loved me and oft invited me," he says, and "questioned me the story of my life from year to year, the battles, sieges, fortunes that I have passed. I ran it through even from my boyish days to the very moment that he bade me tell it. Wherein I spoke of most disastrous chances." The word "disastrous" here carries some of its etymological meaning, meaning under a bad star. The first syllable "dis" originally meant "two" or "separate" but came to mean "bad"; and the second "aster" means "star." A disaster is something that happens under the influence of a bad star, in the astrological sense. Desdemona, though her name means "fearing bad luck," is attracted to Othello by his disasters rather than by his successes. Othello describes some of these disasters: terrible risks by land and sea, narrow escapes from deadly perils, capture and enslavement, all of which he endured. He also recited a "traveler's history" of wonders, from towering mountains and vast deserts to fantastic cannibals and men with faces in their chests. And throughout it all, Desdemona hung on every word she could, though always called away by her household duties.

Where is the witchcraft, the black magic? The witchcraft, of course, is that Othello has lived an extraordinarily romantic life. In that sense, he's lived magically, but the magic is in the poetic narrative of the life that he's lived. Othello seduced Desdemona because of his poetic power. It's not just that he happened to live such a dangerous and adventurous life. It's that he happened to be able to tell the story of that life in such a magical and romantic way. He enchants Desdemona exactly as Shakespeare enchants us. "With a greedy ear" Desdemona comes back to "devour up my discourse," says Othello, and this description of Desdemona's desire is clearly intended to have a sexual undertone to it. Othello notices Desdemona's passionate interest, and they find a time when he can tell her the whole tale without interruption. (Notice Shakespeare's nice touch in showing that the full romance requires an escape from normal domestic duties.) She's heard the story by bits and pieces, but now she wants to be able to sit down and just get the whole story without distraction. "I did consent," says this master storyteller, "and often did beguile her of her tears when I did speak of some distressful stroke that my youth suffered."

Here is the key moment: Desdemona is most attracted to the story of Othello's *suffering*. This is not primarily a story of Othello, the self-sufficient perfect soul, the free maker and absolute agent of his own life. This is a story of Othello as suffering, of Othello as the patient of his life. "My story being done," Othello says, "she gave me for my pains a world of kisses." What connection to Othello was Desdemona expressing with these passionate kisses? Not a love of his achievements, but of his sufferings, for she says of his story that it was "pitiful, wondrous pitiful." It's Othello's ability to present his hard life as a pitiful life that draws Desdemona to him. I suggest the tragedy of the play is moved by Othello's second thoughts about that way of proving himself attractive. Can being pitiful, after all, be integrated into Othello's sense of his free unhoused condition? Can he acknowledge that it's exactly his vulnerability, what makes him pitiable, that also makes him attractive to this lovely woman? What he goes on to say about how he enchanted Desdemona indicates he cannot: "She wished that heaven had made her such a man." Such a wonderful ambiguity of that line! When Desdemona wished that heaven had made her such a man, one thing she does is flirt with Othello, saying, "Oh, the man in those adventures – I wish I could meet a man like that." Of course, a man like that was sitting right there; how convenient! "The story of your life is so interesting," a woman says to a man, "I really wish I could fall in love with somebody like that." Even a soldier like Othello, who hasn't had much time to learn the subtleties of romance, would get that hint. That's one way to read what she said. But what's the other way? The other way is, Desdemona wishes that she herself had been made by heaven into that kind of man, that Desdemona wishes she could have lived Othello's life. Not the life of prim and proper maiden in Venice, but the hard life of pitiable adventure, of pain and challenge. So on the one hand Othello finds that he's attractive to Desdemona exactly to the extent that he's a man of pain, of vulnerability, lovable insofar as pitiable. And on the other hand, he finds that he's the occasion of Desdemona's own fantasy that she play the man, that she be the agent, and that he be the patient. Desdemona's passion for Othello makes her desire him, but it also makes her desire *to be* him. Can he accept that desire without giving up his own exclusive manliness?

Othello ends his account of how he enchanted Desdemona with a frank statement that pity is the center of her love. "She loved me for the dangers I had passed, and I loved her that she did pity them. This is the only witchcraft I have used." He enjoys her pity, as blind Martin enjoyed and exploited the pity of Celia in *Proof*. But he is also like Martin in distrusting pity, and feeling that it unmans him. I suggest that Othello's second thoughts and misgivings about this pity being the basis of his lovability provide a useful way to read Othello's susceptibility to Iago. If his vulnerability is what makes him lovable to Desdemona, Desdemona is very different from everybody else who loves, indeed admires Othello. They all love him because he's such a great captain, because of his self-sufficiency, because of the way that passion, that passivity cannot shake him. That's not why Desdemona loves him. But Desdemona's pitying love raises the question, Why does Othello love himself? Can Othello love himself for what Desdemona loves in him? So when we hear Othello being so receptive to Iago's slanders about Desdemona, we have, it seems to me, already been prepared for Othello's acceptance of the slander by this particular earlier speech of Othello's, where he tells us the nature of the love between Othello and Desdemona. Could it be that in the end, it's easier for Othello to make of his wife an eternal monument to virginity and at the same time a tomb, than it is to let her be a live, flesh-and-blood marriage partner in all that that implies, including as a sexual partner? Is there instead a challenge that he cannot face in letting himself be pitiable, and in letting his own weak function be at the beck and call of this beautiful young woman? I don't want to insist that this is the only way to read *Othello* as a tragedy of marriage. But it would help to explain why inside of this play, marriage really is a kind of hell.

The lover plays the cynic in Plato's *Phaedrus*

It was not Plato's way to horrify us with a direct portrayal of the violence of skepticism and cynicism. But we find in Plato as much awareness of the violence of the rejection of love as we find in *Othello* and Shakespeare's other great tragic romances. The Greek master and the English master knew the same things about romantic cynicism. But their thoughtful moods are quite distinct, Plato tending more toward the comic. We have already thought about the many timid lovers at the beginning of the *Symposium*, in all their comic stumbling as they look for love while still refusing to abandon themselves to it. In his *Phaedrus*, Plato experimented with a radical rejection of love, rather than merely with its timid avoidance, but even then he has Socrates treat this topic with his characteristic cheerfulness. After the dark of *Othello*, we should welcome a little light.

Plato's *Phaedrus* is named after the same young man we met as the first speaker in the *Symposium*. Phaedrus is again the champion of the beloved, especially in relationships between younger men (like himself, though he is a bit too old to still be a beloved) and older men (like Socrates, though he is a bit too old to be a lover). This very handsome young man is surprised to meet Socrates as they're both on their way to take a walk out in the country away from the city. Plato uses this already old theme – flight from the city into the country – to put Socrates and Phaedrus, and us readers as well, into a honeymoon mood. (Shakespeare likes to use the same device in his romantic comedies, where lovers flee into a forest to be free of the limitations of civilization. We'll think more about this flight into "The Green World," as critics often call it, when we discuss *A Midsummer Night's Dream*.) Socrates is almost never to be found outside the city, because, as he tells

Phaedrus, "I can't learn anything from trees and stones, since they won't converse with me like men will." But today he takes his habitual bare feet outside, and the two men cross a cool stream to recline in soft grass, finding shade under a tall plane tree, called in Greek a *platanos*. Their conversation will take place in Plato's pastoral bedroom. So Socrates is presented to us as already outside his everyday self, with one foot in romantic ecstasy, you might say. Socrates's habitual bare feet here are luxurious and sensuous; in the *Symposium*, they were a mark of his simplicity and toughness, when Aristodemus came upon him uncharacteristically putting on his fancy shoes. Dressed up or nude, Socrates's feet in both dialogues enter the realm of Dionysus and Aphrodite. Socrates may not have entered that realm often, Plato seems to suggest, but when he did, he had a great time.

It turns out, we learn, that Phaedrus has just come from listening to one of the great writers and orators of the day, a man named Lysias. Lysias has been showing off a speech about erotic love, and Phaedrus liked the speech so much, he has gone off to the seclusion of the country to study it and learn it by heart, to memorize it. After some friendly bickering, Socrates commands Phaedrus to read the speech from the scroll hidden in his pocket. Phaedrus is actually happy to be forced, even though he had been acting coy, as if he didn't want to deliver the speech. Plato creates a complex ambiguity, then, about just whom we will be hearing in this speech: Lysias, the original writer; or the hypothetical speaker for whom Lysias wrote the speech; or Phaedrus, quoting Lysias's writing with approval; or Socrates, through his forcing of Lysias's speech from Phaedrus's mouth. (It is actually more involved than this, because there are questions about whether the written text is or is not the same as the writer speaking; but enough is enough!) We seem to assume new identities and lose old ones in the enchanted realm of erotic love, and Plato plays with these unsettled selves. In the speech that has captured Phaedrus's fancy, Lysias writes for someone trying to persuade an attractive young person that he would do better to grant his romantic attentions – by which Lysias means especially his sexual favors – to someone who, like the speaker, appreciates the young man's beauty, but has not fallen in love with him. Take my advice, say the words Lysias puts in the speaker's mouth, and give your erotic favors to a non-lover. And since when people talk about love, they mostly talk about themselves, Lysias is also insinuating, give your sexual favors to me, since I am that someone who doesn't love you. No matter who the "real" speaker is, one can't imagine a more complete and cynical rejection of love.

This speech and Phaedrus's fancy for it immediately raise two questions: How could one argue that a relationship with a non-lover is better than one with a lover?; and Why would a man like Phaedrus, champion of beloveds, find such an argument attractive? Here we have a star case of something that is typical of Plato's genius as a philosopher. He is interested in arguments, of course, and can analyze them as well as any philosopher ever could. But Plato is always interested, too, in why a particular kind of person would be attracted by certain arguments, would *want* them to be true. In fact, later in the *Phaedrus,* Socrates tells Phaedrus that the truly skilled speaker must understand the soul of the person he speaks with. It's not enough for philosophical arguments to stand alone in abstract truth; they must find the student, and move that student toward the truth. The best speaking, Socrates says, is a way of leading souls.

What could suggest such a paradoxical result, that a beloved should prefer a non-lover over a lover? Well, Lysias tells us in great detail why it would be better to avoid someone who has fallen in love with you. The problem, it seems, is that a lover is by nature a madman, someone who's out of his mind. And so to put up with a lover is to put up with somebody who will do all sorts of crazy things. Lysias's speech is to a large extent a cataloguing of all of the stupidities that people fall into when they fall in love. More particularly, Lysias's speech lets us see how inconvenient it is to be treated as the object of somebody's crazy love. Someone who's fallen in love with you, claims Lysias, will be so possessive of you that he will have a bad effect on the rest of your life. He'll try to take you away from your family and friends because he's jealous of your time, and because he's paranoid that your family and friends might think he's not good for you. He wants all of your mental energies focused on him in a kind of self-protective obsession. (So Lysias ascribes to every lover one of the typical strategies of an abusive romantic partner, namely, isolating the other party.) At least as bad, Lysias goes on to say, someone who's fallen in love with you will try to keep you more stupid and less manly than you otherwise would be. Your lover wants you to be completely dependent on him, so he tries to keep you immature in body and mind. As we might say, your lover wants you to be cute. There's really not a Greek word for our English word "cute," but our ambivalence about cuteness points to the same problem Lysias is putting his finger on. Is it a good thing to be cute? Does anyone aspire to be cute? One hopes not. The line between being cute and being stupid is a very thin one. Your lover will think, says Lysias, that the very behavior that in other circumstances you'd be embarrassed by because it make you seem light-headed, giggly, silly, and girlish, is why you're so precious.

As in the *Symposium*, these anxieties about whether love is unmanly are focused in Plato's Greece on young men, but they are anxieties equally for men and women. Does a kind of silliness and immaturity go along with being the object of someone's love? Older people sometimes say falling in love makes them feel young again; but how attractive is a man or woman of mature years behaving like a teenager? (Thomas Mann's novella *Death in Venice*, which we'll consider later, has an excruciating example of how being crazy in love makes an older man lose his dignity.) Do even teenagers really want to come off as immature in these ways? But for some reason a lover is charmed when his beloved lisps like a child, with a body fair and soft, and possibly hairless. So your lover, Lysias all but suggests, will try to shape you into his image of a very agreeable pet. This is true physically, where your lover will tend to find you more attractive insofar as your body stays youthful and adolescent. But it's also true about the beloved's mind. Which will a lover remember and value more, sound judgments or sweet nothings?

So, if you are reckless enough to attach yourself to someone who's out of his mind, crazy in love with you, you will become worse in body and soul, less manly and more stupid. On the other hand, writes Lysias for his speaker, if you give your sexual favors to someone in his right mind, who appreciates your attractiveness but isn't crazy about you, you won't be embarrassed by having someone do stupid things like sleep outside your door at night, or have songs written about your family's heroic ancestors, both of which were traditional things lovers did in ancient Athens – you can supply your own examples of dopey things that people with a crush on you might do to get your attention nowadays. Maybe some of them will still have songs written about you and your family. Taylor Swift, a preternaturally astute articulator of the contemporary world of Dionysus and Aphrodite, could take commissions.

So Lysias claims the non-lover, the rational guy – and of course the speaker is talking about himself – will be your mentor and introduce you into adult society, a nice arrangement that reminds us very much of Pausanias's speech from the *Symposium*. He'll educate you and help you become more cultured, not to mention more connected, more "networked," as we say today. So the non-lover's focus on your soul doesn't ask for you to be a silly, giggly pet, but rather to be a respectable young man (or woman) that the non-lover can present with some pride as a kind of student, as a protégé.

Now, this speech is very much at home in a cultural situation where there's a lot of anxiety about erotic love of the sort we've already explored in the *Symposium*, anxiety that erotic love must involve some loss of control, some dangerous riskiness of identity meltdown. This anxiety seems to me as alive in America as it was in ancient Athens. We hear purveyors of this anxiety proclaim, as boldly as Lysias did, that it is better for a young person who is on the social ascent, a young person of ambition, not to get entangled in all of that romantic nonsense. One might expect these prophets, if their advice were sincerely grounded in the dangers of erotic identity meltdown, simply to preach the avoidance of sex and its enchantments altogether. Pausanias or Lysias or their contemporary versions might have given a speech about love that said, "Really, you should stop having sex and just get an education, start a career." But of course they didn't and don't say that. Pausanias justified getting sex from his beloved by claiming that he was his beloved's educator. Lysias, in his speech as the non-lover, tries much the same move, but it suffers from much the same problem. This insincere preaching forces us to ask, if rational control is really all that great, and if erotic identity meltdown is all that bad, why are you telling this beautiful young man to give anyone his sexual favors at all? If it's really all about his mind, what is your hand doing on his thigh?

It's hard to believe Lysias was entirely serious in this speech praising the non-lover over the lover. Perhaps he just wanted to show off his ability to defend even the most implausible positions. But whatever Lysias may have had in mind when he was showing off this speech, Phaedrus is making his own use of it. That's one of the magical things about a written text: whatever the writer meant by it, it's available for other people to take it up and use it for their own purposes. Later in the dialogue, Socrates suggests rather darkly that writings are promiscuous, willing to play with anyone who lays hands on them. What game is Phaedrus laying with Lysias's speech?

Many romantic invitations are proffered playfully, without being directly acknowledged. This indirection saves face for both parties if the invitation is declined, but it also gives one party the chance to teach the other party what he should say, to teach him his lines in this love story. Shakespeare's richest treatment of this theme, of the teaching made possible by indirect flirtation, is probably *As You Like It*. Rosalind disguises herself as a man with the androgynous name Ganymede, and actually volunteers to teach her love interest, Orlando, how he should go about wooing his love interest, which is Rosalind herself. But this sort of indirection can be as simple as a woman saying to a man, or even just within his hearing, "I heard about this new restaurant that sounds interesting." If he takes the hint, she has succeeded in teaching him exactly how to assume to himself the words to make a romantic opening to her, namely, "Would you be interested in having dinner at the new restaurant?" Notice that the indirection is still ongoing in the man's response, because all that has been directly expressed is a mutual interest IN THE RESTAURANT, even if the undertext of flirtation, of interest in each other, is present though unacknowledged. Much less indirect would be the woman saying, perhaps ruefully, "I wish someone would be interested in taking me on a date," since the man needs to assume to himself the words "interested in you," not just "interested in the restaurant," if he is going to respond. If the woman wanted to be more direct still, she could say, "Let's go on a date," where the man cannot silently decline to assume the offered words, and must either directly accept or decline. But this bluntness wouldn't teach the man his proper lines, and indirection has the advantage of avoiding unmediated rejection and the potential loss of face and the embarrassment that goes with it. Of course, the disadvantage of flirtatious indirection is that the object of it may not take the hint. What one interested party thinks is an invitation so thinly veiled as to be all but a naked proposal, the object may find so wrapped in doubtfulness that he cannot see how to take up its words. The flirtatious invitation constructs for its object an identity to assume, but anything from lack of desire to fearfulness to cluelessness can leave the invitation unaccepted, the role unplayed. But negotiating one's way through the tangle of identities on offer is no small part of the exhilaration of romance.

Phaedrus's game of indirect flirting has much in common with the version played between Desdemona and Othello. Othello, though he presents himself as a military man unaccustomed to the games of love, shows himself to have some erotic talent. He has noticed how Desdemona hangs on the stories of his adventures, receives them "with a greedy ear," when she hears them by bits and pieces during his audiences with her father. So he makes the first indirect move, still leaving plenty of space for mutual deniability. He manages to get her to ask him – "to draw from her a prayer" – to tell his story fully and without interruption, which will have the convenient consequence of requiring that they be alone, if not outside the city, then at least outside the normal routine of their duties, military and domestic. Like Phaedrus by Socrates, Othello figures out how to be forced by Desdemona to give the very speech he most wants to give. When he had finished the whole beguiling tale, Desdemona "wished that heaven had made her such a man," Othello says, and she tells him, "If you have a friend that loves me, just teach him how to tell your story, and that will woo me." In other words, Desdemona invites Othello to own his own speech, to become his own friend, as an act of seducing her. She constructs the role he can assume, and encourages Othello to acknowledge his own speech, his life story, as a lover's speech, as an act of wooing. All you have to do, Othello, is to mean what you say. "Upon this hint," a hint with so thin a veil Othello need be no visionary to see through it, he makes an explicit proposal to Desdemona. The tragedy lurking behind what looks like a successful climax of indirect flirting in acknowledged love is that Othello will not accept the role Desdemona's pity plotted for him, and he falls instead under Iago's malevolent direction.

Plato has staged a yet more elaborate version of this masterful mutual seduction. Socrates happens upon Phaedrus as they're both on their way for a walk out in nature, where they'll be alone. In this romantic setting, conducive to a honeymoon mood, Phaedrus knows Socrates has a greedy ear – Socrates says himself he is sick with the love of speeches – and Phaedrus can count on this demonic man to "devour up the discourse" he is carrying in his pocket. Now, Othello had in his "pocket" the story of his own life, which made himself attractive to Desdemona when he managed to get the speech forced from him. Phaedrus has a speech at one more level of indirection. The speech he allows Socrates to force from him isn't intended, as Othello's speech was, to present the speaker, Phaedrus himself, as attractive. Instead, it offers an identity Phaedrus thinks Socrates might be willing to assume, as non-lover, to make a romantic offer to Phaedrus. He knows Socrates is a philosopher and famous for his self-control and rationality in addition to his love of discourse. Socrates will not make any romantic overture that isn't appropriate for a man upholding this philosophical identity. Lysias's speech praising the rational non-lover delights Phaedrus because, if he responds to Lysias's words from Socrates's mouth, Phaedrus will be able to accept Socrates's invitation while leaving Socrates with his cover story, his professed identity, of being self-controlled, rather than crazy in love. Phaedrus is like Othello in being the one "forced" to speak; but he is like Desdemona in being the one teaching the other party how to tell a story that will woo him.

Phaedrus gets Socrates to force him to give the very speech that Phaedrus would love to teach to Socrates, so that Socrates could use it both to maintain his own sense of identity and to seduce Phaedrus. The different levels of deniability here have been managed with real erotic genius. I was tempted to try to set out all these indirections in a diagram, like the London Underground map; but they are erotic, not geometric, necessities, after all. Phaedrus has in effect said to Socrates, "I am ready to give you my romantic attentions if you say Lysias's words to me, acknowledging those words as your own words." But Socrates is not as willing to assume the identity of "rational non-lover" as Phaedrus thought he would be. Perhaps Phaedrus did not know Socrates's identity as well as he thought, or he may even think that in the game of love, all identities are at play, so that he and Socrates would have no settled identities that would block erotic satisfaction.

Socrates responds to Phaedrus's complex offer by making a counter-offer of his own. After criticizing the disorder he sees in Lysias's speech, Socrates provokes Phaedrus to invert their relationship. Phaedrus insists that Socrates give a better speech, if he finds so much lacking in Lysias's, and he uses the same language Socrates had used against him, forcing Socrates to out-Lysias Lysias himself. But Socrates intensifies the flirtation by removing one veil of indirection, because he does not give a speech of a non-lover at all. Socrates says being a non-lover is just a pose for his speaker. He will propose a speech appropriate for a lover pretending to be a non-lover to seduce a hard-to-get beloved. Socrates, speaking as an intensified Lysias, will say, in a more orderly way, many of the same things Phaedrus had quoted, but he will really be constructing a role to be assumed by someone crazy in love, even while pretending to be a rational non-lover.

The professed rationality of Socrates's speech, then, is nothing more than a rationalization, a mask for an erotic passion that the speaker refuses to make fully public. Socrates's new and improved, more rational version of Lysias's already rational praise of the sane non-lover, is a mask for erotic madness. The surface control projected in Lysias's speech, and in Socrates's improved version of it, is revealed by Socrates to be false, a vehicle for erotic identity meltdown, for a loss of control. Phaedrus offered Socrates a speech that would give Socrates a way to approach Phaedrus without admitting he is in love. Socrates responds with a speech that gives the beloved plausible deniability that he is attaching himself to a madman, even while letting the veil slip enough for the observant beloved, like Phaedrus, to see the deception. Socrates keeps the lover behind the veil of indirection, but the veil has worn much thinner. Phaedrus has only to reach through that veil to touch the speaker, Socrates, not just as some person who *might* give such a speech to seduce an attractive young man, but as the very man who *is* saying it, to seduce Phaedrus.

One passage in particular jumps out of Socrates's revision of Lysias's speech. Recall that Lysias's speech argued that the crazy lover wants the beloved to be made effeminate and adolescent, both in soul and in body. Socrates has his speaker, the lover playing a non-lover, make a much more pointed version of this charge against the lover. The lover, says Socrates for the lover disguised as a non-lover, will deprive the beloved, not just of intellectual cultivation in general, but specifically of *philosophy*. Every negative of the lover implies a complementary positive for the non-lover, so indirectly Socrates takes Lysias's charge that a lover will cause you to be silly, effeminate, and immature, and transforms it into an invitation: form a relationship with a non-lover, and you will be initiated into philosophy. This explicit mention of how the non-lover will make you philosophical all but pulls away the veil, and almost becomes a direct proposal by Socrates to Phaedrus. Socrates never directly says, "At this very moment, Phaedrus, I'm thinking of you and me"; but surely Phaedrus was thinking it, when he heard the word "philosophy" in Socrates's mouth, even if Socrates was speaking his part behind the double veil of the lover playing the non-lover. Upon this hint of philosophy, who could blame Phaedrus for thinking Socrates is saying something deeply personal and extremely candid about why Phaedrus should be attracted to him? Without the veil, Socrates seems to be saying he wants to be Phaedrus's lover, so long as Phaedrus allows him to keep up the cover story of being the rational non-lover.

But Socrates couldn't give such a speech in his own name, and he doesn't mean what he is about to say. "So I don't get distracted by you, Phaedrus," he says, "I'm going to cover my head with my cloak while I'm speaking." So this whole speech of the pretend non-lover is delivered with Socrates's face physically veiled in his cloak, a dramatization of his refusal to own these words.

What is Plato up to in this complicated play of mirrors, where we can't tell who owns which words or who is seducing whom? And why does philosophy provide the punchline when, with his head veiled for maximum deniability, Socrates intensifies Lysias's claim that only a non-lover can be good for your mind? On the surface, Socrates seems to have given the honeymoon away, falling in with the anti-romantic, macho, abstemious excluders of wine and women of the *Symposium*. But Plato's darker purpose is to expose the philosophical cynic as a pretender. Lysias's speech, made more pointed and intense in Socrates's veiled speech, praises reason and philosophy by slandering love. Its mood is more comic than Othello's violent rejection of love, but its spirit is much the same. The Moor and the non-lover, Shakespeare and Plato show, are both hiding a lover beneath their cool exterior, pretending they want knowledge, when really they just fear love and lust for control.

Plato searches for a way for philosophy to embrace romantic love rather than to reject it. The cynic seems tough-minded, and can even seem to be pursuing a perfect soul when he harshly rejects silly nonsense, rather as Apollodorus tried to imitate Socrates by abusing his friends. But here as in the *Symposium*, Plato rejects the violent skepticism of that image of philosophy, and when Socrates revises Lysias's non-lover as a hidden lover, the first two speeches of the *Phaedrus* do what the opening of the *Symposium* did: they cast a shadow of weakness and dishonesty over philosophy's noisy insistence to tell the unadorned truth about erotic love by policing the boundaries, keeping Dionysus's intoxication and Aphrodite's pleasures outside its limits. Both dialogues, as we shall see, move toward a more adequate view of love, and of philosophy. In the next speech in the *Phaedrus*, Socrates will uncover his head and tell a story of why we should abandon ourselves to the dangers of love, and give up our safely cynical selves to accept the ecstasies of erotic identity meltdown, with the hope of finding a truer identity, an identity we can only find when we look in the eyes of our beloved.

Love trumps truth? Alan Rudolph's *The Secret Lives of Dentists*

The cynical non-lover wears the mask of the philosopher. Like jealous Othello and blind Martin, the cynic thinks himself devoted to truth. But his demand for truth veils his rejection of love. His slogan is, I won't believe without proof; but his secret motive is to avoid trust. The cynic's perfection and self-sufficiency – at least he claims to be free and impossible to pity – means more to him than any beloved, and this incurable distrust puts a demon in his heart. He lives constantly in the hellish state that the French philosopher Descartes famously recommended as philosophy's starting point: under the hypothesis that we are being deceived by an evil demon.

Othello and the non-lover both make a demand for knowledge and control that is inconsistent with the abandon of romantic love. I want to end these thoughts with another of my favorite movies, *The Secret Lives of Dentists* (2003), directed by Alan Rudolph and written by Craig Lucas, from a short story by Jane Smiley, "The Age of Grief." This movie presents us with a man, a dentist named Dave, who is the perfect opposite of Othello. Othello demanded evidence so he could kill love. Dave refuses evidence so he can keep love alive.

The movie opens with dentist Dave (Campbell Scott) and his dentist wife Dana (Hope Davis) with patients at the dental offices they share. Dave is meeting a new, rather difficult patient, whom we know only by his last name, Slater (Denis Leary). Slater is a jazz trumpeter, and he doesn't want Dave's repair of his teeth to disturb his ability to play his horn. Slater also will not obey Dave's directions not to bite down on his repaired tooth. In the other room, Dana is talking to a patient about Giuseppe Verdi's opera *Nabucco*, in which Dana will be performing in the chorus for a local production. *Nabucco* is the story of the captivity of the Israelites in Babylon, and it is probably relevant to the movie that the most famous piece from this opera, a version of Psalm 137 known as "Va, pensiero" ("Fly, thought"), is a lament for lost freedom, sung by the chorus of female Israelite slaves. The opera, Dana says, is "all the things you can't really say in life, lifted and purified by the music." Jazz and opera may be different kinds of music, but the movie sees them both as expressions of freedom and beauty. Already this first scene sets us up for the movie's central question: Can we expect married love to live up to the standard of music, of art? The actress Susan in Dubus's "Falling in Love" wanted just such a life, and sacrificed child and husband to have it.

Dave and Dana have three young daughters, played well by the young actresses and directed brilliantly by Alan Rudolph. We see them at the dinner table before Dana goes off to the final dress rehearsal, Dana telling the girls how inspiring she finds the music. When Dana gets home very late, she seems rather sad and distracted. It doesn't help her mood that Dave wakes from sleep barely long enough to say, "I love you." Her marriage has fallen into a boring routine, where I-love-yous are just empty sounds got between sleep and waking. We hear the frustration in her voice when Dana says, "Remember when a year seemed like a long time?" To come from the intensified beauty of the opera, an opera about slaves longing to be free, makes her real life weary, flat, and stale. "Real life," we call it: but perhaps reality is her moments on stage? Might the exhilaration and ecstasy of playing a role be more real than dragging oneself through a plotless marriage? Dana's boredom depresses and sullies her spirit, and she longs to be uplifted and purified.

The next evening is the performance, and Dave and the two older girls drive with Dana to the theater. Dana gives a last explanation to the girls of what the chorus will be singing – "We're all singing for redemption" – and joins the cast, while Dave parks the car and takes the girls to their seats. But before the show starts, Dave realizes Dana has forgotten a good luck token the girls had given her, a rabbit's foot. Dave goes backstage to bring it to his wife, but he stops suddenly when he catches a glimpse of Dana, apparently being kissed by another man.

This is the Othello moment in the movie, only Dave has rather better evidence than a lost handkerchief. During the performance, in a moment of sudden thought, his mind races through all those events that have made up their life together, from first meeting as students, to Dana pulling her first tooth, to buying their first house and the birth of their daughters. All of it, years of growing love, now at the stake of a single glimpse of a kiss. After the show, he takes the girls backstage, where the Italian conductor congratulates Dana warmly, but ignores Dave. Of course, Dave suspects this is the man he glimpsed kissing his wife earlier.

How will Dave respond? Dave is the sort of man who would prefer to avoid conflict. We have just seen an example of his distaste for conflict when he and the girls took their seats before the performance began. Slater, Dave's disgruntled patient, had suddenly appeared in the audience, loudly berating Dave for his ruined tooth repair. Dave is embarrassed but stays calm, and asks Slater to come back for another repair. But the example of Slater starts to work on Dave's mind as he ponders what to do about his suspicions about Dana's infidelity. There is a part of Dave that would like to be more assertive, to take charge, to fight back. In Dave's mind, an unconscious thought takes shape: maybe I should be more like the rude, blunt, manly Slater, this jazz musician who isn't constrained by politeness. So Dave is torn between avoiding conflict and being more manly and combative, between what his regular Dave self would do and what his secret Slater self would like to do. Which part of Dave will win out?

When they come home from the performance, Dana is more depressed than ever. "I can't believe it's over," she says. "It's so beautiful. I could sing it every night forever." Dave, in typical male fashion trying to comfort Dana by giving her advice rather than by acknowledging her pain, tells her to cheer up, there will be other chances to sing. You might as well cheer a parent mourning for a dead child by saying, "You can always have another one." Dana responds with understandable anger, "I don't want to sing *other* things"; she wants this experience, this very feeling of exhilaration, to be her normal state, to return day after day and night after night. In short, she wants her life to come up to the standard of opera, a life composed by Verdi. Dave feels inadequate to this woman's grief, tries to change the subject, mentions being insulted by Slater, looks uncomfortable and incompetent; and his wife ignores him. "It's a waltz," she says, still musing on the opera and on the way it let her be a truer self, but only inside the theater. "That's what's so tragic. You could dance to it; but you can't."

The next morning, Dana is up early, and says she's leaving to pick up a newspaper. But why is she so nicely dressed, and why is she gone unusually long? Is she "dancing" with her sexy Italian? Dave is seeing more things as evidence, more ocular proof. But at night in bed, he isn't ready yet to let the Slater self out, and he avoids a conversation Dana starts to open with him. "I wish we were closer," she says, but Dave pretends to be asleep. Back at the dental office the next day, Dave says to his wife as she leaves rather early in the afternoon, "See you around six." Is Dana being evasive when she answers, "Six-thirty, sometime"? Has she planned a little "meeting" with a lover? Back home, Dave is having dinner with the girls, when Dana finally arrives, an hour late. "Oh, good, Mommy's home!" Dave says cheerfully to the girls. But his mind flashes back to the glimpsed kiss backstage.

The evidence is getting harder to avoid, and Dana clearly has something she wants to say to Dave. "Do you like me?" she asks him one night, as she watches a movie on television after the girls are in bed. "I mean, if you weren't sleeping with me, would you want to talk with me and have lunch with me? Do you think we're friends?" Dave doesn't know what to say, but he begins fondling her as she speaks; sex, not conversation, is his answer to her question about whether he would want to talk to her if they weren't sexual partners. We are forced to answer Dana's last question: No, you are not friends with your husband. But is that the right standard for a marriage? Is it perhaps too much to ask? As they drift toward lovemaking, Dana voices her dispirited thought, that she expected her marriage to be "more like a movie." Of course, her marriage is a movie, the movie Alan Rudolph is showing to us, a movie with a plot about how real life doesn't have the same intensity and beauty as scripted life. The scene asks us viewers to consider whether the fantasy of having a "movie life" is destructive of the only life we have. Expecting marriage to be as romantic as a movie, and your spouse to always be as fun to talk to as your best friend, might be a sure way to put yourself into a sad story. The next morning, Dana leaves early again.

Dave is reaching a crisis where he must decide what to do about his suspicions, and take a side in the dispute between the conflict-avoiding Dave self and the conflict-confronting Slater self. From this point, the movie presents this crisis to us by taking the Dave-Slater dispute out of Dave's mind, and putting it into the world. Slater starts to appear to Dave, to give him advice and to urge him to be more of a man, to take charge of the situation. (This movie came out just after a more famous movie, *Fight Club*, had used the same device, taking a voice from a character's head and making it appear as a real person, giving advice and urging to manliness. I find Rudolph's comic use of the device more effective than the more earnest use in *Fight Club*.) The first Slater appearance happens after Dana has again left the office rather early, and Dave is driving to pick up the girls from school. Slater is in the car, and to challenge Dave's manliness, says, "You're kind of like the mommy here." When Dana arrives home rather late, Slater is there, coaching Dave to be assertive. Under Slater's direction, Dave kisses Dana, and Slater puts Dave's hand on Dana's breast. But when Dave asks Dana what she's been doing, she again seems evasive. "Just the usual," she says. "The usual," Slater mockingly repeats to Dave, "isn't that nice." Slater forces the thought on Dave that "the usual" is probably meeting her lover. During the family's dinner, Slater keeps pushing Dave to let his anger show. The youngest daughter refuses to eat, and overturns her plate. "Where's the booze?" Slater says, and Dave carries the girl away, as we hear him shouting at her while the other two girls and Dana fidget over their food. When Dave comes back to the table, Dana criticizes Dave for being so harsh with the little girl. Slater urges Dave not to tolerate this challenge to his manliness. He puts a fireplace poker next to Dave on the table, and says, "Kill her; I would." (Slater's offer of this particular weapon is funny because a poker is a cliché weapon in old murder movies.) Dave snaps at Dana, "Admit that every day is worse." Under his breath, but loud enough to stun Dana and the girls, and himself, too, for the first time he lets a Slater thought slip out into the open, in his speech: "I could kill you."

Of course, Dave doesn't really mean this, does he? The mild dentist hasn't become a murderous Moor, right? He tries to smooth over the shock, telling the girls, "You can't control your thoughts, but you mustn't act on them." Dave drives off in the car to clear his mind and gather his thoughts, and Slater is in the passenger seat. He stops at an empty part of the city, gets out of the car, and screams. Slater screams too, and asks Dave what he really wants. "I wish my wife loved me," he answers, "I wish she'd look at me with desire instead of regret." Slater prods him, "Why don't you come right out and ask her? Personally speaking, I'd rather know one way or the other." Slater at this crucial point, the fulcrum of the movie, has become the voice of reason, the voice of knowledge, the voice of Othello's philosophy. You are like a blind man, Dave, refusing to look at an incriminating photograph; how can you refuse to develop it? Proof, proof, proof; kill, kill, kill. But the Dave self has an answer to Slater's insistence on knowing the truth. I am avoiding asking my wife about her infidelity, Dave says, because "then I have to do something about it." It is hard to decide if Dave is being a weak man, or a good husband and father, when he gives this answer. Maybe he is being both.

Dave decides to try one of the traditional ways a couple rekindles their romantic spark: he suggests that the family head out to the country for a little vacation. Dana approves of the plan, but she says she will come later, and Dave drives to their country house with the children. Slater, of course, tags along, and Dave can't escape Slater's insinuations about why Dana didn't come with them. "What do you suppose he's doing to her right this second? Maybe she's dead," says Slater, and Dave imagines Dana with various lovers, then identifying her dead body from her dental records. Like Othello, he is tortured by fantasies of his wife's sexuality and fantasies of his revenge. But unlike Othello, Dave takes extraordinary measures to avoid having proof. Dana arrives very late that night, as Dave hides outside the house. "I know you're out there!" she calls, but he does not answer, he tells Slater, because "she's determined to tell me; see that look on her face." He wakes early the next morning and keeps busy with such noisy activities Dana can't get a chance to talk with him, cooking breakfast, mowing the lawn, and using the leafblower. When they return home, Dave imagines a happier conversation they might have had when Dana arrived late to the country. In his fantasy, she says, "I missed you so much today. I love you." She explains she had to stay late because a pipe burst at the office, and she comforts him, "Did you think I was having an affair?" But when Dave awakes from his dream of renewed love, Slater is there again. "Somebody's throwing her the bone, big boy," says Slater's crude voice. The Slater in Dave fantasizes about escaping all this domestic turmoil, wife and children both. "These children should be struck," says Slater, and every parent will recognize the sound of that irritation.

"If I let her tell me about it, we'll have to do something about it," says Dave, so he continues to play for time, to be patient. He is tempted when Slater, trumpet in hand, invites him, "Dump the evil bitch; put the kids up for adoption. Come on tour with us. You know you want to." After all, there is a part of Dave, just as there is in Dana, that would like his marriage to be like a show, an expression of beauty and freedom rather of work and commitment. The evidence has become so clear that people at the dental office are starting to talk. Dana cancels her afternoon appointments, and one assistant whispers to the other, "Do you believe me now?" At dinner that evening, the oldest daughter asks where Mom is, and Dave puts the girls to bed without her returning. It is the first time Dana has been gone overnight. Slater can't understand how Dave puts up with this final insult. "Why are you so devoted to this?" he asks. Dave reflects on all his efforts to avoid knowing, and on what he is willing to do to live with his wife and children. Living with these people, his own family: it's the only answer he has to why love is more important to him than knowledge. "To have this, what I have," he responds to Slater. In the morning, Dana returns and sits down at the table, site of so many family moments. "Until last night," says Dave "I thought I might be misreading the signals. No?" Dana doesn't answer him directly; her thought goes beyond this moment of revelation to her husband to its potential consequence for their family, and she asks, "How are the girls?" Dave (with some prodding from Slater, the last advice Dave will receive from him), responds "I'll ask the questions. Are you leaving or staying?" Dana's one word says everything Dave needs to know: "Staying." The youngest daughter calls for her daddy, and Dave responds, "Just a minute, sweetie," then turns to Dana and says, "I don't want to know who it is; I don't want to know what you did." And with that, the Slater voice disappears. The truth of love is trust, not revelation.

I've talked with many viewers, including many of my own students, who dislike this movie. They are as frustrated with Dave's avoidance of knowledge as Slater is. Such viewers are, I suppose, making a certain sort of philosophical demand on human life. But I worry they are more like Othello than Socrates, clutching knowledge as a tool or weapon, looking to get control over love, even at the cost of spouse and children. Beneath this veil of toughness, though, I think they are lovers, too; and I have hope they will live with more abandon than their words will own.

Chapter Four
EMPTY WOUND AND FULL HEART

Plato begins the *Symposium* by dramatizing ways we avoid the exhilarations and ecstasies of love, clutching to a false self-sufficiency. Like most people in his place and time, and many in ours, Plato's characters defend this false ideal as a narrow manliness. Of course, the false image can be embraced by women as much as by men, something Woody Allen brings out well in the character of Hannah. Being tough rather than soft, silencing the flute and keeping the wine in the bottle: philosophy has always played with this self-image. But Aphrodite and Dionysus can't be kept out of romantic love forever, and it should be no surprise that the next two speakers, the theater men Aristophanes and Agathon, bring the gods roaring back in. Both break through the all-male atmosphere Phaedrus and Pausanias established, and laugh at the silly claims to scientific control of love made by the medical man Eryximachus.

To compete with the manly ideal of Achilles presented by Phaedrus, these two devotees of Aphrodite and Dionysus present a new ideal, the ideal of the *androgyne*. The word "androgyne" combines the Greek word *andro-*, meaning "man" in an emphatically male sense, and *gyne*, meaning "woman." Aristophanes and Agathon celebrate the integration of the male and female into one romantic life and one personality. They also both return to a model of the experience of love that we saw playfully introduced in the banter when Socrates first arrived at the drinking party: the model of fullness and emptiness. Agathon had arranged for Socrates to recline on his couch, hoping some of Socrates's wisdom would flow into him, like wine from a full goblet into an empty one. Aristophanes sees romantic longing as the sign of our emptiness: love is a form of need. Agathon takes the opposite view, and celebrates love as an overflowing fullness of the human heart. In this and the next chapter, I want to focus on Aristophanes's views. Agathon, you'll remember, had challenged Socrates to a contest in wisdom, to be judged by Dionysus, god of wine and theater. So we'll think about Agathon when we return to Socrates's own speech.

The wounded androgyne

For many readers, the speech of Aristophanes is the highlight of Plato's *Symposium*. It penetrates to the heart of our own ideas about love, ideas that emphasize the emotional bond and intimacy of lovers. Plato emphasized how important Aristophanes's speech is in a number of ways. Most important is that Plato lets Aristophanes tell the very best story in a dialogue full of good storytelling. Aristophanes makes up a myth about where human beings come from and why sexual love is so important to us, a story so interesting, so funny, and so wise, that if the few pages where Plato has Aristophanes tell this story were all that the wreckage of the centuries had left to us of Plato's writings, we would still know he was one of the great masters. Second is that in his own speech, Socrates responds more pointedly to Aristophanes's speech than to any of the others. And third is that Plato has discreetly contrived to make Aristophanes's the central speech in the whole dialogue. Plato often made the central position in his dialogues especially important. In the *Symposium*, he has given us a hint of this by having the order of the speeches brought into prominence. Aristophanes would have given the third speech, but because he has hiccups his speech is delayed, and he and Eryximachus switch spots. This exchange of speaking positions is stressed by both Eryximachus and Aristophanes. This rearrangement allows Plato to do something particularly interesting. It will turn out that there are seven speeches. By having Eryximachus and Aristophanes change places, it makes Aristophanes the fourth speech and therefore the central speech. Now, the dialogue in effect has two centers: one is the central speech based on counting all of the speeches, and the other is the center based on the length of the entire dialogue. So by drawing our attention to the order of the speeches, Plato is able to show us that in a certain sense this dialogue has two centers, and Aristophanes is one of them. The other center, of course, is the speech of Socrates, a speech that he says he learned from a woman named Diotima. Aristophanes's hiccups, we've seen, are a kind of comic response to Eryximachus's own sense of the medical art, as the art that can control the experiences of love. Now we see that these hiccups also allow Plato to control the order of the speeches and make Aristophanes's speech the central speech. As he begins his story, Aristophanes himself marks the fact that his speech is discontinuous with the previous speeches. The dialogue is in a way making a new beginning with Aristophanes's speech.

Aristophanes is different from Phaedrus, Pausanias, and Eryximachus because Aristophanes gives no analysis or theory of love. His speech is taken up wholly with telling a story. More precisely, Aristophanes tells us how to think about love by telling us a myth. Now, to call Aristophanes's story a myth is not to say that it's false or that it's untrue. Of course not. A myth teaches us truths by the way the story works, rather than simply by making a series of claims on us. Aristophanes tells a very common type of myth, a mythical history of human origins. Such origin myths about how humans came into being help us think about human nature, about how we are. Myth uses history to capture essence. In this case, Aristophanes thinks about erotic love by telling a story about how we humans became sexual creatures from an earlier state of existence in which we were not sexual. This story is the way Aristophanes analyzes something that's simply natural to us, something essential to us. And this is a typical way that myth makes itself thoughtful: by telling us something as history it shows us something about who we are right now. After all, when we read Aristophanes's myth we're not provoked to ask questions about what things were like in ancient times; far from it. The story about human origins is in fact a story about how we live right now.

So Aristophanes's mode of thoughtfulness is mythical, and this thoughtful storytelling shows us something about human nature that itself isn't mythical at all, no more mythical than we are. But by casting this thoughtfulness into the mode of myth, Aristophanes also develops another theme we saw in the earlier speakers, the theme that there's something divine or sacred about the human experience of love. Because myths are usually stories in which humans interact with divine beings, myths are especially suited to think about how certain human experiences – falling in love and being in love, for example – lift us from our everyday selves into the abandon of a self in contact with something divine in us.

Aristophanes, of course, was a great comic poet who produced comedies, not tragedies. And it's perhaps not surprising then that his story is so funny. But he makes a distinction just before he gives his speech. He says to Eryximachus, "It will be appropriate if the speech that I give, the story that I tell, is funny, if it makes you laugh. But yet I don't want it to be merely ridiculous." So that the humor of Aristophanes's speech is intended to be a deep and thoughtful humor, not merely an entertainment, not merely a joke. As Aristophanes sees things, then, the comic is itself a mode of deep thoughtfulness. The comic isn't the opposite of the serious. The comic is one mode of serious thoughtfulness. In fact, I suspect that in the realm of love, any good thinking, any insightful thoughtfulness will have to be alive to the humor of erotic experience. If I read a very sober-minded analysis of the nature of falling in love, I always suspect the lack of humor goes along with some failure of thoughtfulness. A description of something that has its funny side, but that isn't funny itself, has missed one of the main features of the thing it's trying to describe. So that a speech like Pausanias's, say, that is so sober, so serious-minded about love, might by that very feature show that it's lacking as an analysis of love. Aristophanes is making a claim for comedy, a claim that comedy itself might be part of what's necessary for us to understand love. If we get too serious, we might also end up squinting our eyes so that we can't really see the very phenomenon that we're trying to analyze. So Aristophanes's mode of thoughtfulness is both mythic and comic – a combination perhaps we're not so used to, but the more myth that one reads the more you see how often there's a comic dimension to mythical storytelling.

"Once upon a time, human beings weren't like we are now,"

Aristophanes begins his story. Instead, in the beginning, when we originated, human beings were round, like a big sphere. In our original state, we were much more powerful and self-sufficient than we are now. We originally had one neck, with two faces on it facing opposite directions. We had one big round body, and we had two pairs of legs and two pairs of arms. These original humans also had a pair of genitalia, on the outside of their spherical bodies. Such was our original nature; what we are now, is nothing more than a broken half of the original perfect form of human nature. These original creatures were, by the standards of us broken creatures, extraordinarily powerful and self-sufficient. The fact that they're spherical is an image of this original self-sufficiency. As Aristophanes puts it at the beginning of his myth, the sphericity of these whole natures was an image of the divine heavenly bodies, either of the sun, or of the earth – the sun, Helios, being a male god, and the earth, Gaia, a female god – or of the moon, Selena, which (though a female god for the Greeks) is in one aspect earthly and in another aspect more sunlike, and so has both female and male attributes. So these original human beings, these whole human beings, are made in the image and likeness of gods. Their round shape and also their mode of locomotion was an image of those divine bodies. They could walk like we do, but for them walking was a kind of unhurried, underpowered way of moving. When they wanted to move quickly, they could stick out all their arms and legs and just roll in a circle, like an acrobat doing cartwheels or like a tumbleweed. Such powerful locomotion is an imitation of the eternal circular orbits of the divine heavenly bodies. So in both their shape and their mode of life, we might say, the original human beings were an image of something divine.

This picture is so vividly described in Plato's text that you would think painters and other artists would have tried their hand at putting the words of the myth into physical images, but there is not, I believe, a single famous representation of Aristophanes's original human beings. But there is an entertaining cartoon version of Aristophanes's myth in the song "The Origin of Love" from the movie *Hedwig and the Angry Inch* (2001) – though this version does take the liberty of introducing the Norse god Thor into the Greek story!

Now these original human beings did not come in the two sexes we are accustomed to, male and female. Instead, original human beings came in three types, though none of the types were exactly sexes, as we will see. The sun-type was wholly male, both faces and both genital organs. The earth-type was wholly female, with both faces and genitalia of corresponding form. The moon-type, though, was androgynous, with one male face and male genital organ, and the other face and organ female. Aristophanes mentions that the only trace remaining of this third type of human being is the word "androgyne," which, he says, exists only as an insult. This is Aristophanes's first little dig at the excessive masculine focus of the previous speakers; they would think of someone who had (what they think of as) the feminine characteristics of softness and tenderness mixed into a masculine personality as effeminate, and the word "androgyne" would be used to insult such a person as a womanish man, a failed man. But Aristophanes is resuscitating the word as the name of a complete, self-sufficient, ideal human being, at least as perfect as an all-male or all-female type. Indeed, without ever directly saying so, Aristophanes seems to present the androgynous type as a better model for us modern day humans than the models of pure masculinity or pure femininity.

As we now think of sexual differentiation, into male and female, we would be tempted to describe these original human beings as having two halves, either both of one sex or one of each sex. But the myth is trying to unsettle this way of thinking of sexual identity. These original beings weren't two creatures stuck together. They were integrated wholes. What then are we, with only two arms and legs, a single face, and one genital organ? How did we become such diminished versions of the power, divinity, and self-sufficiency that originally belonged to human nature? Through this rather comic picture of the original beings, Aristophanes has already made a serious, thoughtful point: human beings in their integrity are an image of something divine. Insofar as we are broken pieces of that original image, we are diminished images of something divine.

Now it turns out, Aristophanes says, that the great power of these original spherical human beings also filled them with great ambition. They were led by this ambition toward impiety, and they tried to displace the gods. They were not satisfied with merely being created in the image and likeness of god. They wanted instead to usurp the place of the gods, to take over their privileges and their powers. (Notice the idea of divinity implicit in this aspect of the myth: gods are characterized primarily by power and dominion. A different understanding of what defines a god – for example, creativity or generosity – would produce a different way for humans to be imitators of gods.) Humans were, we might say, dissatisfied that their self-sufficiency was merely human, as if the gods who made them had deprived them of something rightfully theirs, namely, equality with the gods. And so our original ancestors tried to attack the Olympian gods in their mountain fortress. For this impious aggression, the original humans were punished by Zeus, the father of gods and men and leader of the Olympians. The punishment took the following form. Zeus did not want to simply annihilate the humans, though he was very angry with them, because the gods enjoyed the sacrifices and honors offered to them by humans. But Zeus devised a plan to prevent the assault on the gods, and yet still preserve the human race. The round humans were punished by being divided in two by Zeus's thunderbolts. Zeus sent Apollo, the god of healing, to reconstruct human bodies after they suffered this terrible calamity. In our original round form, our heads faced in the same direction as the roundest part of us, what would now be our buttocks. (So the original beings were asses, as well as spheres; just the kind of crude joke we might expect from a comedian!) But after Zeus had severed us, Apollo turned our head around, so that it faced the broken part of us, this open wound. He pulled the skin together to close that wound, and then sealed the skin and held it together with a small button, so that our navel is the one place we still notice Apollo's repair of the wound. So the original round part of us that's on the outside, our buttocks, is now behind us because our head has been turned around. But in your present state you're ass-backwards. The head has been turned around so that now we face the visible emblem of the punishment of our impiety. We have fallen from our original, integrated, perfect self-sufficient state and been punished by the gods, and we are constantly reminded by the form of our own bodies of the punishment for that impiety.

But this reconstruction of the human body is not the final chapter of the transformation of the original spherical nature into our present condition. The original state, the first phase of human existence, is the perfect round sphericity of the original beings, whether all male, all female, or androgynous. These beings could form alliances, as they did against the Olympians, but they had no longing for each other, and they did not fall in love. As a result of our impiety, we fell from that state, and we're punished by the gods with a terrible woundedness. But, Aristophanes says, at this stage human beings aren't yet just like we are now. In this broken state, with our heads turned around, facing backward, as the original beings would say, or forward, as we would say, these broken human beings spent all of their time searching desperately for their other half, the one from which they've been severed. When they would find that other half, they would throw their limbs about each other along the cut – what we now call the front of the body – and hold each other as closely as they could in an attempt to overcome their wound, to heal their brokenness. If their original half died, they sought after another broken half of the right type to complete them, whether male or female. And so powerful was the longing that they had for each other, they would perish of hunger and of thirst, neglecting everything else in life except reunion. Nothing was as important to them as trying to be together again. And so, to the gods' consternation, the human race was in danger of dying out. This, the reader understands, is Aristophanes's answer to Phaedrus's death test. anes agrees with Phaedrus that we will die for true love, but he does not see this death-devoted longing as heroic, an imitation of Achilles and his courage. We embrace death because love is a despairing attempt to escape brokenness.

Notice that the way Aristophanes tells this myth, there's a challenge to Pausanias's sharp dichotomy between body and soul.

These lovers aren't primarily trying to get their *souls* back together, nor are they merely trying to get their bodies back together. The myth doesn't think of humans as a composite of two things, body and soul. The wholeness they seek is equally physical and psychological. So there's not the kind of valorizing of soul over body in this particular speech that there was in Pausanias's speech.

The origin of sexual love, then, was this terrible longing to be repaired from being severed. But the physical intertwining the broken humans achieved in this state was only quasi-sexual. It was not yet sexual intercourse. Why not? Because, says Aristophanes, their genitalia were not in the proper position for intercourse to occur in these quasi-sexual embraces. Remember that in our original integrated state, our genitalia would have been on the outside. In the severed state, Apollo had closed our wound, but our genitalia had not been rearranged. Lacking mutual genital contact, humans were never satisfied with these quasi-sexual embraces, and continued to neglect life's necessary business. So, Aristophanes says, Zeus thought up another idea, one that would both make humans less distracted and keep the race going. He sent Apollo back, and this time he had Apollo move the genitalia to the other side of the body, what used to be the inside of our bodies. This final reordering of our bodies produced human beings like we are now. And now, Aristophanes says, when human beings seek reunion through physical intimacy, they will satisfy to the extent possible for us in our broken state their longing for their other half. We still pursue someone who can be our other half, and cure our wound. From the merely human point of view, this reunion is the main thing we pursue in sexual love. The fact that Zeus and Apollo have put our sexual organs into position to join together in the unifying embrace makes the embrace more satisfying than before, a less imperfect approximation to our original perfection. This satisfaction is enough to stop us from being so obsessed by our brokenness that we perish from longing. But from the divine point of view, the human desire for reunion can now serve the higher purpose of reproduction, of preserving the human race. The physical expression of desire for union with the other half is truly sexual, because the erotic embrace now fulfills both the human purpose of union and the divine purpose of procreation.

This is a very funny picture of human romantic life. We frantically seek a good mate, trying to get as round as possible, and as an unintended consequence making babies. But the myth is also profoundly serious. Reflect on three ideas Aristophanes has built into his myth. First, he has challenged the macho, masculine orientation of Phaedrus and Pausanias, and of the drinking party as a whole. Remember that both of those speakers diminished the love of men and women, praising instead love between men, as more heroic and heavenly. But it's clear Aristophanes's myth makes the androgyne, the being that integrates the male and female, the exemplar of the human imitation of the divine. Only the reunion of halves from an original androgyne would serve the divine purpose of procreation. Aristophanes allows for the possibility that male-male couples and female-female couples exist in our present condition, but the paradigm human couple, the one that gets closest to our original perfect nature, is the androgynous couple of a man and a woman. Before human beings were broken, Aristophanes says, we reproduced asexually, self-sufficiently, by casting our seed into the ground, and we were earth-born rather than born from human parents. Now, in our new state, we have lost our divine self-sufficiency, but in its place we have the comfort of human sexual love, providing both unity and reproduction. Second, Aristophanes has made central to his speech a clear rejection of Pausanias's claim that the soul is simply superior to the body. In romantic love, Aristophanes suggests, there is no sharp distinction between soul and body; indeed, in his myth, Aristophanes never makes that distinction. Lovers are as much body-mates as they are soul-mates. This view makes the physical expression of love – especially sexual intercourse – much more important and meaningful than it appeared in the earlier speeches. Third, in this myth the human erotic drive is a drive for reunion alone. But superimposed on the physical expression of that human longing for reunion is a divine purpose of procreation. The human desire and the divine purpose are two distinct things. The shattered human beings do not have sexual intercourse with each other because they seek procreation. Procreation is a divinely ordained consequence of the expression of human erotic desire, but it is not part of the very structure of human erotic desire. Socrates will challenge this separation of human desire and divine purpose, and suggest that procreation is as important to erotic life as intimacy.

So Aristophanes's myth is structured around three stages of human erotic history. Our original, integrated, wholesome healthy state is non-sexual. By nature, before we fall into imperfection, we are self-sufficient, asexual beings. Sexuality is the most powerful mark of our brokenness. It comes into the world only with our punishment. Sexuality itself is not a punishment, but it's the result of the loneliness we feel because we've been punished. Notice the radical intimacy that this story conceives of your lover as having to you. Your lover is not like your arm or your leg. Your lover is a much more intimate part of you than any mere limb. After all, somebody who's lost an arm or a leg, by accident or disease, is still a whole person, a whole organism. But in this myth, it is a romantic couple that makes a true organism. The couple, it turns out, is more truly what is really human, originally human, than any of us can be as an individual. After all, wholeness and procreativity belong to the couple, and it's in and through erotic love that we return, to the extent possible for us in this limited world, to the original state in which we were an undiminished image and likeness of the divine. Even love leaves us with our wound, and lovers always feel something of the absurdity of being a severed limb.

Are you one of the ones?

What we really want when we fall in love is obscure to us, even a mystery, says Aristophanes. His myth is supposed to shine a light into these obscure erotic mysteries. We have an aspect of divinity that love longs for, his myth tells us, and though a lover does not make us whole, he or she at least cures our wound as much as it can be cured in this life – and as a happy bonus, babies are produced, too! If you want to understand how absolute our desire for union can be, Aristophanes says, consider this thought experiment.

Suppose the blacksmith god, Hephaestus, came down and visited two lovers who were in their bed together, and said to them, "What is it you really want out of your love life?" The lovers wouldn't know what to say. They would feel the potency of their erotic desire for each other, but they wouldn't know how to articulate the ultimate goal of that desire. Erotic desire is not a clear and simple message, telling us, "This is what you want." Instead, desire is like an oracle from some divinity, full of a meaning that eludes us. We need some kind of divination to interpret the oracle of our desire, to point us toward the fuller interpretation of what we seek. Aristophanes, through Hephaestus, offers to be just such an interpreter of obscure erotic oracles for us. When Aristophanes talks about Hephaestus as a god of love, he is really talking about himself.

When the lovers are at a loss for words, Hephaestus gives them the words they need. "Is this what you want?" the god asks, "that you two be welded together into one being, so that you live as one, and die at the same instant?" The lovers would be delighted to hear this offer from the god, and would recognize this was in fact what they've wanted all the time, the fulfillment of their erotic desires. They would not have been able to articulate it themselves – it's difficult to articulate – but when Hephaestus/Aristophanes gives the appropriate interpretation, they would be able to recognize it. The god's gift of language overcomes the limits of their previous erotic world. And we see again how Aristophanes gives a more mundane or humane interpretation of Phaedrus's death test for love. It isn't Achilles's heroic sacrifice to avenge a lover's death that is the proof of love, but the more human sense that when a lover dies, we die, too. Bereavement is a form of death, and we mourn our lover because a real thing, the romantic couple, has died. To be so unified with a lover that there can be only one death: this is the fulfillment of love, suggests Hephaestus. The god and the comic poet could almost have taken their view from the traditional wedding vows of the Christian tradition: for better, for worse, till death.

All this talk of "becoming one," and of unity, and of "being completed" by our lover: it is all very romantic, and this language is still popular today. One of the most quoted phrases of romance in the last couple decades is "You complete me," from the Tom Cruise movie *Jerry Maguire* (1996). Not many people who say it realize they are indebted to Plato's Aristophanes, but they are! But there's a question about this romantic picture of finding the one who completes you. Aristophanes's speech points to this question, although he doesn't himself focus on it. Think back to the myth when the original humans have been broken but before the structure of their bodies was rearranged to make intercourse procreative, the quasi-sexual state. In Aristophanes's story, these broken beings seek for their other half. But if their "other half" dies before they die, they don't just kill themselves or waste away in mourning. They go look for another half to throw their arms and legs about and embrace. They live a life of constant distraction in trying to return to that original whole state. Those who come from an original all-male look for another male. Those who come from an all-female look for a female. Those who come from an androgyne look for the appropriate complementary half. What model of erotic completion are we to understand is operative here? Well, one way to understand it is that there is a *unique* other that will make us whole insofar as we can return to that original state. From this point of view, the focus of Aristophanes's speech is on the way one other complementary special person will be the fullest satisfaction of all of our erotic longings. But other passages in this myth make it sound like our erotic longings are not so finely delimited, not so tightly defined, so that what we seek for is really simply *some* person of the right *type*. (Of course, these severed halves are not really persons; they're horribly scarred half-persons.) If we understand Aristophanes's myth in this way, focusing on types rather than unique individuals, sexual complementarity or erotic complementarity allows for a lot more diversity of object than it would if we think of looking for just that perfect other half.

It's interesting to go through Aristophanes's telling of the myth and ask yourself which passages seem to assume more a uniqueness model of erotic satisfaction, and which seem to assume more the type model of erotic satisfaction. I take it that for us, we mostly adhere to something that's closer to the unique individual model of erotic complementarity, of romantic longing. At least when we're in love, we do. But when you're more of an observer of romance than a participant in it, are you quite as devoted to the uniqueness of erotic objects? One of my students told me that when she went away to college her grandmother gave her only one piece of advice: she said to her, it's as easy to fall in love with a rich boy as a poor one. Grandma wasn't anti-romantic; she wanted this student, her granddaughter, to fall in love. But Grandma didn't seem to think her granddaughter's romantic choices should be limited to a unique individual! Or suppose your friend comes back distraught, perhaps this very evening, from "breaking up" (a strikingly Aristophanic phrase) with his or her unique other. Will any of you offer comfort that's basically of the form, "There are a lot of fish in the sea"? It's easier for an observer than for a participant to say these sorts of things. Which perspective gives a truer view of love, the inside view or the outside view?

How many fish are in your erotic sea? When you give advice, or comfort after a break-up, why does the advice or comfort tend to go in the direction of a more type-oriented conception of erotic complementarity? Whereas when you're in love, you want that beloved to be utterly unique. You don't want to hear that your girl-friend looks like her sister. You don't want to hear that your boyfriend buys presents like every other guy who reads the same magazines. You want to think that there's something unique about your relationship. And if it's hard to think of your lover merely as a type rather than as a unique individual, it is even harder to think of yourself that way. But do you fall into erotic patterns? I had a friend who dated four Jennifers in a row. I've even known some men who've had a whole string of blondes or redheads as the objects of their erotic interest, or women who were attracted only to men with broad shoulders. Now, they didn't think of their romantic interest in this type-oriented way. They didn't say to themselves, I'm hoping to meet some redheads tonight – and they surely don't say it to the redheads! It's not comfortable to think we like someone as a type, nor flattering to think we are liked as a type. But maybe the world should get used to the idea that we love and are loved as types, rather than as individuals. Imagine if a store that sells cards for lovers to give to each other on Valentine's Day tried this experiment. They'll stock the typical cards that say "You complete me" and "You're the One," in a section called "Inside View." But they'll also have an "Outside View" section. Here you will find cards that say things like "You're My Type," or more explicitly "You're One of the Ones"; and for the mathematically inclined, "You Are in my Maximal Erotic Set." Which section will sell more cards? One advantage of the "Outside" cards over the "Inside" cards: you don't have to fill in the name until later. You just bring it with you to a singles bar, or wherever you meet the right type of people, and wait for an opportune moment! But if you're worried about how a potential romantic partner will respond to an "outside" view of their attractiveness, you could try this strategy: shape your heart to the type model of erotic complementarity, and shape your words to the unique individual model. Tell each one of the ones "You're the one." And you won't quite be lying. This strategy flatters the fish, while expanding the sea.

The question of uniqueness or individuality in love is a central question, and it's a question that I do believe we feel very differently about when we're inside of a love affair and when we're observing love from the outside. The question is, which of those views tells us something more true about the structure of our own erotic desire, about the structure of our own erotic needs, and about what might satisfy them.

The perfect couple in Patrice Leconte's
The Hairdresser's Husband

I mentioned that something like Aristophanes's account of lovers as each other's "other half" is a part of popular culture, and can be heard repeated in songs and movies. The most perfect contemporary Aristophanic love story I've found is *The Hairdresser's Husband*, a 1990 French movie, from the distinguished director Patrice Leconte. The movie tells the story of an unusual couple, Antoine (Jean Rochefort) and Mathilde (Anna Galiena), whose union is an extreme version of the self-sufficiency of Aristophanes's original humans. I am tempted to say that Patrice Leconte has made an entire movie by thinking through what it would mean for two lovers to be granted Hephaestus's wish and be melded into one being.

Let me begin with a brief summary of the movie before we discuss its themes and some particular scenes. The movie moves back and forth between Antoine's life as an adult and his childhood, because his childhood experiences have made him the man he is. His childhood, we might say, is Antoine's origin myth, the history that tells us his essence. The founding poet of English Romanticism, William Wordsworth, famously said, "The child is father to the man," and this movie takes that idea to heart.

The movie opens with Antoine as a boy, on the beach where his family vacations every summer. He is dancing to North African music, in a comic style that will still be with him as an adult, with wild arm gestures and swaying hips. In a voiceover, adult Antoine reflects on the wool swim trunks his mother forced him and his brother to wear. Wool doesn't dry easily, so the two brothers were constantly chafed and sore from the damp trunks, which they hated. But, in the first hint of how deeply adult Antoine has been made by young Antoine, the adult thanks his mother for the hated wool, because, as he says, it drew his attention to his genitals. Adult Antoine's sexual self is the fruit from seeds planted in the boy.

The scene shifts from the sea to young Antoine's home. The boy is off to have his hair cut, but really he wants to see the voluptuous hairdresser who runs the shop. She shampoos his hair, and he enjoys the sensuous pleasures of the salon, with its lotions and colognes, its textures and scents. As she bends over him for the shampoo, a button accidently pops open on her shirt, and boy Antoine silently gazes on her large breasts. That evening, at dinner with the family, Antoine's father asks his sons what they want to be when they grow up. The older brother wants to be a civil engineer, but Antoine catches his father and mother off guard when he responds, "Later on, I'll marry a hairdresser." His father is so shocked by this answer – he probably realizes his son has a crush on the voluptuous hairdresser – that he slaps Antoine. Antoine runs to his room, and his father comes to apologize. "Do what you want in life," he tells his son, and the boy Antoine knows his plan to marry a hairdresser is safe. Notice how young Antoine exemplifies the tension in Aristophanes's speech between the individual and the type as an object of love. His crush is on this individual hairdresser, but she represents a type for Antoine, the type that will define his romantic desires.

After this introduction to the young Antoine and the experiences that establish the pattern of his erotic desires, the scene shifts to adult Antoine, reading a newspaper in a hair salon, speaking with the beautiful and buxom hairdresser (we later learn her name is Mathilde). Mathilde notices one of her regular customers is aging, and becoming careless of his appearance. It is the first of many instances in the movie where we see Mathilde's worries about the passage of time. The story flashes back to a younger Mathilde, taking over the hair salon when the previous owner, an elderly man we are told is a homosexual, decides to retire. (The owner's homosexuality is relevant to the story because it means he has no children, a theme that becomes central to the movie.) "Liking solitude, she ran the shop alone," we are told. One day, Antoine happens to see her, and he instantly knows this is the hairdresser he has looked for all his life. It is an Aristophanic moment, an experience of a complete connection that represents all that Antoine has been made by his past. He has a vivid memory of a moment with his father on the beach. His father struggles with a difficult crossword puzzle, and young Antoine asks why this struggle is enjoyable. His father laughs, and thinking as much of love as of crosswords, he teaches Antoine a motto the boy holds to as an adult, too: "The more they resist, the sweeter the surrender." Young Antoine pulls up his wool trunks, and adult Antoine smiles at the memory, and thinks of his father's slap: against all odds, he is doing what he has always wanted in life. He will be the hairdresser's husband.

Antoine enters Mathilde's salon and makes an appointment for a haircut later that day. As she bends over him for the shampoo, just as the voluptuous hairdresser of his youth had done, he notices Mathilde's shapely breasts. Another storm of memory comes over him, and we see the awful and defining event of Antoine's youth. Young Antoine gazes into the salon, and discovers the voluptuous hairdresser sprawled on a couch. Her body falls onto the floor, and he realizes she is dead; she has committed suicide. The complex memory lodges deep in Antoine, and connects sex and death in his desires for the rest of his life. Director Leconte is following the same path to unsettling erotic desire that we saw in Atom Egoyan's *Exotica*, where discovering the murdered girl in the field is inseparable from the romance of Christina, Eric, and Francis. Like Phaedrus, like Aristophanes, for Antoine love must pass a version of the death test. What premonition does adult Antoine have of his future with Mathilde?

Antoine sits through his haircut in silent ecstasy and exhilaration. As he pays Mathilde and prepares to leave, he stuns her with a question: "Will you marry me?" She says nothing and gapes at him, as he mumbles "Forgive me" and leaves. But adult Antoine has not forgotten the lessons in perseverance his father taught him. He remembers a time on the beach when he and a group of boys tried to build a dam in the sand to hold back the tide. Their little shovels could not accomplish the task, but young Antoine becomes a hero when he spots a man on a bulldozer down the beach, and persuades the bulldozer to push enough sand for the dam. "No dream is impossible," young Antoine believes, and adult Antoine believes the same thing. Three weeks later, too soon to need a haircut but as long as his desire lets him wait, he is back at the salon. When Mathilde finishes his shampoo and haircut, she fulfills his fantasy. "If you weren't teasing," she says, "I will marry you." Mathilde's acceptance is as sudden and mysterious as Antoine's proposal, and viewers may scoff at it. But do falling in love and being in love, having a vision of another as the fulfillment of your desire, really become less mysterious merely if they take more time? The suddenness emphasizes the mystery, but it does not cause it.

Antoine and Mathilde sit in the salon and plan their future together. "We'll stay here," Antoine says, "the past is dead." Except for a short honeymoon at the beach – adult Antoine wants Mathilde to see where child Antoine fathered this man she loves –

they spend all their time in the salon and the little flat upstairs. They even have their wedding reception there, with Mathilde in her wedding dress and Antoine's brother, his wife, and the retired owner of the salon. The brother brings the old pair of wool trunks, and a childhood picture of Antoine and his father at the beach. "Mathilde had no family," we are told. Antoine asks to see childhood pictures of Mathilde, but she has none because they make her sad. "Time flies too fast," she says. Adult Antoine is a man made completely by his past, whereas Mathilde is a woman with no living past at all. Later, Antoine does his childlike dance to his exotic music, and invites Mathilde to join him. He holds her close, and we hear Antoine in a voiceover that could have come straight from the god Hephaestus: "We'd be so closely welded that nothing cold or evil could slip between us."

Antoine and Mathilde, then, have become Aristophanes's perfect couple, a self-sufficient whole with no needs outside themselves and the salon. They pass the death test: they live completely in each other's desire, and would die outside of it. The movie drives to its conclusion by considering the consequences of this enclosed perfection. One set of scenes focuses on how this self-sufficient couple is different from couples for whom children are an intrinsic part of their relationship. Another set focuses on the threat that time and its changes would bring to the perfection of such relationship. As the movie sees things, a relationship that wants to be unchanging and timeless, like Antoine's and Mathilde's, will also find children a distraction or even a threat. At the least, such a "perfect couple" will understand procreation to be outside of their own desire, just as Aristophanes's broken half-humans did. Reunion is desire, procreation is unintended consequence.

The question of children arises twice. In both cases, the children seem to be obstacles or threats to a relationship. We see a man run into the salon, trying to hide from his wife. He asks for a haircut and tries to remain hidden under the apron Mathilde puts over him. But his wife walks in a moment later, strides to the customer, apologizes to Mathilde for interrupting, and slaps her husband hard across the face. She leaves, and the man concedes he deserved her slap, and praises her, particularly noting what a good mother she is to their three children. In a scene a little later, he returns, and we see his children outside. He has come back to tell Antoine and Mathilde that his wife has left him, and he is caring for the children. In the second child scene, one of the comic highlights of the movie, a woman arrives pulling a whining and unkempt boy into the salon. The boy, we learn, is her adopted son. She wants Mathilde to cut his messy hair, but they can't calm him down, as he resists sitting in the chair. Antoine comes to the rescue with his dancing. "I'll show you something you've never seen," he says to the awful boy, and puts on some music and starts his comic dancing. The boy sits down, enchanted, and sits quietly while Mathilde cuts his hair and his mother looks on astonished. We hear Antoine in a voiceover, "We've no children. We've no friends. What could they add to our lives?" Mathilde's flat belly, he says, will never be deformed by pregnancy. He goes on to suggest that when couples spend time with others, "it's a proof that their love is lacking." As the boy and his mother leave, she says to Mathilde and Antoine, "Never adopt." Afterwards they dance together to Antoine's music, and Mathilde says to him, "I'm scared that someday you won't want to dance with me. I've never belonged to anyone." Antoine tries to reassure her. "I ask nothing of you," he says. They are, at least from Antoine's point of view, so complete as a couple that nothing, not even a child, could contribute to their life.

The more general issue of time and change comes up over and over again in scenes where Antoine has a cheerful optimism about their relationship, but Mathilde has a melancholy fear. We see Mathilde reading a magazine, telling Antoine about an advertisement for weight loss. Antoine responds by caressing her voluptuous breasts and playfully saying, "Lose half a pound, and I'll throw myself under a bus." Mathilde gives an unexpectedly serious response: "The day you don't love me anymore, don't pretend you do." A little later a regular customer arrives, who always recites short bits of poetry, hanging onto them as long as their beauty doesn't become stale. "Some last, others vanish," he says. As Mathilde cuts the hair of this beauty-seeking customer, Antoine surreptitiously caresses her.

We understand the point of the scene: as the customer seeks to keep his experience of poetic beauty ever fresh, so Antoine's desire for Mathilde is always renewed.

One night, after the only argument they have, Antoine says, in their ten years together, Antoine is smoking in the salon. Antoine thinks back to a time he and his brother were smoking and drinking while their parents were out. Mathilde comes down and smokes with him, and Antoine says, "We should smoke more often." They make cocktails from cologne – don't try that at home, reader! – and spend the night drinking and dancing. The morning after, they awake with terrible hangovers – just like the *Symposium* – and the camera shows us Mathilde with a very pale face, lying next to Antoine. Antoine's voiceover says, "None as happy; nothing but death could part us," and his memory goes back to the boy peering into the salon and discovering a suicide.

While they were dancing, Antoine had noticed a crack in the ceiling. Why did the director Leconte give us this small detail? We find out in the next scene, when Antoine and Mathilde visit the retired salon owner, now living a dispirited existence in a retirement home. They chat about the salon, and Antoine mentions that he plans to repaint the ceiling. The ceiling crack, revealed even in Antoine's timeless dancing, is a symbol of the passage of time into decrepitude. As they leave the retirement home, Antoine walks into the street cheerfully, but Mathilde gazes back at the closed gate with an anxious look on her face. Back at the salon, the aging customer who attracted Mathilde's concern at the beginning of the movie reappears. As he leaves, Mathilde notes, "He's more stooped every day," and Antoine replies, "He's a bit older every day." It is the last reminder Mathilde can stand about the passage of time. She looks outside and says, "A storm is coming," and soon thunder and lightning fills the salon. "Sit where you always sit," Mathilde says to Antoine, and they make love. Suddenly Mathilde leaves in the midst of the storm, runs to the river, and jumps from a bridge into the rushing water. For the second time, Antoine's hairdresser has committed suicide. In her final note, she tells him she did not want their desire and passion to cool into affection and friendship.

In a voiceover, the only time she takes on the authority of the narrator, we hear the words of Mathilde's suicide note: "I kiss you now, so tenderly I'll die of it."

In the last scene, Antoine sits alone in the salon. The aging customer gazes in at him and leaves. A man enters, and Antoine gives him a (rather poorly executed) shampoo, puts on some of his music, and dances. The customer joins him until Antoine turns off the music. "The hairdresser will be back," he says, and sits down again. After all, hairdressers are just his type.

The Hairdresser's Husband is focused on the place of memory in erotic life. More generally, the engine of this movie is a reflection on the issues of temporality and eros, of time and of love. I mentioned earlier Wittgenstein as one of the great philosophers of the last century. Another giant of last century's philosophizing was Martin Heidegger. And one of the things Heidegger is famous for, or notorious, is his discussion of the importance of death. Heidegger believed that forgetfulness of death is forgetfulness of being. To live a life in forgetfulness that it's a mortal life, is to live in a way that's not fully human. This movie is a thought experiment about living a life that doesn't experience time within mortality. Antoine, the male figure, doesn't experience time as linear, as passing. He experiences time as cyclical, as repeating. So for Antoine, temporality does not bring with it mortality. He is, so to speak, in a constant state of youthfulness, a constant repetition of something the beginning of the movie shows us is a part of his childhood. There's something rather comic about a grown-up, an adult, repeating his or her childhood. The movie shows us some of this comedy with the theme of the wool swimming trunks. The adult Antoine is grateful to those awful, never-drying swimming trunks because they drew his attention to his genitals. On the day that he's married, his brother digs out the old bathing suit and gives it to him as a wedding present, so that we have a visual mark of this repetition. And of course the movie also shows us how his schoolboy crush on the local hairdresser formed for Antoine the structure of his own erotic desire down into adulthood. Every woman Antoine will love will, in a certain sense, be the same woman. He will always be the hairdresser's husband, and who that hairdresser is, you might say, is of only secondary importance. In this respect, Antoine is an embodiment of the type interpretation of Aristophanes's myth. But notice that Antoine is not, so to speak, merely born with that type. The type instead comes through memory, through lived experience, so that in *The Hairdresser's Husband* what makes us of a particular erotic type is our history. It's our history that individualizes us, that makes us a particular person when it comes to love, and determines whom we'll fall in love with, for good or for ill. Antoine is capable of unusually powerful erotic attachment, in no small part because the childhood experiences that founded his erotic desires were unusually powerful, and were also in an unusual way bound up with death, and more particularly with suicide.

So, the figure of Antoine is a figure who flees from temporality into a kind of timelessness, timelessness through repetition. What would this movie look like if we reversed the gender roles? Antoine is a middle-aged man – the actor Jean Rochefort was in his late fifties when he played the part. He is not particularly handsome, and is actually rather odd-looking. Certainly when you watch this movie, you wouldn't think, "Wow, that Antoine, what a hunk! He is really hot." In fact, he's absolutely drab, a kind of everyman living out a male fantasy. He's very funny, so he might be attractive in that way, but he's not physically attractive. But the woman who plays Mathilde, Anna Galiena, is almost impossibly gorgeous. She might as well be named Aphrodite. And of course she's noticeably younger. She's not exactly young (the actress was in her mid-thirties), but she's noticeably younger than Antoine. Imagine if the movie were inverted, so that the female figure were middle-aged and frumpy, and the male figure was a young, hunky Dionysus. How would the movie work? I think that, at least in our place and time, the movie is thinking that the male experience of temporality is different from the female experience of it. The female experience of temporality feels the passage of time as more of a threat to erotic attractiveness. So it's much easier for us to think of male actors who, well into their fifties, even their sixties, were still leading men: Paul Newman or Robert Redford in an earlier generation, Sean

Connery and Harrison Ford, and now Tom Cruise and even the new James Bond, Daniel Craig, who continued in this romantic lead as he became closer to fifty than to forty. It's much more difficult to think of women who've been able to command the screen, to be the focus of romantic fantasy, into their fifties and sixties in anything like the way men have. So the movie is thinking about that.

This gulf between male and female temporality comes out especially powerfully in a scene I mentioned earlier, my favorite in the whole movie. We start out with Mathilde reading a diet advertisement in a magazine. Antoine, after she unbuttons her dress and he's caressing her, says to her, "Lose half a pound and I'll throw myself under a bus." Now, what does Antoine *think* he's saying when he says that? He thinks he's saying, Mathilde, you don't need to think about diets, you shouldn't have any worries. I love you completely. There's nothing for you to change. I can't imagine loving you any more than I do right now! I love you so much that any change that you try to make wouldn't make you any better for me. Things are perfect! But what Antoine *thinks* is not what Mathilde *hears*. The thought that goes through her head in response to Antoine's words is, "The day you don't love me any more don't pretend you do." So he says, "You're perfect. If you lose a pound I'll throw myself under a bus." And she thinks that he commanded, "Don't change. If you change, I won't love you anymore." What he *means* to say is an expression of timeless repetition in a perfect romantic bliss. And what she *hears* is a threat to their relationship as the inevitable changes of time weigh upon them, and most particularly on her. So the very thing that Antoine thinks he can say to reassure her turns out to put words on her deepest anxiety, the anxiety about the mortality of their love.

This gulf between the male and female experience of love and time goes along with a number of other things in the movie. You'll remember earlier when they are in their wedding clothes in the salon. Antoine's brother is there and brings the wool trunks and a childhood picture of Antoine with his father. So the scene flashes us back, as the movie does so many times, to Antoine's childhood, to the way that for Antoine the child has been the father to the man. By contrast, when Antoine asks Mathilde if he can see childhood pictures of her, she says she has no childhood pictures because they make her sad. She says time flies too fast. There are a number of other places in the movie where this issue about the two different perceptions of time is central to the drama. So that in all these rather sweet, concrete scenes there's a very deep and threatening theme. This theme doesn't become fully conscious for us, the threat doesn't come down on us fully, until toward the very end of the movie when Mathilde finally reaches the logical conclusion of her fears of temporality.

The scene about the awful adopted boy – it's a scene that always has a particular shock value to somebody like me, since two of my three daughters were adopted – inserts a theme into the movie that questions the relationship between romance and children. The interpretation of children that this scene gives is a lot like the interpretation of children in the speech of Aristophanes. Children form no part of the erotic union that this couple seeks. Children indeed can be nothing but an intrusion into that kind of relationship. An especially cruel mark of this rejection of children is Antoine's comment that Mathilde's body will never be deformed by pregnancy. His image of "the lovable Mathilde" does not include what Mathilde would be as a mother, a fact she knows and dreads. Antoine's peculiar childlike dancing seems to me the only "child" such love allows: be your own child. It is the symbol of his timelessness, of his ability to, so to speak, live so completely in the moment that he doesn't experience the moments as passing.

I mentioned that when Antoine says to Mathilde, "We'd be so closely welded that nothing cold or evil could slip between us," the very word "weld" seems to be drawn from Hephaestus's question to the lovers in their bed about what it is they most truly want. This couple, Antoine and Mathilde, know what they most truly want. For Mathilde, though not so much for Antoine, death is the threat to that enduring relationship. The awful boy is soothed by Antoine's dancing, who says, "I'll show you something you've never seen." And in the voiceover, Antoine says, "We've no children, we've no friends. What could they add to our lives?" He says that when couples spend time with others it's a proof that their love is lacking. Antoine and Mathilde form a perfect couple, a couple that's perfect. They satisfy each other's needs so well and in such a complementary way that they really are each other's half. But they also form a perfect couple because they're a closed couple, not an open couple. You may have noticed that when one of your friends is in the throes of falling in love or establishing a romantic relationship, they often seem to disappear from view for a while. They go into a kind of romantic cocoon. Their friends complain, "Hey! You never go out with us anymore." They smile sheepishly, but they prefer their new lover's company to their friends. There's a kind of enclosure that at least a certain stage of romantic love seems to offer to us, to invite us into. Antoine and Mathilde are trying to live out that life of enclosure. It doesn't mean they're impolite or hostile to other people, of course. New lovers are often unbearably cheerful! But it does mean that everything except themselves is exterior to the nature of their erotic love. And most particularly, children are exterior to it. As they understand their love, if their acts of sexual consummation were "unprotected" (what an unromantic word world that term comes from), they might end up with a baby or two, and the demanding little things would be distractions and impediments to their singular focus on each other. They have to protect their closed love from the openness of new life. How many movies can you think of, where a central aspect of the romantic attraction between two lovers is their desire to have children through each other's bodies? Children in a romance are almost always the cause of comic impediments to the lovers' romance. They are virtually never the expression of, or the culmination of the lovers' romance. The erotic cocoon is so tightly closed that even the children of a particular romantic couple count as intruders.

I suspect many younger adults would be surprised, not to say mortified, to find out how much of the time that their parents spend on dates (and yes, even old married people do still go on dates, whether their children like to think about it or not) they spend talking about their children. I ask my students to ponder, do your parents experience you as an intrusion into their relationship? Or do they experience you as such an integral part of their relationship that when they're together, trying to have the kind of intimacy a good conversation provides, the most natural topic of that intimate conversation is their child, their children, you? So much so, that people without children can have a hard time connecting with people who have children, because they're so boring, talking about their children all the time. Now among people with children, it's not so bad, because you can let those people brag or complain about their children for a while and then you get a turn to do the same about yours. It's a bit like Dubus's Susan Dorsey, who needed a lover so she could talk about her own gratitude for her creative talent. – It's even worse with grandchildren.

So the movie is focusing on the way that children are perceived as intruders within this Aristophanic model of the welded, enclosed couple. The structure of the actual desire for union between these two human beings has no space for a desire for procreation or reproduction. Pregnancy becomes deformity, and fertile sex becomes "unprotected." The movie focuses on the romantic cocoon, the enclosed couple, but this focus reveals on its blurred exterior, we might say, another possibility: the possibility not of a closed couple, but of an open couple, procreatively open. The movie does not give us a healthy model of that kind of couple. It's a question whether there are ANY romantic movies that give us a healthy model of that procreatively open couple. Of course there are family joke movies, about people who have so many kids that it's hilarious, movie versions of the nursery rhyme, "There was an old lady who lived in a shoe who had so many children she didn't know what to do." The movie *Monty Python's The Meaning of Life* (1983) has a very funny, rather anti-Catholic song, "Every Sperm is Sacred," making fun of large families. When I was growing up, how many kids did you have to have before you were comic? About eight. Now, if you have more than two you look like a large family. When my three girls were all little, say under the age of five, if I'd go to the mall with them and their mom wasn't there, people would come up and talk to me like it was amazing I could manage three of them at once. You'd think I was juggling them in the air like balls. People used to think that was light child-work. So there's something about children in our place and time, in our culture, that this movie is really getting at. And more generally, I think it's reflected in what kinds of movies there are about romance. How hard it is to find a good movie where the desire for children is a central part of people's love life!

Because his own sense of romantic possibility is so thoroughly male, Antoine doesn't think of time as a threat to his romantic potential. But Mathilde is constantly working with the anxiety that what makes her the perfect person for the man she loves, Antoine, will be diminished, even destroyed, with the passage of time. This is why she has such a different relationship to her childhood from Antoine. Far from repeating her childhood, she suppresses it. She wants no reminders of it. When Antoine and Mathilde go to visit the former owner of the salon, in the old folks' home, it's not Antoine, it's Mathilde who turns to look back with a look of horror on her face, because the retired owner's present is her future. For Antoine, that's not a problem. Being old, for Antoine, is just another temporal accident. It's not something that changes his life in some fundamental way. The movie codes this as a male/female difference. We wouldn't have to code it the same way, but I do think the movie would be much harder to make if you tried to invert the gender roles. There's something that the movie is capturing, whether it's just a passing part of our culture or something more permanent in human nature. It's a theme that we can see in the *Symposium*, especially in Agathon's speech, the theme of youthfulness within the economy of romantic love. In *The Hairdresser's Husband*, the last word on the nature of our erotic desire comes from Antoine, who says enigmatically enough, "The hairdresser will be back." He can say this because Antoine is always dancing, always living in the mode of repetition. For him the hairdresser will always be back. He's dancing, dancing, dancing, all the way to the grave.

Chapter Five
UNION AND PROCREATION

We saw in the last chapter that Aristophanes's myth of the origins of sexuality picks up a number of themes introduced by the earlier speakers – especially about the integration of masculine and feminine aspects of romantic love, and the openness of erotic experience to something beyond the everyday human level, to something sacred or divine. But Aristophanes also introduces new themes of his own, especially the themes of union and neediness as essential aspects of love. Perhaps the most important new idea introduced by Aristophanes, though, is that the human erotic drive has a dual aspect, and combines something that we might call merely human, the desire for union or reunion, with something divine or sacred, a divine purpose, the purpose of reproduction or procreation.

The speech of Aristophanes uses a mythical *history* of human origins to think about the actual *nature* of human love. An origin myth gets at human nature, at the essence of human beings, by giving us a history of human beings. The most important myth about human nature and sexuality in Western culture still remains the Adam and Eve story from the Book of *Genesis*, the beginning of the Old Testament (which some scholars prefer to call the Hebrew Bible). This story is beautiful, compact, and open to many different interpretations. The interpretation I'll be suggesting is very much influenced by some brief words of Jesus Christ, as reported in the nineteenth chapter of the *Gospel of Matthew*, in the New Testament. (Similar reports appear in the gospels of Mark and of Luke.) Adam and Eve, and the whole story of the Garden of Eden, are still a part of popular culture, even among people who recognize no religious authority in the Bible. I want to turn to this story of Adam and Eve, seen through the perspective of Jesus, with an eye to how it compares to Aristophanes's myth of human origins and the nature of human love. So in a sense I won't be treating the Book of *Genesis* as a religious book at all, or at least no more so than we were thinking of Plato's *Symposium* as a religious book. Of course, both Plato and Jesus, and the anonymous authors and editors of *Genesis*, think we will understand romantic love more fully if we acknowledge that such love goes beyond the merely human, and has about it something sacred. But openness to the sacred is the natural inheritance of philosophy in Western culture, as I see it. At any rate, gratitude for this openness is presupposed by Plato's writing – and by mine!

This comparison between the *Symposium* and the Bible is made more palpable and delightful when we think about it in literature and movies from our own time. Before returning to ancient myth, I want to reflect a bit on modern love in the movies, and on the problem children cause for movie romance. In particular, I'll develop some thoughts about the fairy tale romance between the elf princess Arwen and the human king Aragorn in Peter Jackson's movies based on J.R.R. Tolkien's famous novel *The Lord of the Rings*. Then we'll turn to the Adam and Eve story, and complete this chapter on union and procreation with our second discussion of a short story from Andre Dubus's *Dancing after Hours*, "All the Time in the World."

The child and the death test in
Peter Jackson's *The Lord of the Rings*

In the last chapter we discussed the movie *The Hairdresser's Husband*, with its vision of the perfect couple. Romantic perfection in that movie, and in almost every romantic movie, is purely a matter of the union or intimacy of two people. I am tempted to say that such movies are all conceived under the spell of contraception. When these movies think of a man and a woman who fall in love and have an enduring sexual relationship – a marriage, in the best case, when their desire avoids the weakness of dishonesty and impatience – they hardly notice that a natural consequence of making love is making babies. I mentioned that it is very hard to find a movie where a defining aspect of a couple's being in love is seeing themselves as parents together. In modern romance stories, children are never the happy ending. In fact, children are usually comic obstacles or interruptions to romantic union; the challenges of raising a child together aren't the business of being in love, but a distraction from that business.

I think this oddly contraceptive way that movies see human life is unreal, that it doesn't reflect the way men and women experience their own mutual power of fertility in a sexual relationship. A couple may be in awe of this procreative power, or fearful of it, or even wish it weren't in them, but they will not usually be as forgetful of their life-giving powers as the movies make it seem. Of course, there are many unreal things in movies, from how physically attractive the actors are to how a body reacts to a car crash or a gun wound. So I don't criticize all romances for being under the contraceptive spell. But wouldn't you expect to find more movies that see children as the goal of love, or at least a goal, rather than as obstacles to love?

It is against this background that the central romance in Peter Jackson's *The Lord of the Rings* is so astonishing. Jackson's three movies (released in 2001, 2002, and 2003) were of course based on the three volumes of J.R.R. Tolkien's extraordinary novel (published in 1954). Tolkien is a very deep well, and we can draw only a few buckets from it here. The book has long attracted a devoted community of readers, among whom I count myself. When the news arrived that Peter Jackson was making the novel into movies, many of these readers were skeptical about the whole project. I admit I was among the skeptics. When you love a book, you often become protective of it, and you are a bit hostile to any changes a director might make to the story to adapt it for the screen. But five minutes into the first movie, *The Fellowship of the Ring*, all my doubts were swept away. Jackson certainly changed important parts of the story, but a movie is not just its plot. Jackson found a way to realize aspects of Tolkien's writing in what I would call the visual vocabulary of the movie, as well as in its powerful, Wagnerian music, composed by Howard Shore. The movie captured many aspects of Tolkien's imagination in this rich visual and musical vocabulary, compensating generously for the ways it had to simplify and adjust the plot, to fit within the confines of a watchable movie. Especially effective, it seems to me, were the decisions to use musical ideas from Richard Wagner's operas, and visual ideas from British painting, especially from the so-called Pre-Raphaelites. This late nineteenth-century aesthetic world fits well with Tolkien, who was deeply influenced by these ideas. So the music and the visual images compensate for some losses at the level of plot.

Of course, some fans of the book complained about favorite plot details or characters that were cut from the movie version, but to satisfy them all, the movies would have to be ten times longer than their already long nine hours or so. But stronger complaints came not from what was excluded, but from what was changed. I wouldn't defend every change, but one major change seems to me to have been a brilliant success: the romance between the elf princess Arwen (Liv Tyler) and the human king Aragorn (Viggo Mortensen). This story is present in Tolkien's novel, though most of the details are relegated to one of the many appendices Tolkien added to the book to fill out the long fictional history presupposed by the novel itself. Its basic outline goes like this. Elves and humans are different races, but in a few rare and historically crucial cases, they have married and produced children of mixed elvish and human nature. The fundamental obstacle to such marriages is that humans are by nature mortal, while elves are immortal, though they can be killed by violence. Elves eventually will grow weary of their unending lives on earth, and they have the privilege, when they choose, of sailing away to The Undying Lands, where they can live in close community with the gods. Arwen's dilemma is that her elven father Elrond (Hugo Weaving, the blind man in *Proof* much earlier in his career) encourages her to sail to safety and immortality, while her love for Aragorn leads her to cleave to him in his dangerous war to establish his kingdom on earth.

For two humans to accept each other in marriage is a radical thing to do; as the traditional wedding vows say, they marry for better, for worse, till death. But for an elf to marry a human is an even more radical choice, for an elf must give up her immortality to marry a mortal man. This is a much more extreme version of Phaedrus's death test even than Achilles had to pass. The Greek hero chose a short life over a long one, but he was not forced to choose between death and unending life. Not only would Arwen's choice to marry Aragorn mean giving up her own individual immortal life, it also means being forever severed from her elven family and kin. Arwen does choose to marry Aragorn; as she says to him in the movie when she declares her love, "I choose a mortal life." There are some fascinating connections between Tolkien's version of this choice by an immortal being of mortality and human love and Richard Wagner's version, in the story of Brunhilde and Siegfried in Wagner's opera cycle *The Ring of the Nibelung*. Tolkien based his novel on the same northern European myths that Wagner used in his operas.

Peter Jackson and the two women who were the other principal writers of the movies, Fran Walsh and Phillipa Boyens, greatly enlarged Arwen's part in the movies, to create another strong female role and to give the romance subplot more prominence. They wanted to emphasize the crisis Arwen faced when she had to choose between the safe escape her father urged upon her and the sure death that marrying Aragorn would bring. For the second movie, *The Two Towers*, they created a beautiful and haunting scene where Elrond gives Arwen a vision of what a bitter experience mortality will be for her, when in the end, even if Aragorn wins his war and lives a long life, he must finally die, and she be left to mourn for him. (By the way, one of the designers of this scene, John Howe, mentioned that he drew on Pre-Raphaelite paintings to imagine it.) This, too, is a death test, the test of being forced to outlive your lover rather than to die for him. Arwen weeps at this painful future, and she decides to leave and sail to The Undying Lands. Yet something changes her mind, and in the third movie, *The Return of the King*, she marries Aragorn after all. Yes, she loves Aragorn, but is that enough to explain why this immortal being would pass the death test? Can union with her lover be enough?

The two women writers, at least, felt that they hadn't given Arwen a strong enough reason to explain why she decides to stay. And so they wrote one of the most beautiful scenes in all three movies to give the explanation. Arwen is riding a horse through a forest, escorted by a troupe of elves, on her way to the harbor where she can board a ship to take her to The Undying Lands. Suddenly, she has a vision of her own, to compete with her father's vision of her pain at the death of Aragorn. She sees Aragorn, older now with graying hair; but running into his arms is a little boy. As Aragorn lifts him and both smile and laugh, the boy turns to gaze at Arwen, and she realizes she is having a vision of the son she may have with her husband. She turns her horse and rides back to confront Elrond. "What did you see?" she demands of her father. "I looked into your future and saw only death," he responds, but her own vision of love has shown her more than this. "But there was life, too; I saw my child." Elrond does not deny the possibility, and he mutters, "Nothing is certain." But now Arwen will cleave to her mortal love rather than to her own immortal life and that of her kin, abandoning even her father. Her vision has revealed to her that the bitter harvest of mortality brings with it a most sweet fruit, the fruit of a new life, sprung from the union of the two lovers. She gives up her own immortality for a mortal man, but sees this love as itself a participation in another kind of immortality, through procreation.

Why did the writers find this open love for new life a sufficient explanation of Arwen's death test, when her partnership in a closed couple was not? It would be a mistake to think Arwen would love her child *more* than she would love her husband, and so find it easier to accept death for the little boy than for the aging man. No; her love for the boy is bound to her love of the man, is an aspect of the same love, so that union (with Aragorn) is itself a commitment to an openness (to her son). Arwen's vision of the son she and Aragorn beget at last helps her understand the fullness of her commitment to her husband, and his to her. Only this full commitment, both unitive and procreative, allows her to leave her father and kin to marry Aragorn. The union she seeks is essentially an open union, not a closed one. And so this movie makes its habitation in a deeper realm of the heart than did *The Hairdresser's Husband*, where, as Antoine said, children could add nothing to the perfection of his relationship to Mathilde. Indeed, Arwen goes beyond even the severed humans of Aristophanes's myth. For them, union was the whole of their erotic need, and it was only a happy divine accident, we might say, that the physical expression of union in sexual intercourse also produced children and preserved the human race. For Arwen and Aragorn, procreation is an aspect of the human desire for union, not just a divine consequence of it.

By feeling their way toward this deeper motivation in Arwen, the writers of the movie discovered for themselves and their viewers a view of romantic love that is in fact very ancient. It is a view that becomes visible when we consider some comments of Jesus about marriage, and about how marriage requires us to put away our fears and our attempts to control love, to tame it.

Aristophanes versus Adam and Eve

Chapter 19 of the *Gospel of Matthew* has a special focus on Jesus as a teacher, and it starts particularly from a teaching about marriage. Some teachers are content to work from the outside of their students, you might say. They are rather like Eryximachus, offering information and advice, but not noticing whether the listeners are taking the lesson to heart. Socrates and Jesus were the better type of teacher, the kind who work from the inside. These teachers were never content merely to say true things; they always wanted to say things the student could feel to be true, things the student felt as a demand. Indeed, strictly speaking, what I receive from the best teachers is not so much instruction as provocation. Their words to me become my words to myself.

One day, Jesus was with some of his students – we call them "disciples," which just means students – when some professional experts on the law, called Pharisees, came and tested Jesus by asking him, "Is it lawful for a man to divorce his wife?" Jesus answered them with a question of his own. "Have you never heard the saying, 'The creator made them from the beginning male and female'? And 'For this reason a man shall leave his father and mother and be made one with his wife, and the two shall become one flesh'?" Of course Jesus knew that these experts would recognize these two passages. They come from the first few pages of the Bible, in the Book of *Genesis*, and they are essential moments in the Bible's myth of human origins and the origins of sexuality. Jesus goes on to draw his uncompromising conclusion from these two passages. "It follows," he said, "that they are no longer two individuals, they are one flesh. What God has joined together, man must not separate."

Part of what's so striking about Jesus's model of marriage here is that he combines two passages that are presented separately in *Genesis*. The first passage, "The creator made them from the beginning male and female," comes from the creation myth that opens the Bible. In this familiar story, God creates the world in six days. On the last of these days, God creates the living animals that populate the earth, and last of all creates human beings, male and female. This myth of human origins is very lofty and impersonal, rather like Pausanias's Heavenly Aphrodite. It seems to focus more on God's purpose in creating humans as both male and female than on the human experience of this difference. The second passage Jesus invokes, "For this reason a man shall leave his father and mother and be made one with his wife, and the two shall become one flesh," comes a page or two later in *Genesis*, from a second myth of human origins, the Adam and Eve story. This myth is much more earthy and human, like the earthy Aphrodite, and gives a memorable account of Adam's reaction when he first sees the woman Eve who's been created for him. So in Jesus's teaching here, two things that in *Genesis* are presented separately are integrated. Jesus teaches that to understand what marriage really is, we have to combine things that we might have thought of separately. So let's turn our attention to *Genesis* and see what it is that this particular teacher is putting together when he teaches people about what marriage would be.

The first passage comes from the larger account of God's creative activity that opens the Bible. The creation of human beings is the capstone of this creative action, and we have a special share in God's creative power. First God says, "Let us make man in our image and likeness to rule the fish in the sea, the birds of heaven, the cattle, all wild animals on earth, and all reptiles that crawl upon the earth." This verse does not yet hint that in order to be an image of God, human beings will have to be sexually differentiated. You might say that if we read no farther, we would expect the foundation myth in *Genesis* to be more like the myth in Aristophanes, where the original perfect human nature is self-sufficient, unitary, and asexual. The all-male, the all-female, and the androgynous beings in Aristophanes's myth of human origins are all unified images of human nature. In Aristophanes's story, human beings become sexual only after they are punished for their impious attempt to usurp the place of the Olympian gods. *Genesis* continues with this unitary language for a little longer: "So God created man in his own image, in the image of God he created him." But suddenly the reader is in for a surprise, for the next phrase says, "Male and female he created them." Suddenly we have sexual distinction. The language starts out by emphasizing the way humanity, all humanity, images God. But when we get down to the most articulated description of how humanity images God, it's through maleness and femaleness together. One is not more an image than the other; indeed the image is incomplete without both. Only as a couple of man and woman is the human image of God at its most complete, for only the couple images God's creative power. In this respect, too, we're reminded of an aspect of Aristophanes's myth, the notion that in our current state, we are simply broken halves, we are not wholes. It's our sexuality, our erotic potential, that can return us to a state of wholeness. But there is this crucial difference between Aristophanes and *Genesis*: the original whole human being in Aristophanes is self-sufficient, and is an image of the self-sufficiency of the celestial gods, the sun, moon, and earth; whereas the couple in the *Genesis* myth images God through imaging creative power, not self-sufficiency, and the original beings are radically incomplete without each other. In Aristophanes's myth, the gods see to it that human sexuality serves a divine purpose. But that divine purpose of human procreativity, human fertility, is not itself an image of anything found in the gods themselves. Sexuality in Aristophanes's speech, you might say, is a purely human concern. It serves divine purposes, but it is not itself part of what makes us an image of something divine. We image the divine in Aristophanes's speech through our sphericity, our self-sufficiency.

Procreation is not the only aspect of the human image of God in this passage of *Genesis*. The text goes on to say, "God blessed them and said to them, be fruitful and increase. Fill the earth and subdue it. Rule over the fish in the sea, the birds in heaven and every living thing that moves upon the earth." One of the ways, then, that humans are images of God is by being able to rule, to manage, to be stewards of the earth. But at its most basic, to image God here is to image what God is doing throughout this hymn to creation that begins our Bible, that is, to be creative, to be procreative. To image God is to be fruitful. It's in human fertility that humanity most deeply or most directly images this creator God. So we see why the emphasis on humanity imaging the divine has as its punchline, its capstone, the notion that it's human sexuality that allows us to image this aspect of the divine most potently, most fully.

So one verse that Jesus draws on for his own teaching about marriage, marriage under the threat of divorce, emphasizes that human sexuality is essentially connected to fertility, to creativity or procreativity. The second verse that he draws on comes from the second origin myth in *Genesis*, about the creation of human beings in the Garden of Eden. Now, in this myth first there's a man, Adam. When God sees it's not good for the man to be alone, he decides to provide a partner for him. All of the animals are created and are brought to Adam as potential partners. But Adam gives names to all the animals, a sign that all of the animals are subordinated to man's cognitive power, to his command over language. None of them is a fit partner, because all of them in some way are subordinate to human purpose. In light of this human specialness, where can humanity find something that relieves its loneliness and makes possible a life of partnership?

Contrast the situation of Adam in the Garden of Eden with the emergence of need and loneliness in Aristophanes's myth. In this *Genesis* account, humanity has not yet fallen. Humanity has done nothing wrong. It's intrinsic to our natural, healthy condition that we need partnership. Our incompleteness is not a punishment for anything. Adam is not broken or wounded. He simply needs partnership. In this mythical history, unlike Aristophanes's, our need for partnership is a part of what human perfection is. It is not a falling off from some original state of human self-sufficiency. Now, while God has seen that it isn't good for Adam to be alone, Adam himself doesn't yet really understand what he is missing. He only understands after God puts Adam into a deep sleep and constructs a woman from a part of Adam's body (his rib). God doesn't make an animal for Adam, constructed in such a way that it's subordinate to the man, but rather a partner that's so equal with Adam that she's created from his own body – another striking resemblance to Aristophanes's broken beings. Adam has not had the experience of partnership before, and behold! this woman is brought before him, naked as he is naked, barefoot in the soft grass. The experience overwhelms him, and his language, an expression of the pure joy of finally understanding what he needed all along, is a barely grammatical exclamation: "Now this at last, bone from my bone, flesh from my flesh." And in his now open heart he says, "This is a partner! This is not something subordinate to me. This is me, but it's outside of me. My partnership, my union with this being is as intimate as my partnership with myself – except she's beautiful." And it's after this babbling joy of Adam in seeing what a real partner would be for him that we have the passage, the commentary from which Jesus quotes. "That is why a man leaves his father and mother and is united to his wife, and the two become one flesh."

So at this moment, we have a radical distinction between any kind of subordination the animals might bear to Adam, and the true partnership that would fulfill him. Now to be sure, Adam, like lots of men, will be tempted in various ways to treat his wife as a subordinate. The Bible has lots to say on these sorts of issues. But subordination within the marital partnership will be understood as something that occurs after the Fall. That is, the subordination of women to men is a part of human imperfection, not a part of human perfectibility.

Think back to Aristophanes again. In Aristophanes's myth, the human sexual drive, the restless erotic life, is driven by reunion. It's that sense of re-union, of a perfect partnership that makes us fully integrated and whole again, that's behind the sexual drive. So too, in this story about Adam and Eve, about the original man and woman. After all, Adam does not say, "Here is the woman who can be the mother of my children." What he says is, "Bone of my bone, flesh of my flesh." He focuses on the intimacy of the union, the intimacy of the partnership possible with this other being. So right at the beginning of the Bible, within a couple pages of each other, we've got two stories about maleness and femaleness. In the one, the emphasis is on fertility as an imaging of God's creativity. In the other, we have a story about the intimacy of partnership, of union. What Jesus does is to put these two ideas right next to each other, as a teaching about the possibilities of marriage, about what a marriage could be. Aristophanes's myth also considers both of these aspects of human sexuality, the unitive and the procreative. But in Aristophanes's way of telling the story of human nature, these two drives are kept separate.

Jesus and the deaf heart

Now, when we return to Matthew 19, we learn something more about bringing together union and procreation in marriage. When we put together the passages the way that Jesus does, the picture of the union possible for a man and a woman that we get from *Genesis* looks very demanding. And that's the way that both the legal experts, the Pharisees, and Jesus's own disciples, his students, experience this teaching. They have heard Jesus say, "The intimacy of this partnership and the imaging of God in this partnership is so complete that there's no such thing as divorce." With Aristophanes in mind, think of marriage and divorce this way. You've become one whole organism when you marry. Divorce would be like cutting yourself in half, and then deluding yourself into thinking you've made two whole organisms, when in fact you've just made one broken organism. If you decided that there should be more people like you, and you take an axe and cut yourself through the middle of your head down through your groin, you've made a terrible conceptual error. You're not a worm; you can't double yourself that way. What Jesus is suggesting is that it's that bad of a mistake conceptually to think you can divorce your spouse. A married couple is now one thing. Again, there's something in this story that's a lot like Aristophanes's story. It turns out the way we are now, uncoupled, is something that has to be seen as incomplete, that's completed by our coupling. And so to break an erotic couple is itself to return to a state of brokenness, not primarily to a state of freedom, a state of self-sufficiency.

To say the least, this teaching about marriage and divorce can seem hard, even inhuman. Then as now, a lot of people heard what Jesus said and thought, "Well what if my wife turns out to be a bitch? What if my husband is a drunk? You mean I'm stuck with that? I'd hack off even my own arm if it was a drunk; or at least I'd cut off my little finger if it whined at me every morning. You mean there's no escape hatch?" Jesus knows this is what both the legal experts and his own students are thinking, and he addresses this objection head-on, so there won't be any doubt that he means what he says about marriage. Jesus notes that in the law, inherited from Moses, a man was allowed to divorce his wife with a formal note of dismissal. Of course the social context here is that it's the woman who's much more likely to be abandoned by her husband, who decides that maybe he'd like to go back to the original state of brokenness after all. So the law seems to grant married people, or at least men, a freedom that Jesus denies to them, the freedom to become single again. Jesus has a really interesting answer. Jesus says, Here's why Moses gave you the escape hatch. "It was because of the hardness of your hearts that Moses gave you permission to divorce your wives. But in the beginning it was not so." Jesus is thinking back to the passages from *Genesis* he just quoted. The mythical original condition of man and woman, one flesh, one life, is the standard he uses to measure our lives now. The time has come, Jesus teaches, to accept a higher standard than the compromise Moses allowed for your hard hearts. He asserts his own authority to revise and bring to fulfillment the law of Moses, and he says, "I tell you, if a man divorces his wife and marries another, he commits adultery."

The key to this challenging passage is the beautiful Greek word we translate as "hardness of heart," *sclerocardia*. The first part of this word, *sclero-*, is where we get medical words like sclerosis of the liver, or arterial sclerosis. It's a word that means hard, or hardening. The second part, *-cardia*, is where we get other medical words like cardiac. It's the word for heart. So what Jesus says is that the Mosaic law compromised with your hardness of heart, your *sclerocardia*. Now, we think of the heart as the seat of feeling and affection, which is why we decorate Valentine's Day cards with hearts. But in ancient Semitic culture, the heart was not primarily an organ of feeling or affection the way it is for us. It was primarily an organ of perception. When Jesus says that the Mosaic law allowing divorce was a compromise with our *sclerocardia*, he is suggesting that Moses was making allowances for something we weren't ready to understand fully. When you want an escape hatch in your marriages, you're hard of hearing, you're not listening to something. In particular, you're not listening to what you really wanted out of marriage in the first place. Look at the sparkle in the eyes of a couple on their wedding day, when they say those vows, for better, for worse, till death. Perhaps then you perceive that they really want to mean what they're saying. But a kind of fear, a timid withholding of the self, makes us not quite hear the very words that we're saying as we're saying them. It is as if at the very moment we say those bold words that pledge us till death, for better or for worse, we mutter an undertone of "maybe later, but not quite yet." The undertone is our *sclerocardia*, our hardness of heart. And what Jesus says here is that the time has come to stop muttering, to mean what we say; the time has come to listen to our own hearts.

Now, the reaction of the disciples is disbelieving. The disciples, some as young as college students, some of them quite a bit older, were all men. I picture them standing there, rather enjoying watching their hero Jesus show up the legal experts. But when they hear what he says about divorce, they glance nervously at each other out of the side of their eyes. "Did you hear that?" they whisper, "what the hell's he saying?" And so one of the disciples, asking the question out loud that many of them have in their minds, said to Jesus, "Well if that's the position with husband and wife, it's better not to marry." This disciple is thinking, "I've seen some wives who are awfully hard to put up with; I don't think I'd take the risk of being stuck with a woman like that, Jesus!" The disciples feel their fear talking: "Marriage without the possibility of divorce sounds like an imprudent or even mad course of action. Nobody could pledge himself to be married no matter what. There's got to be an escape hatch. You wouldn't build a building without a fire escape. It's against the building codes of marriage, somehow. Jesus, you're a fine teacher, but you're making marriage uninhabitable." This is a typical response from the disciples to some challenging teaching of Jesus. They were slow learners, as slow as we are! The Gospels don't show us the disciples as heroes and saints, as heavenly men better than us. They are earthy and stumbling, led by love but limited by fear, and so we identify with them and are given hope that we too may rise from our own deafness to an acute listening.

How did Jesus respond to this display of *sclerocardia*, a kind of moral deafness? He looked his students in the eye and said, "Not everyone can accept this teaching, but only those to whom God has appointed it. There are others who have renounced marriage." So the disciples are thinking, that sounds better. If there's no divorce, I think I'm going to renounce marriage. I don't think God could have appointed me to something as difficult, risky, and even crazy as marriage for better, for worse, till death. It really is better not to marry, rather than to accept such an open commitment. But Jesus has no intention of leaving his students settled in this comfortable avoidance of love. In effect, he says to them, "You know, you might be right. You might not be the kind of guy who should get married. You might not be man enough to get married! Why did you think everybody was big enough to get married? A lot of you might be very little men right now. You're going to have to grow quite a bit before you can get married." What the disciples would consider prudence, Jesus would consider fear, something to be challenged, to grow out of.

But Jesus goes even farther than this. He won't allow his students to renounce marriage just to stay settled, but he does invite some to renounce marriage to become even more unsettled. You might be called, Jesus suggests, to renounce marriage "for the sake of the kingdom of heaven." This abandonment of marriage is the opposite of settled comfort. When a student looks into his heart and says, I can't marry someone without having the escape hatch of divorce, Jesus doesn't say, Okay, just don't get married. What he says is, "You are partly right and partly wrong. It may make sense for you to decide that marriage isn't the way of life for you. But don't do this because you're going to hang on to your hard heart. Do it because you're going to open your heart even more than marriage does. Give up marriage for the sake of devoting yourself to the kingdom of heaven – not for a less demanding ideal, but for one that might be even more demanding, that requires you to open up your closed heart even further." The openness of marriage becomes then a sign and a symbol of the possibility of an openness that hadn't even entered the disciples' minds: the possibility of a complete openness that doesn't have within it the satisfactions of a private family, but that devotes one entirely to service of the kingdom of heaven.

Jesus realizes there's something frightening in what human beings want from each other when they desire marriage. In a fearful mood, marriage seems to take on too much risk to be prudent. But Jesus also suggests that a lot of life is like this. It's not just marriage that asks you to take on the task of really meaning what we say. It's everything about following his teaching, for example, in the radical way of life a vow of celibacy might require. But from the point of view that Jesus has just preached here, it turns out that a married man or a married woman is more like a celibate priest than like an unmarried man or an unmarried woman. It turns out that when you get engaged you've entered the seminary. There's a continuity between the life of celibacy and the life of expressed sexuality in marriage, because both of those commitments require an overcoming of *sclerocardia*. It's no wonder that the disciples found this all a little surprising. It's not like they all ran over and gave Jesus a hug and said, I'm so glad you made all that about marriage and celibacy clear; I feel much better now. In fact, the very next scene seems to have been designed by the writer Matthew to show what slow learners the disciples were. (Matthew is a very funny Gospel if you're in the right mood. Why shouldn't good news be funny?) Matthew reports that people were bringing their children to meet Jesus and to have him pray over them. The disciples found this irritating, and rather a waste of the Master's time. "Take those kids away! Jesus is busy." But Jesus said to the disciples, "Let the children come to me. Do not try to stop them, for the kingdom of heaven belongs to such as these." So right after the disciples wish there were an escape hatch in marriage, they don't understand children. Now, Jesus has just told these men that if they think through what marriage is, they'll see what an open life that would be; and they'll see that an even more open life might give up even marriage for the kingdom of heaven. Jesus gives them an example of what "living for the kingdom of heaven" might be: openness to children.

The myth of marriage that's embodied in the beginning of *Genesis*, as seen through the lens of Matthew's Gospel, has many points of contact with Aristophanes's myth. The myth of marriage in Matthew is more demanding, but on the other hand, it's much more optimistic, because the myth in *Genesis* does not make human sexuality a function of our imperfection. Human procreativity, based in the distinction between man and woman, is an expression of our perfection, of the way we image God. In Aristophanes, sexuality is not a punishment, but it's the result of a punishment. In *Genesis*, sexuality has nothing to do with punishment; it is a part of the Garden of Eden. It's a part of what it would be to be as perfect as a human being can be.

There remains, then, a striking philosophical issue raised by the competition between Aristophanes's myth and the *Genesis* myth: does the human erotic drive combine a desire for union with the desire for creation? Like those lovers in their bedroom when the god Hephaestus comes down and visits, we're trying to articulate a mystery at the heart of romantic life. Aristophanes introduced the theme of reproduction, of procreativity, into the *Symposium*, but in Aristophanes's myth union and creation are kept separate, and the human erotic drive focuses only on the one, on union. In the *Genesis* myth, at least as interpreted by Jesus in Matthew's Gospel, there is an integration of those two into one form of human desire, a form that we can listen to only if we can overcome a certain hardness or a certain fearfulness. It is not until Socrates's speech in the *Symposium* that Plato also tries to integrate union and procreation into one unified form of human erotic desire.

The Garden of Eden in Andre Dubus's America

In the contemporary world, the most consistent and prominent promoter of the view that romantic love correctly understood includes both union and procreation has been the Roman Catholic Church. This view, in fact very old and the shared tradition of all major Christian denominations, became a focus of worldwide controversy in 1968, when it was defended in a famous encyclical written by Pope Paul VI called *Of Human Life*, usually known under its Latin title *Humanae Vitae*. The second of Andre Dubus's short stories telling the story of the romance of Ted Briggs and LuAnn Arceneaux, "All the Time in the World," is itself a deeply Catholic piece of literary thinking. It never mentions the controversies around the encyclical, but the story is best understood against that background. So let me start out by talking a little bit about *Humanae Vitae*.

In May 1968, the country France almost ceased to exist. Now, for most of us this comes as quite a surprise. We think of France as more or less a permanent part of the earth's geography. But of course, that's really not true. In May 1968 a general strike spread throughout France and brought down the government, and they had to bring the old World War II hero General Charles DeGaulle out of retirement to put things back together. It was a time of great social and political ferment in the United States as well. This of course was during the Viet Nam War, and it was right near the beginning of what was known as the Tet Offensive, a great escalation in the violence of the war due to a new military offensive coming from North Viet Nam. It was a time when revolution was in the air, when people expected, or at least feared, great and uncontrollable cultural and political change. With all that going on, in July 1968 Pope Paul VI issued his encyclical *Humanae Vitae*, and despite the war in Viet Nam, despite the recent near-collapse of France, this little pamphlet made headlines all over the Western world. An extraordinary thing for a papal document that, in truth, simply repeated what the Catholic Church had been teaching for two thousand years.

It is a great pity that this encyclical provoked so much controversy that its actual teaching was obscured by much thoughtless polemic. The core of the document is an understanding of marriage, and of the way sexual intercourse between spouses expresses both natural and supernatural dimensions of the union of man and woman. But this core was almost completely neglected, by opponents but also by supporters, to focus instead on the less enduring but more contemporary issue of artificial contraception. Not only the Catholic Church, but nearly every Christian denomination until around 1930 had held the same doctrine about contraception, about birth control, as the doctrine enunciated in *Humanae Vitae*. The tradition clearly condemned contraception, seeing it as a denial of the fundamental meaning of married sexuality. But changing technology, especially the invention in the late 1950s of hormone-based contraceptive drugs, known simply as "The Pill," shaped a more general change in social attitudes toward married sexuality. By 1968, many Catholics thought that severing procreation from union in marital sexual intercourse might be morally acceptable, and even hoped the Catholic Church would solemnly change its age-old teaching. But the teaching did not change, and *Humanae Vitae* reaffirmed the Christian tradition that openness to new life is an essential aspect of sexuality. This was not so much a prohibition on artificial contraception as it was a challenge to a certain sort of marriage; but this challenge was lost in the fog of the war about contraception. Notice that the focus of debate at this time was still about the sexual relations of spouses within a marriage. But within a very few years, the question of whether spouses might have good reasons to sometimes make their sexual acts artificially infertile, had given way to the much more radical question of whether everyone of sexual maturity had a right to make themselves infertile to pursue sexual pleasures without the threat of pregnancy.

Pope Paul VI did not do anything particularly radical, particularly revolutionary, in issuing *Humanae Vitae*, unless you think repeating something the Church had been saying for two thousand years sounds revolutionary. Paul VI's encyclical came at a historically very volatile time, a volatile time particularly for sexual mores, for sexual culture. Dubus's short story "All the Time in the World" is his attempt to think his way down into the new social world that had been created by the promise of cheap and effective contraception. The widespread availability and acceptance – two quite different things – of cheap, effective contraception around 1960 does not, it seems to me, compare to some other important inventions of the twentieth century, inventions like the airplane or the hydrogen bomb or the automobile (although the automobile did provide more market incentive for the use of contraceptives, as a car became for unchaperoned young adults a mobile bedroom). Contraception is less like those technological innovations, important as they are, than it is like the moment in human history when human beings mastered the use of fire. Contraception, accepted as the normal practice of people in sexual maturity, is something much more basic than the invention of any of these modern technologies. Human sexuality has been essentially changed. Before there were cheap, effective contraceptives, the link between sexual intercourse and procreation, reproduction, was as natural as the force of gravity. Not many of us would wake up on a given morning and throw our feet over the side of the bed and complain, "Damn, gravity's here again. I wish I could have floated up to the ceiling this morning." And very few people complained, after they got up out of their conjugal bed, "We made love last night, we might have a baby in nine months." The "risk" of a baby was an acknowledged feature of the habitable erotic world. But sometime around half a century ago the limits of that world changed. And now each and every act of the conjugal embrace was shadowed by a question, a shadow cast over sexual life in a way that Dubus's story tries to bring out. Because now the question arose about each and every act of sexual intimacy: will we allow this act to be procreative as well as unitive?

As I say, I think this is a fundamental change in the structure of human life. It is not simply another technological invention. It's changed something as basic to us as anything could be, for beings like us, incarnate beings, not souls driving around in bodies, but embodied souls, animated bodies, the thing that we really are. So the new possibility of severing sexual union from procreation has produced an entire population of young adults who defertilize themselves in order to live sexualized lives. The sexual world changed for everybody, not just for married couples who wanted to control how many children they had. The offer of severing the procreative from the unitive has had a much more pervasive impact on human sexual culture than many people at the time predicted that it would. Imagine a technological innovation – of course it's possible, we can do it now with the means that we have – that had this kind of effect on another basic incarnational human activity: eating food. Suppose the people who govern my university or other corporations devise a new plan: "We can make our human resources, students or employees, more productive, increase their productivity, if we can only get them to waste less time in the dining halls and cafeterias. We're going to get rid of the whole notion of dining. Why do you spend so much time there chatting with your friends? You could be in a computer cluster! You'd be searching the web for information! You could even be posting your resume! If only we could get you to stop dining. It's dining that's the problem. Of course you've got to eat, but let's get rid of the dining halls; even the phrase "dining hall" sounds too much like a place for a leisure activity. Let's instead have nutrition stations, and in three minutes you can stick a needle in your arm and get all the nutrition you need. It will be the fastest fast food there's ever been!" And so the whole ritualized human culture that surrounds food and eating together and dining can be done away with technologically. We have the means; all we need is the will. We can change ourselves. Think how different our world, your world, would be, if we separated the nutrition function of food from the companionship function of food. (The word "companion" has as its root the Latin word for bread, *panis*. A companion is literally someone with whom you share bread, someone with whom you dine; in our imagined new way of seeing things, someone with whom you waste your time.) It's possible to sever the nutritive from the companionable.

It was also possible to sever the procreative from the unitive. It's an offer that Paul VI rejects in *Humanae Vitae*. Instead, he suggests that the connection between the unitive and the procreative is what makes of human sexual expression something that's conjugal, something whose natural home is in marriage, in a lifelong commitment both to the union of the spouses and to the fruitfulness of that union, shown in being willing to raise children. From the point of view that Paul VI represented in *Humanae Vitae*, the unitive and the procreative are different aspects of one and the same thing, and that thing is sexual intercourse. The meaningfulness of sexual intercourse, the longing in human beings that's responded to fearlessly through sexual marriages, is a longing for a complete, unreserved, mutual self-giving. Now, any gesture toward a completely unqualified mutual gift-giving naturally will provoke our fear. Paul VI was working very old ground, ground we've already explored in Matthew's Gospel, with another teacher who talked of the way marriage overcomes our hardness of heart. Continuing in that tradition, Paul VI saw sexuality as an expression both of our unitive desire to be with another person in complete unqualified intimacy, and of the unfolding of that complete commitment to union into an openness to new life. This openness involves a lack of a kind of control, a gesture of optimism to an uncontrolled and open future with children. Pope Paul VI sees that as an interpretation of what our heart most wants when we fall in love with another person, when we want that person to become our sexual partner. So, at least, did the pontiff read the oracle.

I think Andre Dubus tries in his short story to continue something that he tried to do in "Falling in Love," the first short story
we considered from *Dancing after Hours*. In "All the Time in the
World," Dubus now tells us the story from the point of view of a
woman in her twenties, LuAnn Arceneaux. LuAnn was a student
at a Catholic college based in Boston, and she lived before AIDS.
For those of you who are young, I think it's very hard for you to
appreciate how much the sexual culture of America changed due
to the AIDS epidemic. AIDS wasn't really fully understood until
well into the '80s, and it changed the sexual behavior not only of
homosexuals, but of heterosexuals as well. LuAnn Arceneaux's story
in her twenties is a story before sexuality had that particular threat
or that particular fear to confront. Of course, there were the diseases of Aphrodite, venereal diseases; but none of them were as
mortal a plague as AIDS was. So the story has a certain historical
value. It's clearly placed primarily in, let's say, the later '70s and
early '80s. LuAnn Arcenaux is a woman who pursues love, but she
pursues it in a partial way, a way that she discovers is not honest
to her own deepest desires. One thinks here of the way (in "Falling
in Love") Ted Briggs pursued a sexual life, a life of sexual intimacy,
in its way a loving life, but pursued it without fully realizing what
his own commitments were. He didn't realize that for him, if sexual
life resulted in procreation, he couldn't reject that new life to maintain his current life. Ted lived as if he accepted with Susan Dorsey
an implicit contract to sterilize the sexual expression of their love.
But when the moment came, and he discovered that his child and
her child was growing inside her body, he was not able to stick to
his part of that sexual contract.

LuAnn goes through some similar experiences. She discovers a
growing feeling of emptiness or hopelessness in her own pursuit of
a "relationship," as she calls it. Dubus has a fine paragraph on
what relationships are and of how the language of relationships
seems invented in part to cover over, to hide from us, our own
deepest heart's desires in sexual relationships. She realizes that the
men who sincerely believe they love her, who love her all the way
into bed, all of these men, even the most tender and gentle of them,

have abortion as the secret but necessary condition of their love affair. And she doesn't want to live that way anymore. She's unwilling to accept that condition – "If you get pregnant, we'll pay for an abortion together" – because she wants to give more of herself than that condition on her sexuality allows. And what she does is to stop dating, because in her own experience, it's also a condition of serious dating that one be willing to establish a sexual relationship.

LuAnn stops dating for a time, sorting out her aspirations and experiences. One Sunday after Mass – she has always been a serious Catholic, even when she was living a sexual life the Church would condemn – she stumbles on the steps outside and breaks the heel on her shoe. By a lucky chance, a chance the story invites us to interpret as providential, she meets a man who wants something more. As she looks at the broken heel, she hears a voice say, "I could try to fix it," and when she looks up, there is handsome Ted Briggs, also coming from Mass. They go off to brunch, and Ted surprises and delights her with something he says: "I want a home with love in it, with a woman and children." LuAnn's response is to almost laugh out loud. Instead of laughing, she smiles and says, "My God!" Accidents happen in real life but they don't happen in a well-written short story. That moment when she says, "My God!" is an important moment. For the first time, she knows what her heart had always wanted in her relationships: to hear a man say, "My connection to you is a part of my own search for a family. It's not just that you're beautiful, that you're sexually attractive, though I'm thrilled that's true. I want that sexual attraction to grow into more than just the two of us. I want it to open us up to a future together." When she hears that, she spontaneously reacts by putting a name on what it is, and it turns out to be a divine name.

When a writer has a character talk about writing, he's likely to be talking about himself. There's a line in this story that I think shows you what Dubus's own ambitions as a short story writer must have been. He's telling us the story of how LuAnn got her first job in insurance. Insurance is an indispensable responsibility of adulthood, but most young people aren't interested in it. When you're young, you don't have a vivid sense that you're going to die, so you don't think about buying life insurance. One of the things adults discover is that the first time you have a child, or the first time that you and your lover are pregnant, suddenly you will be very interested in life insurance. Because when you have a child, you go from thinking you'll never die to thinking you might die any day. Death becomes very real to you, at exactly that moment when you've brought a new life into the world – another version of the death test. Well, LuAnn's first job was with insurance. And she's a good worker. But she could feel her spirit bleeding away in this job where every day she put on a happy face, a happy face that wasn't really supported by any internal interest that she took in this particular job. "LuAnn appreciated the practical function of insurance," Dubus writes, "and bought a small policy on her own life, naming her parents as beneficiaries. But after nearly a year with the insurance company, on a Saturday afternoon while she was walking in Boston, wearing jeans and boots and a sweatshirt and feeling the sun on her face and hair, she admitted to herself that insurance bored her." (Insurance isn't as interesting as philosophy, after all.) Soon she was working for a small publisher. She moves from insurance and money to writing, to literature. "She earned less money but felt she was closer to the light she had sometimes lived in during college, had received from teachers and from books and other students, and often her own work." Now she was trying to sell literature. And then Dubus gives you a description of his own aspiration as a writer: "Literature, the human attempt to make truth palpable and delightful." This story is trying to make a truth palpable to you, concrete, touchable, tangible; the truth about union and procreation, as Dubus and Paul VI saw it. But Dubus also strives to make this truth delightful by presenting a delightful young woman who finds this truth. LuAnn Arcenaux is somebody who discovers the truth about her own sexuality after a Catholic Mass, where she is a regular participant in the Eucharist, in what Catholics believe is the body and blood of a very physical God. The incarnate Jesus is her Dionysus and Aphrodite. LuAnn Arcenaux finds the same sacred truth in her bedroom she finds in a church. That's how she knows that her sexual life is living out the commitments that are deepest in her own heart. Andre Dubus's literature is an attempt to bring out that sacramentality of sexuality as LuAnn Arcenaux experiences it.

One of the general features of Dubus's writing is the way that his Catholicism creates a world in which sacraments happen all the time, not just on Sundays. So much of ordinary life turns out to be extraordinary, turns out to have a sacred dimension. We occlude that sacred dimension through distractions of money, of worry, of ambition. Dubus is grateful for those moments where the sacramental breaks into our consciousness, and he tries to give us an example of that epiphany, that breaking through of the voice of something sacred or divine, both in what happens to LuAnn Arcenaux and in what happens to Ted Briggs. When Ted Briggs saw this beautiful young woman with the broken heel on the steps outside of Mass, his heart thought, "This moment is a gift that's been given to me." It's true that he isn't very smooth in trying to seize that moment, thinking up an opening line no better than, "I could try to fix it." It's an incredibly stupid thing to say, but LuAnn found him attractive enough to put up with it, and just says, "What are you going to fix it with?" He blushes and says he was just looking for an excuse to talk to her, which probably would have been a much better opening line anyway. I don't suppose many men would be tempted to try out Ted's seduction strategy from this story, I mean, to try out in a first conversation, "I want a home with love in it, with a woman and children"; probably not many more men than would try "Bone of my bone, flesh of my flesh" when they first see the woman they want to marry. Speaking those words in a public place, getting to know an attractive woman: for many men, it would feel like Gandalf in Rivendell, uttering the words of the Black Speech of Mordor at the Council of Elrond. They are words that have never been spoken there before, and the lights would flicker as you said them.

But why? Is Dubus right about where your heart really lies, about what it would be for you to find a language that articulates what it is that you open into when you find somebody sexually attractive? Is what you want a kind of intimacy with another person, an intimacy that creates within us a fearfulness, a fearfulness because we're being taken somewhere we don't control, and whose end we do not see, an end for better, for worse, till death? If that is what is in our heart when we find another human being erotically potent for us, then the question of how we can open our heart enough, how we can overcome the hardness of our heart's hearing, to live that path, to move that way, becomes a central question for us. It's not just a philosophical question. It's a question that has to be made palpable and maybe even delightful for us to take it seriously.

Chapter Six
THE PHOENIX OF LOVE

After Aristophanes tells his story of the original human beings, and their fall from self-sufficiency into mutual dependence, a dependence we live out in romantic love, it is the turn of Agathon, the other great poet and man of the theater, to give his praise of love. And of course Agathon praises himself. He's the youngest and best-looking man at the drinking party, sharing a couch with the oldest and, as it happens, much the ugliest of all the party-goers, Socrates. Agathon gives a speech about how the god Love (in Greek, Eros) is young and beautiful, just like Agathon. It is wrong, he says, to try to give prestige to the god Love by presenting him as old – as Pausanias did with Heavenly Aphrodite, making her older than Earthy Aphrodite. Agathon was also notorious, a bit of a public scandal, for flaunting his own androgynous, effeminate personality. Like the mythical Orpheus of Phaedrus's speech, and like Dionysus, the patron deity of Agathon as a tragic dramatist, Agathon was soft and musical, the opposite of the tough manliness Phaedrus and Pausanias praise in their speeches. The god Love, says Agathon, is a soft musician and poet, just like me. Aristophanes is all wrong, suggests Agathon, to think romantic love is about filling a need; love is instead about overflowing in joyful fullness. The exhilaration and energy beautiful people like me feel, says Agathon, makes us kind, friendly, and attractive to everyone. You might say Agathon gives the world's first theory of love as consummating in celebrity: the eye of the world turns toward the beautiful people, like himself, and all admire the perfection the celebrity seems to represent. This attractive celebrity is beyond the everyday judgments of good and evil, morality and immorality, and attractiveness trumps virtue when it comes to love; and everything does come to love in the end, because it is the most powerful motive for human beings, certainly more powerful than merely being good.

Agathon's very funny yet quite serious and rather immoral speech returns to two points about wisdom we noticed in the opening scenes of the *Symposium*, when Socrates first entered Agathon's house. Remember the challenge Agathon gave to Socrates: "We'll take up the question of which of us is wiser later, and then we'll let Dionysus judge." Agathon and Socrates had also speculated on whether wisdom flows from the full mind into the empty mind; now Agathon presents himself, like the god Love, as complete fullness, ready to overflow into others. This beautiful young theater person is much like Susan Dorsey, Andre Dubus's beautiful young theater person: both need a lover who lets them experience their own fullness. And so Agathon has praised his own poetic wisdom, and made a claim that ugly, old, empty Socrates can't know about love the way young beautiful Agathon does, full with the poetic inspiration and the attractiveness of love. Agathon has also intensified the androgynous challenge to manliness that Aristophanes's myth had already begun. The two theater men have undermined Eryximachus, the medical man, who had wanted to avoid Dionysus and Aphrodite, wine and women. But these tricky gods keep sneaking in.

The last two speeches in the *Symposium* will accept Agathon's challenge to be judged by Dionysus. Socrates responds to Agathon by giving an account of love as neither full nor empty, but as the constant striving of what is empty to become full. This picture of the life dedicated to love as restless striving: like all the other speeches, it is a piece of self-praise, a remarkable self-portrait painted by Socrates. It is also a further exploration of love's integration of the male and the female. So Socrates's speech will touch on themes from all the earlier speakers, and bring these themes to a higher level. Socrates's speech, while it acknowledges need and limit in human life, is overall a very cheerful speech, and almost makes invisible any of the anxieties and frustrations that falling in love and being in love are subject to. Plato leaves the task of chastening Socratic cheerfulness, with an explicit account of the pain of imperfection, to the final speech, by Alcibiades. Philosophy should both cheer us and chasten us, and Plato never fails to do both. We will conclude this chapter with the third of Andre Dubus's stories about LuAnn and Ted, "The Timing of Sin." It is a story that puts into a contemporary idiom the double business of cheering and chastening – and besides, it makes LuAnn beautiful, funny, serious, and rather immoral.

Immortal longings and the Socratic androgyne

Agathon had arranged things so that Socrates would share his couch at the dinner party, and during his speech he takes advantage of this situation to make a joke at Socrates's expense. "The god Love," says the beautiful young man, "isn't old at all, as some people say" – he means Pausanias – "in fact, love flees as fast as can be from anything old, and always is found among the young." Agathon sees love as many people see it now, especially young people: romance is primarily a business of youth, and if romance can exist among the middle-aged or the old, it is often something rather cute or silly, and perhaps a little disgusting. Agathon holds this view because he thinks the essence of love is what makes someone attractive, which surely doesn't include looking older. There is a good reason magazines and movies are filled with fresh young faces, not to mention bodies, rather than with faces lined with experience and bodies sagging with gravity. Everyone at the party, and none more than Socrates, must have chuckled at how well these words of Agathon applied to the older man reclining next to him.

But Socrates is as ready to praise himself as any other speaker in the *Symposium*. But instead of starting his own speech immediately, he asks the whole group permission to ask Agathon "a few questions," his regular way of forcing someone to defend his views against Socrates's own powerful critique. Permission granted, Socrates forces Agathon to concede a crucial point, which becomes the central idea around which Socrates will build his entire wonderful account of erotic love. Agathon had presented love, says Socrates, as if being loved were the most important experience. From that point of view, of course being beautiful and perfect looks like the center of love. But this is a mistake, says Socrates. The central experience is not *being loved* so much as it is *loving*. This is a natural mistake for a good-looking young man to make, but it's still a mistake. The real question, Socrates goes on, is not What makes us lovable, but Why do we love? Someone so perfect and fulfilled, such a full cup, you might say, has no reason at all to love anything else. Socrates is implicitly using an idea from Aristophanes's myth of the original human beings. Spherical and self-sufficient, they did not fall in love; erotic desire entered their lives only after their terrible punishment, when they were split in half by Zeus. Agathon thinks of the god Love, and so of himself, as a self-sufficient being like these original beings. So Socrates makes Agathon concede this point: If love is a *desire* for something, it must also be a *need* for that thing, based on a *lack* of that thing. Love must be rooted in our imperfection, not in our perfection.

If love requires imperfection, Socrates will be the ideal lover, not Agathon. Because Socrates is willing, even eager, to admit his own imperfections and neediness; in fact, he insists that he is lacking the most important good of all, namely wisdom, and so his whole life is organized by his erotic desire for wisdom above all other things. After he gets Agathon to concede the central point linking erotic desire and neediness, Socrates gives the dialogue a curious turn. He lets Agathon go, and says he will now tell the story of how he came to learn everything he knows about love and romance. "I learned it all," says Socrates, "from a woman," a woman named Diotima. Agathon has presented himself as soft and musical and effeminate, but Socrates goes farther: he presents himself as a woman's student.

This story of Socrates's erotic education begins after he has interrogated Agathon. But oddly enough, his own story begins with Diotima putting Socrates through much the same interrogation Socrates has just given to Agathon, though she is less playful and more harsh. "Agathon, I used to have views about love a lot like you do," Socrates says, "but then I met somebody who taught me what the nature of erotic love really is." Now, why does Socrates present the erotic education he got at the ungentle hand of the woman Diotima as the model he uses to give an education to Agathon? We remember the exclusion from this group of sober men at the beginning of the drinking party of Dionysus and Aphrodite, and of all things musical and feminine, the wine and the flute girl. Socrates, at least in speech, now does something that confronts that exclusion. He introduces a woman as his own guide into the truth of erotic life. In this respect, Socrates intensifies the focus on integrating the male and the female introduced by Aristophanes's speech. You remember that Aristophanes introduced the notion that at least some important part of human erotic life cannot be all male. We have to allow for the female, and in particular we have to allow for the integration of male and female in the androgyne. Socrates takes that theme and turns it into autobiography. Socrates himself has learned everything he knows about Eros from a woman. Diotima examined young Socrates, and now old Socrates examines young Agathon: Socrates puts himself into the role now that in his autobiography was played by Diotima. In other words, Socrates projects himself onto a female model. However manly he may be, he enacts in the sight of all these men at the *Symposium* the fact that he has just done with Agathon, what a woman did with him. The theme of the interpenetration of something we would normally think of as masculine with something we would normally think of as feminine is then a part of the drama of Socrates's own speech.

Phaedrus's speech introduced the death test as the measure of erotic love. Someone in love with you, claimed Phaedrus, will be more willing to die for you than anyone else, even than a father or your closest friend. This willingness to confront death is the basis of the heroism of the beloved. This theme of the connection between love and some confrontation or overcoming of mortality is also front and center in Socrates's own speech. Socrates learned from Diotima that erotic desire is a kind of neediness, but what kind? When we desire a good, Socrates teaches Agathon as he was taught by Diotima, we become aware that we cannot possess that good completely. To desire full possession means that the possession must be secure, lasting, permanent. Now, for beings like us who will die, that means that erotic love looks to stretch out beyond ourselves, beyond our own life, so that a central part of erotic desire, an aspect of the desire itself, is some aspiration to live on beyond the bounds of our mortality. This is one of the central ways, then, that Diotima sees erotic desire as linked to the divine. The human way of making contact with the divine is through an erotic reaching out to the immortal. It is the experience captured so memorably toward the end of Shakespeare's *Antony and Cleopatra*, when the doomed queen tells her servants she has "immortal longings," as she prepares to join her husband in a glorious death. She will live on with her Antony, either in an actual afterlife, or at least in the imperishable fame their heroic love and death will gain them. But the most real escape from mortality, as Socrates and Diotima see things, is not in fame. It is procreation, the immortality of passing on ourselves to new life. Plato, by thinking through his female character Diotima, arrived at the same place as the female writers of *The Lord of the Rings* movies, who made Arwen's future child her way of immortality after she abandons the personal immortality of the elves for love of the mortal man Aragorn. The form of immortality in human beings is reproduction and creativity.

Now, it's striking how Socrates's emphasis on procreativity picks up and transforms the themes of Aristophanes's speech. You remember in Aristophanes's speech human erotic desire for the intimacy of reunion was fundamentally separate from a divine purpose that had been superimposed on the physical expression of that erotic intimacy, the purpose of reproduction. Aristophanes's eroticized broken human beings do produce human offspring when they unite. But the desire for offspring in and of itself is not, in Aristophanes's speech, a part of the erotic drive. By contrast, in Diotima's account of the erotic drive, the sort of union we seek with another human being in erotic life has within it this search for immortality, this overcoming of the bonds of death within which we live. So that as Diotima sees erotic love, when we look into the eyes of the beloved and feel that rush of emotion and desire that we call falling in love, if we could fully articulate what's behind that rush of desire, we would find that it includes creativity, reproduction. So, a topic that Aristophanes's speech had brought into the conversation is now developed to a much higher level of erotic intensity by Socrates's own speech. By the way, this is also a way that Socrates's speech makes use of Agathon's preceding speech. Agathon's speech had presented the creativity of the love poet as a central aspect of the human experience of the erotic. Socrates in his speech takes that up, and inserts it into Aristophanes's picture of a fundamentally androgynous romantic existence.

Agathon, of course, had presented the god Love as the youngest and most beautiful of all the gods. Diotima teaches Socrates differently. It turns out that love is not a god at all, though love also isn't something simply mortal. But if Love is neither mortal nor immortal, Socrates asks in confusion, what sort of being is he? Love, Diotima answers, is a *daemon* between the human and the divine, a being between the mortal and the immortal. This is the same Greek word at the root of Desdemona's name. Since modern English doesn't have an equivalent word, I will use the word "spirit" to describe this sort of "between" being, and say that love makes us "spiritual," in the precise sense that Diotima explains to Socrates: Love is the mediating force that lifts humans toward the gods and allows gods to descend toward humans. Here again we see the theme of divination, of our erotic life as somehow intimately bound up with the possibilities of human transcendence of the mundane or every day in the direction of something understood as sacred, as godly. Doctor Eryximachus had introduced divination, but as something medical science could control and manage. Aristophanes laughed at the pretensions of science to control erotic life, and suggested instead that a kind of divination, like an interpretation of the dark riddles of an oracle, would be needed to articulate what lovers really want from each other; and as Hephaestus, Aristophanes offered to solve the riddle. Diotima and Socrates are more like Aristophanes than Eryximachus, and think of man's opening to the divine, and the divine's graciousness to man, as the mystery at the heart of love.

As Diotima presents the spirit Love, it turns out that the most erotic life is a philosophical life. Of course, the Greek word "philosophy" means just "lover of wisdom," and Diotima applies her conclusion that love and desire imply neediness and lack. "No god philosophizes or desires to become wise, for a god is already wise," she says. Nor would someone who is completely ignorant love wisdom, because such a person wouldn't realize his own lack of wisdom. Only someone who knows that he does not know – Socrates's famous description of himself – is in a position to love and desire wisdom, to be a philosopher. The philosophers on Diotima's picture are the exemplary case of an erotic life, because they're restlessly bound to a constant search for wisdom, a search never abandoned nor fulfilled. This picture of a restless seeker of wisdom is clearly modeled on Socrates himself.

Diotima paints her picture of the erotic life, as the reader expects by this point in the dialogue, by telling a myth of her own, the story of the origin of the spirit Love. Once upon a time, she says, the gods were having a party to celebrate the birth of Aphrodite. One of the gods, a male god named Plenty, had too much to drink, and stumbled outside to sleep. Outside the doors of the party lurked the wretched goddess Poverty, hoping to beg from the other gods. When Plenty fell asleep, Poverty saw her opportunity, and lay with him, becoming pregnant. The divine child produced from this mating of Plenty and Poverty, says Diotima, was the spirit Love (Eros). This spirit shared in the natures of both his father and his mother, and so is between the fullness and perfection of his father and the emptiness and neediness of his mother. Bold and resourceful like his father, he is also tough and enduring like his mother, and is always scheming and striving for the beauty he himself lacks but still desires. Though Diotima doesn't say so directly, this offspring of Plenty and Poverty is an image of Socrates, who combines the luxury and softness of the father with the toughness and need of the mother. Socrates, we've noticed earlier, had the striking habit of almost always being barefoot. He enjoyed the cool stream and soft grass under the Plato tree in the *Phaedrus*, and near the beginning of the *Symposium* Aristodemus was startled to find Socrates putting on fancy party shoes. In a delightful comic touch, Socrates here reports that Diotima described the spirit Love as always barefoot, an aspect of his tough poverty. So Socrates like all the other speakers in the dialogue is presenting the divine being Love in his own image and likeness. This spiritual Eros, this Eros that's in between the human and the divine, is itself an image of the philosophical life as Socrates experiences it, as he lives it out.

The philosopher's life is the most erotic life, and the philosopher is the most extreme lover: so, at least, is the story Socrates tells by telling the story Diotima tells. The most extreme lover, as this dialogue presents him, is the lover who gives up his life for the beloved, who passes the death test. Diotima's spirit of Love passes the death test in an especially subtle way. As with Love's bare feet, which were the clue to Love's identity with Socrates, so Plato gives the reader a subtle clue about another mythic identity taken on by Socrates and Love. Diotima says that the integration of fullness and emptiness in Love makes him constantly alternate between being filled with life and being emptied of it. This restless, unsettling cycle happens over and over; it is the very essence of the erotic life. And so in a single day, she says, this great spirit will die and be reborn, as plenty or poverty dominates. What is this image of a being whose life is in fact a cycle of birth, death, and rebirth? Plato loved to set the reader puzzles like this, and he has given us the clue in a small detail right at the beginning of the dialogue, a detail that at the time seemed trivial, even meaningless. The dialogue began with a friend of Apollodorus coming up to him on the street and asking him to tell him about the drinking party when Socrates and Alcibiades were giving speeches about love at Agathon's house. Apollodorus says he was just asked the same question the other day, by someone who wanted more details, but who had heard a little about it from another man. Who was that man, the other source for the story of this fateful drinking party? His name was Phoenix. Plato does not force this fine detail, this surprising name, on the reader, and he does not make an explicit reference back to that passage here in Socrates's speech. But he does use the image of the mythic phoenix bird as a wonderful image for Socrates, and more generally for the erotic life of philosophy. The philosopher is dying all the time, chastening himself by acknowledging his own ignorance, but also being reborn in his enduring and cheerful aspiration to rise toward wisdom. The philosopher passes the death test, not because he will die for someone else, but because he dies constantly to himself.

Notice how this myth of Love's parents has inverted the assumptions about male hardness and female softness that have been present since the very beginning of the dialogue. In Diotima's origin myth, the female principle is the tough one, and the male principle is the soft, indulgent one. Socrates crosses all the wires and shorts all the circuits with his wildly androgynous image of the restless spirit of Love. It's striking to notice that Diotima's myth also directly contradicts Pausanias's speech. You remember that Pausanias presents us with two goddesses named Aphrodite, a heavenly Aphrodite whose parentage is wholly male, and an earthy Aphrodite whose parentage is both male and female, androgynous. Diotima's story takes the side of the younger and earthy Aphrodite, since it tells the story of the goddess's birthday, from a father and a mother. That is, Diotima's Aphrodite is the androgynous one Pausanias had tried to exclude, in his obsession with manliness.

This theme of the integration of the masculine and the feminine is intensified when Diotima, or Socrates through Diotima, describes love as "giving birth in the beautiful." Socrates is puzzled, as is the reader, by this claim, and he tells Diotima it would require divination to understand what she means. The notion, as Diotima develops it, is that we have a profound desire for creativity. We all feel erotic desire for beautiful people, but not just to enjoy being with them. We want to procreate with them, too, whether physically, by producing children, or spiritually. And we experience a provocation to and an energy for that kind of creativity when we're in the presence of someone we consider beautiful. On this view, a lover does not desire merely the possession of the beloved. That would be a rather poor, a rather vulgar version of erotic desire. Erotic desire instead is propelled by our desire to give birth in the company of somebody beautiful. We experience our beloved as that person with whom we can give birth. The language that Diotima uses for this "giving birth" is a striking combination of male images of sexual climax, and female images of giving birth. Diotima presents the idea that we're all pregnant, either physically or spiritually, "and as it were already bursting with the load of desire," ready to release what we have inside us, "on account of the great pain of retaining that which we have conceived." So this sexualized image of pro-creativity is meant to be neither primarily male nor primarily female. It's meant to combine the male and the female into one potent image of an erotic life that can't be fully controlled within the macho categories originally introduced by the speakers in this dialogue. We need a set of categories that bring directly into erotic desire the aspects of reproduction and pregnancy that were originally introduced into this dialogue by Aristophanes's speech.

Socrates has inherited much from Aristophanes's speech, but Diotima also emphasizes a fundamental difference. The question is, in erotic desire do we desire what is good or do we desire what is our own? Diotima says to Socrates, "It is asserted by some that lovers are seeking the lost half of their divided being. But I assert that love is neither the love of *half* or of *whole*, unless love meets with what is *good*." Her point is that Aristophanes made union and intimacy the ultimate goal of love, when intimacy is really only a means or a consequence of a higher goal. Evidence of the greater importance of pursuit of the good over union and intimacy comes from our attitude to our own bodies, surely as intimate a part of us as anything could be. "Men willingly cut off their own hands and feet," claims Diotima, "if they think their limbs are the cause of evil to them." (I seem to recall another teacher agreeing, and even suggesting plucking out an eye, if it be a stumbling block unto thee.) Union and wholeness cannot be our ultimate goal if we accept such amputations. And will we not also cut off ourselves, even though the pain may be great, from lovers we think are bad for us? When I fall in love with somebody and think that person is my soulmate, or when I say to my beloved, to use the line from the Tom Cruise movie *Jerry Maguire*, "You complete me," do we mean that the other person simply returns us to some state of wholeness, without any regard to whether that state of wholeness or completeness would itself be a good thing? When we fall in love with somebody, are we simply looking for someone who, so to speak, puts us in our comfort zone, who makes us feel at home, so that we're not lonely anymore? But of course, not being lonely is perfectly consistent with being incredibly lazy. It may well be that we settle down with a lover exactly when that person does not provoke in us any restless aspirations to be better, to be as good as we can.

Do you, reader, seek a lover, a beloved, who prods your ambitions and expands your aspirations, as Diotima presupposes will happen in true love in her critique of Aristophanes? Do we look for a love that is an opportunity for restless seeking, the opportunity of a self that's not fully realized yet, something that lies latent in our potential? Diotima sees this restless focus on the good as a challenge to Aristophanes's emphasis on erotic wholeness. Aristophanes says love heals our wounds, Diotima says love fuels our aspirations: Does love settle us or unsettle us?

The famous conclusion of Diotima's speech, known as "The Ladder of Love," is introduced as an initiation into a religious mystery. "Your own meditations, Socrates," says Diotima, "might have initiated you into all these things I have already taught you about love" – she means the ideas of love as need, as immortal longing, as phoenix, and as birth in the beautiful – "but now I come to the highest mysteries. Strive to follow me, though I'm not sure you will be able." Remember that Socrates is the one reporting this speech, so he is using Diotima's words to suggest how difficult these higher mysteries will be for his audience to understand, by putting his audience in the same position he says he was once in with Diotima, his erotic teacher. "Strain all your attention," she told him, "to trace the obscure depths of the subject"; and now Socrates gives his audience the same challenge. The notion that love has "obscure depths," as difficult to articulate as a religious mystery, is again an inheritance from Aristophanes's speech. The god Hephaestus came down to the bedded lovers and asked them to tell the truth of their desire for each other. But this truth escaped their ability to use speech, and only with the help of the god, and of the comic poet himself, could lovers understand the deep heart's core. Here, too, Diotima tries to help Socrates find words for something that goes beyond his unaided capacity. She gives her famous account of "The

Ladder of Love": of how, with the right erotic guide, someone like Diotima or Socrates, our erotic interest in one beautiful individual will gradually expand. As we climb the ladder of erotic desire, we move from attraction to the body of one beautiful lover, to our lover's soul, and then expand to the social world that nourishes the soul, to an interest in laws and institutions, as well as in knowledge and education more generally. Diotima traces a path of ascent that many married couples have traveled; first a romance narrowly focused on themselves, but then an expanding civic and intellectual interest, in their own child, in schools, and in citizenship. This growth into adult responsibilities is also an expansion and elevation of our capacity for love, a love whose seed was that intense moment of falling in love with one beautiful person. The aspiration to climb this ladder of love is most powerful when we're lovers and beloveds. Diotima suggests that this entire experience of ascent and expansion has a peak we never quite reach, but whose summit we can glimpse in sudden revelation, like the top of a cloud-shrouded mountain seen in a fleeting glimpse when the clouds part and the sun, for just that moment, shines through. This sudden and partial vision of something ultimate and sacred orients the entire climb and makes all the effort worthwhile. If we become the lovers Diotima and Socrates would have us be, we will never rest comfortably with what we've already attained.

Diotima presents a beautiful but terribly demanding ideal. We talked earlier about how Aristophanes's speech raised the issue of whether we love a particular individual or whether we love a type of human being. The ladder of love passage intensifies this question in a very potent way. Many readers of this passage are unsettled by the ascent of the lover from the love of one particular beloved toward the love of something that looks as abstract as the sacred, highest objects of platonic knowledge, whatever they may be. Won't this ascent leave behind any real affection for the particular individual who was merely the seed, the first step on the ascent? The journey to the top of the mountain gets colder and colder, an ascent into impersonality. So that by the time we're at the top, the beloved is no more than one drop in "the great sea of beauty," as

Diotima describes it. There is some truth in this anxiety. But it's important to remember that one result of making this erotic ascent is the profound desire for creativity with someone we love. This creativity has as its image the physical reproduction of children, but is expressed more perfectly when our procreativity is also spiritual, for example, in the pursuit of philosophical understanding, something best done, as Socrates's whole life attests, in and through conversation with those we love. So while it's true that there is an impersonal aspect of this erotic ascent, Diotima and Socrates think this erotic ascent produces the most intimate relationship that one could have with another human being. That intimacy is predicated on the notion that the truest self, both of lover and beloved, is something that must be achieved, something that's never merely there to be discovered. When we want to be most completely known, most exposed, most naked before the gaze of those we love, we don't seek merely to be discovered in what we are now. Rather, we want to be seen with the eyes of a lover, the eyes of a lover who sees within us something more divine than we ever would have seen in ourselves unaided.

So Socrates's speech, the speech he learned from Diotima, integrates themes from all the preceding speeches in the *Symposium*. The challenge of whether love, by being aspirational, will also be depersonalized, indeed dehumanized, is a challenge that Plato acknowledges. And the concluding speech in the dialogue, the great speech of that charismatic drunk, Alcibiades, is Plato's attempt to meditate on the costs and the benefits of an aspirational erotic life.

The judgment of Dionysus

Alcibiades was the sort of man Ralph Waldo Emerson described as "carrying the holiday in his eye": wherever Alcibiades was, that's where the party was happening. He was also the most dangerous and charismatic man in Athens. Popular with the people, he was no democrat, and hoped to become the dominant power in the city. He was a bold political and military leader, and inspired deep devotion from his friends, but no deeper than the hatred he provoked in his enemies. He was handsome, witty, shameless:

everything that makes the modern celebrity or the classic Hollywood leading man. In fact, I find it puzzling there are no movies made of his life story; there is no life from the ancient world as cinematic and romantic, not Alexander the Great, not Mark Antony (though Cleopatra gets him close). And Alcibiades was one thing more: the besotted lover of Socrates.

Plato ends the *Symposium* with a beautiful, drunken speech by this dangerous man. In fact, this speech of Alcibiades seems to have been the main reason at the beginning of the dialogue that Apollodorus's friends sought him out to hear his story. "Tell us about the speeches about love given at the party at Agathon's house, when Socrates and Alcibiades were there! Do you really know what they said, Apollodorus? Let us in on the secret!" Plato does not directly say what happened to suddenly make this story of a drinking party that had taken place many years earlier – Plato is careful to give us enough information to figure out the exact date – of such intense interest again in Athens. I think in this as in other cases, though, Plato gave the careful reader enough clues to guess. I suggest Apollodorus is getting these questions from his friends because Socrates has just been arrested, on the charge he has corrupted the young men of Athens and disparaged the city's gods. Socrates was arrested and executed in 399 BC, seventeen years after Agathon won his first victory at the tragic festival, a date we know from other sources. The events narrated in the *Symposium* are suddenly relevant again because everyone realizes that Socrates has been arrested in no small part because of his past relationship with Alcibiades. The political enemies of Alcibiades, who by this time was dead, are using the vague charge of "corrupting the youth" to get back at Socrates for his particular intimacy with a man notorious as an enemy of the Athenian democracy.

I have described Alcibiades as shameless. The first speaker, Phaedrus, had made shame the central motive force of love. Alcibiades returns to this theme, but now with all the complexities introduced by the other speakers, and especially by Socrates. Socrates's speech was throughout cheerful and hopeful, as if the challenging life of Socratic love would produce much more pleasure than pain. But Alcibiades chastens this cheerfulness. He shows us how erotic love for Socrates brings with it ecstasy and exhilaration, but also the deep pain of shame. And no man can feel the pain of shame so deeply as a man habitually so shameless, so immune to shame, as Alcibiades.

The *Symposium* is the kind of work that one wants to linger over or return to from a number of different perspectives. So rather than simply reading it straight through, which of course has its own virtues, I would prefer to keep going back to it to look at it in new contexts, with new ideas, to juxtapose it with the different texts or different movies. So when we come to the final speech, it's important for us to remind ourselves of the entire movement of the *Symposium* that has brought us to the point of Alcibiades's speech.

You'll remember that when Socrates entered the house of Agathon, Agathon and Socrates engaged in some banter about who was wiser. Socrates poked some fun at Agathon, who had just won first prize in the tragic competition. Socrates talked about how wise Agathon must be to be confident in displaying his wisdom before tens of thousands of people. Agathon sees that Socrates is raising a question, a doubt about whether that kind of popular entertainment is an authentic vehicle of wisdom, or whether the desire to entertain is stronger for Agathon than the desire to tell the truth. Socrates compares his own insignificant or ordinary wisdom with what must be the extraordinary wisdom that Agathon is so willing to show off before a large popular audience. Agathon says, "Socrates, I'm not going to argue with you about who's wiser right now, but we will have this argument later and then Dionysus himself will judge between us." The god Dionysus of course is the god of both theater and of intoxication. So Dionysus is an especially appropriate god to judge the claim to wisdom of a tragedian, and is also an especially appropriate god to make that judgment at a drinking party, at a symposium.

Before Alcibiades, we've just seen Agathon and Socrates give their competing accounts of the nature of love. Agathon in his speech presents Eros, the god of love, as young, tender and soft, and as beautiful, and most of all as a poet. And with a sly look at the man lying on the couch next to him, Agathon says, "The god of love has nothing to do with ugly, hard, old people." Agathon, the youngest and most beautiful man at the symposium, is clearly getting in his dig at Socrates, the oldest and by far the ugliest man at the drinking party. When Socrates gives his own speech, he tells us that many people make the mistake of thinking that the god of love must himself be beautiful, but that's wrong. Love is in fact neither a god nor a human but something in between, something that interprets the divine to the human and the human to the divine. And this intermediate being, called a *daemon*, a spirit, is the offspring of a father that's plentitude and a mother that's emptiness. The child of these opposites draws together the divine and the human, allows them to understand each other. The child is neither absolute fullness nor simple emptiness. A being defined by erotic love is always looking for fulfillment, but never quite achieves it. And this restless, searching Love, Socrates says, must be a tough hunter, not a tender heart in the way that Agathon presents, and must himself lack beauty because he longs for it so much. And in the end this spirit must be philosophical, must be a lover of wisdom, not having wisdom like the gods themselves do, but always being in search of it.

Agathon presented the god of love in the image of himself. He presented himself as perfect Beauty, as the exemplar of what love can be in its full perfection. Socrates provides an alternative. He says that love is not wholly divine, nor either is it merely human. Instead, Socrates says, love is like me. I am the image of love, a restless philosopher always in search of beauty and wisdom, but never fully in possession of them. This is the competition between Agathon and Socrates. Who then will be the judge of these different views of the way that the erotic enters into human life?

After Socrates finished speaking, the whole assembly praised his discourse. Suddenly they heard a loud knocking at the door outside and a clamor of revelers attended by a flute girl. Agathon tells his servants to see who is knocking. "If there are any of our friends," he says, "call them in. If not, say that we've already done drinking." In other words, this party would have been over after

Socrates's speech, except for this unexpected interruption from outside. An outside power, it seems, unsettles the settled evening of these sober men, who would be content to go home and leave the last word to Socrates's praise of love. If the party had ended here, their agreement to exclude the feminine and to exclude the Dionysian would have been broached in word, especially by Socrates introducing Diotima, but not in deed. The party would have been over without ever having opened itself up to either Dionysus or to Aphrodite. Thank god for revelers!

A few moments later, they all heard the voice of Alcibiades just at the door, "excessively drunk," as Plato describes him. I love that phrase, "excessively drunk," because of course it implies there is a way to be moderately drunk. "Where is Agathon? Lead me to Agathon!" Alcibiades roars, staggering and leaning for support on the flute girl, until his companions lead him in and place him against the door post —he would have fallen over otherwise, and I guess that's what it means to be *excessively* drunk. Alcibiades is wearing a thick crown of ivy and violets and ribbons on his head. A Greek reader would have immediately identified the ivy and violets and ribbons as the marks of the god Dionysus. When Dionysus is leading his followers, he is represented as wearing ivy and violets and ribbons, as they dance ecstatically to flute music. Alcibiades plays Dionysus when he enters into Agathon's house, leading a troupe of ecstatic, intoxicated revelers. It's this Alcibiades/Dionysus who will render judgment on the wisdom and love of Socrates.

Alcibiades bursts into the room where they are all reclining, and shouts an affectionate greeting to them. "My friends," he cries out, "how good to see you!" He looks around at them all, this respectable group who had told themselves at the beginning of the evening, "Let's just be sober tonight and have philosophical discussion instead of the usual wildness of drinking parties." Alcibiades bows to everybody and addresses them very formally, "Gentlemen, I greet you. I am excessively drunk already, but I'll drink with you if you will." Alcibiades's language is polite, in the way someone who has had a few too many drinks will try to be especially correct and polite. But the power of his personality shines through his apparent deference, and his charisma gives the words of his self-effacing invitation – "I'll drink with you if you will" – the force of a command. He means to possess them in the way a god would possess them. "If you don't want me to stay," he says, "we'll go away; but not until I crown Agathon, which is why I came." It turns out Alcibiades couldn't come to Agathon's big victory party the night before, the one that made everyone but Socrates too weak to put up with another evening with Aphrodite and Dionysus. So he has come tonight, because he wants to be a part of the celebration. Like every celebrity, Alcibiades wants to be seen with the beautiful people, to be at the right parties. If he is seen congratulating Agathon, some of the spotlight now on the brilliant young poet will fall on him, too. And he wouldn't turn down a little flirting with this handsome young man, either. "I couldn't come yesterday," he says, "but I'm here now with these ribbons around my temples, so from my own head I might crown Agathon's head who, I hope you will allow me to say, is the most beautiful and wisest of men." And so Agathon's prophecy to Socrates is fulfilled: Dionysus has appeared to judge them for their wisdom. They all laugh and applaud Alcibiades, and he takes control of the party. "Are you laughing because I'm drunk?" he says, "I know what I say is true, whether you laugh or not." And then again he makes his request with the force of a command: "Tell me now, shall I come in or not? Will you drink with me?" Who could turn this Dionysus down? Not even somebody with a hangover; and so the dolphins leap to the sea.

So Alcibiades is invited in, and he plops onto Agathon's couch, between the poet and the old philosopher sharing it. This representative of Dionysus has finally gotten in through the real front door, after sneaking in the back in the speeches, and he brings with him a real flute girl, not just a woman in speech like Diotima. Aphrodite has arrived, the feminine presence of music and poetry. The partygoers abandon themselves to all the untamed divinity that had been excluded by Eryximachus, the sober medical doctor. Alcibiades takes some of the ribbons off his head, and as he crowns Agathon, he praises him as the wisest man in Athens. He hasn't noticed

Socrates is sitting there silently on the same couch. It's amazing what an intoxicated man can overlook. Only after he praises Agathon's wisdom and crowns him does he notice there is a third person on the couch. "Who is this?" he says, and gets a shock when he turns to see Socrates, silent and smiling. "What are you doing here, Socrates?" he blurts out, "you're always sneaking around, giving me a sudden surprise, turning up when I least expect to see you!" Alcibiades is suspicious now. "What did you come here for?" he asks, and like most suspicious lovers, he answers his own question. "Why are you on this particular couch, and not over there, near Aristophanes or some other ridiculous person? No, instead you're sharing a couch with the most beautiful man at the party!" Alcibiades is jealous because he's still in love with Socrates. And he doesn't think it's an accident, any more than we should, that Socrates has ended up reclining on the couch with the most beautiful, the most attractive, the most seductive man available. Socrates asks Agathon to protect him from Alcibiades's jealous anger. "Ever since I became his lover, he hasn't allowed me to speak to another attractive person without getting angry," says Socrates, "so do your best to calm him down, or at least to keep him away from me!"

But Alcibiades can't stay angry with Socrates for long. "I'll punish you another time," he says to Socrates, but then he turns back to Agathon, and taking some of the ribbons back, he says, "Agathon, wise as you are, no one in all of Greece is as wise as Socrates. So I'll have to take some of those ribbons back, and put them on his old head instead." And so he attires the old man's tawny brow, and Alcibiades, Agathon, and Socrates now make a fine Dionysian triptych, decked out in the emblems of the god. The judgment of Dionysus is complete, and Socrates has won.

And now the gaudy night begins. "You gentlemen all look far too sober," says this new leader of the symposium, "and you need to catch up with me." He shouts to the servants to bring him a goblet, but he decides that's too small, and calls for a pitcher. They fill it with wine, and Alcibiades empties it at a shot. "Fill it up again and give it to Socrates," he commands; at this drinking party, as at others I've seen, the most exuberant person sets the standard for how much drinking there's going to be, and other people feel called upon to catch up to the level of intoxication of the most intoxicated person. Socrates doesn't flinch, and empties the pitcher, too. We remember that when Eryximachus settled the rule for moderate drinking, he mentioned that Socrates himself didn't care whether they drank or not, and seemed immune to the effects of drunkenness. His emptiness never gets too full.

So suddenly this very sober drinking party has become a different sort of thing. It's been taken over by Alcibiades, as a sign of the overtaking of philosophy by Dionysus and Aphrodite. Eryximachus tries to keep some control of the proceedings, and he urges Alcibiades to take his turn giving a speech in praise of love, like all the other participants. "But it isn't fair," Alcibiades protests, "to expect an intoxicated man to compete with the speeches of the sober!" But if you want a speech, Alcibiades says, I'll give you a speech – a speech where I tell you the truth about Socrates. Telling the truth about Socrates will be the way Alcibiades praises the god of Love.

When we talk about love, we mostly talk about ourselves. Every speaker in the *Symposium* up to this point has given a speech about himself. But the self-reference of each speech was somewhat indirect or veiled; no one has admitted to simply telling the story of his own romantic life. Socrates did cast his speech as autobiography, when he showed how he learned about love from Diotima. But even Socrates didn't make explicit how the images in Diotima's speech, of love as a phoenix, of the barefoot child of Plenty and Poverty, of giving birth in the beautiful, and of the lover ascending and expanding to the great sea of beauty, are all images of his own life. Socrates never makes explicit that he himself is the spiritual interpreter of things divine to human beings. But as befits a man in his cups, and very full cups at that, Alcibiades is willing to tell direct and indiscreet truths, from his own life and from Socrates's. Alcibiades explicitly tells an autobiographical love story, whereas everybody else was pretending to give a general theory of love, when in fact he was talking about himself. Alcibiades's acknowledged autobiography strips naked every other speaker's unacknowledged autobiography, Plato's way of showing us readers how to read the whole dialogue.

Alcibiades's shameless story is about how he tried to seduce Socrates. A decade or so before Agathon's victory, when Alcibiades was still the best-looking, most sought-after young man in Athens, he had many admirers, but he rejected them all. He would become the beloved only of someone he greatly admired himself, and who would add to his prestige. Alcibiades thought he had found his man when he noticed how much attention Socrates paid to him. Naturally, he thought Socrates had fallen in love with him for his youthful beauty. One night, he schemes to make Socrates spend the night at his house by keeping him up late in conversation. He also arranges to have the servants leave early, so Alcibiades is alone with Socrates. Alcibiades is sure Socrates will say to him the sort of things lovers said to their beloveds; but Socrates is just the same as always, no more changed by night and privacy than he is by wine. But Alcibiades thinks Socrates is just shy, and as they lie down to sleep, he cuddles close to Socrates and makes it clear he admires the older man, and is willing to give him whatever he wants. "Very well," says Socrates, "we'll consider together what would be best for both of us. But we must beware that your offer of your beauty for my wisdom is not a bad bargain, like an exchange of gold for bronze." Alcibiades tells the audience that he was sure his seduction had been successful, but he was humiliated when Socrates simply went to sleep, and nothing happened. "I might as well have been in bed with my father or older brother," reports Alcibiades, to the laughter and admiration of the party-goers – by now the wine had been going around for a while. (Alcibiades's comparison of the cold bedroom partner Socrates to a father or brother recalls Phaedrus's speech, when that young man had claimed a lover provokes more bravery than even a father or a comrade; and yet Alcibiades later reports that Socrates risked his life to save him in battle. So is Socrates Alcibiades's lover after all? Plato discreetly sets the reader the puzzle of comparing the passages.) Alcibiades so prided himself on his physical beauty that he never imagined Socrates's interest in him would not be consummated sexually. But the gold of Socrates's soul was not to be bartered for bodily pleasure, not even for the best body in Athens. Socrates was paying attention to young Alcibiades, not to get him into bed, but to draw him to philosophy.

Alcibiades's experience of this humiliation is complicated. Like any rejected lover, he is angry, and because he is so filled with pride, his anger is more intense than usual for a rejected lover. But there's another part of him that's drawn to admire Socrates in a way that he admires nobody else. Now suddenly he understands something about Socrates's own virtue that he'd never noticed before. In fact Alcibiades goes on to say, "None of you here, no matter how well you think you know Socrates, knows his secrets in the way that I do. I once saw him open up, and I saw inside of him such divine images! It was as if he were filled with statues of the gods." Alcibiades returns to this image of a secret inward divinity in Socrates. Socrates's words seem so plain and everyday on the outside, yet on the inside their true meaning is something so divine and challenging. Socrates's virtues are like his words: Socrates seems like such an ordinary man until you open him up and appreciate the virtues he has. Alcibiades is especially struck by the virtue that he shows when he turns down Alcibiades's sexual advances. So Alcibiades says, "I see the secret Socrates that you all overlook. I've seen what's divine inside of him. I see Socrates the true lover, the lover filled with divine virtue." From Alcibiades's perspective, then, Socrates is far from empty. In his way, Socrates is as full and overflowing as Agathon claimed the god Love to be.

But the fullness of Socrates reveals to Alcibiades his own emptiness. Socrates is a sort of mirror that lets Alcibiades see himself – an image we will consider in detail when we see it in Plato's *Phaedrus*. Alcibiades has seen in Socrates a beautiful potentiality for himself that other people have overlooked or forgotten. But the difficulty for Alcibiades is that his vision of true virtue, this vision that he gets through Socrates, is not strong enough to overcome Alcibiades's attachments to things that are far from divine. Alcibiades is not able to make his own life Socratic, so that his experience of Socrates's perfection is an experience not of joy, but an experience of shame. As he says to the astonished audience, "Socrates can make me feel something that you'd never believe I feel. I'm famous for being shameless, for being exuberant, for carrying the holiday in my eye wherever I go. But Socrates makes me feel shame. Because when I see into what Socrates is, at the same time I see what I'm not and what I could be." Socrates, then, for Alcibiades is both extraordinarily lovable and extremely hateful. As he says, "Many are the times when I wish nothing more than that Socrates would be dead, that I could never see him again and experience this humiliation. And yet if he died I would be completely lost, and I would not know what to do." For Alcibiades, too, as we've seen for other speakers in the *Symposium*, there's a very curious connection between love and death, a connection that is mediated by an experience of shame.

The problem for Alcibiades is not that Socrates has been an unfaithful lover. No; it is Alcibiades who is unfaithful, to the better self Socrates shows him he could be. Alcibiades is exhilarated by this better self, but he is also frustrated by it. The true problem of Socratic love has been Alcibiades's inability to follow where he knows Socrates leads. Diotima taught that the correct romantic love has built into its very structure something that draws us to aspire to a more perfect self, a more perfect self we see revealed to us through something our love reveals in our beloved. If that kind of aspiration is an essential part of our erotic life, then the shame or humiliation, the anger, the resentment of Alcibiades will be a threat in any erotic relationship. To open one's self to the beauty of the beloved will also be to open one's self to the ugliness, the incompleteness, the limitations of one's own self. And it is on this unsettling note, with a Socrates who inspires both love and hate, that the *Symposium* ends. Alcibiades's experience shows the reader that Socratic love avoids the comfortable laziness of Aristophanic love, but at the cost of an unsettling abandonment of a stable identity. Socrates makes everyone he loves into a phoenix, living and dying, living and dying, striving for a perfection we never quite possess. After Alcibiades's speech, Plato added a coda to the *Symposium*, a final conversation after everyone else has gone to bed, or at least passed out on the floor. This final conversation is between Socrates and Agathon, the great writer of tragedies, and Aristophanes, the great writer of comedies. Socrates is trying to force Agathon and Aristophanes to admit that anyone who could write a great comedy should also be able to write a great tragedy, and vice versa. It's Socrates himself who seems to embody that integration of tragedy and comedy, an integration that comes out in Alcibiades's uncanny combination of shame and enduring love. It's this possibility of integration of tragedy and comedy that I'll take up in the final chapter, when we think about Shakespeare's *A Midsummer Night's Dream*.

"Sex is like the weather": Andre Dubus's confession

There is a cost in shame of holding oneself to high standards in love. Socrates's cheerfulness in celebrating the high standard of Diotima is chastened by Alcibiades's frustration and humiliation in falling short of these standards. Andre Dubus's third story about Ted Briggs and LuAnn Arceneaux, "The Timing of Sin," tells a contemporary story of this tension between high standards and shame. Alcibiades saw himself as a failure when he thought about Socrates's virtue and the ways he fell short of such virtue in his own life. But aren't we all failures? Who lives up to the ideals of love? We catch no more than brief glimpses of that high summit, and often the clouds enveloping the peak are so thick, we aren't even sure anymore we are traveling toward a real height. Failure breeds doubt, and doubt gives birth to cynicism. Why, after all, should we keep pursuing a goal we never achieve? Why not just lower our goals?

These are the issues at the heart of "The Timing of Sin." The last time we saw LuAnn and Ted, they had just met outside a Catholic church, and they had discovered they both aspired to leave the dating scene behind and start a life of committed married love. Now we see them as a married couple, with three young children and a settled life. They are happy, and they still are in love, still have energy for each other, still live a romance. But the story hinges on a moment of sudden sexual desire, when LuAnn almost commits adultery. The story is about how LuAnn responds to this surprising failure. She does not become cynical, and tell herself "It could happen to anyone"; nor does she hate herself, and suffer the sort of shame that Alcibiades suffers. She turns to a different resource, to heal the damage and still hold on to her ideals: she confesses her sin and seeks forgiveness. Confession and forgiveness are the necessary supplement to Socratic cheerfulness and Alcibiadean despair.

LuAnn volunteers one evening every week at a home for troubled teenage girls. The girls who live there, with therapists and the residential staff, have had terrible lives, and often they have been sexually abused as children. LuAnn usually reads with the girls, and simply talks with them. (LuAnn is reading the girls short stories by Alice Munro, a subtle recognition by Dubus of a fellow writer. Munro was awarded the Nobel Prize for Literature in 2013, fourteen years after Dubus died. A beautiful gesture.) She sees only a little of how deeply traumatized the girls have been. But one evening, one of the girls leaves the room while LuAnn's reading a story to them. After a few minutes, LuAnn notices another girl looking anxious, and LuAnn goes to check on the girl who left. LuAnn discovers she has locked herself in a restroom. The director of the home, a man of LuAnn's age named Roger, rushes to the locked door and starts to talk to the girl inside. When the door is opened, they find the girl stabbing her arm with a pen, drawing blood; she responds to the stress of her past abuse by abusing herself still, with self-mutilation. Dubus is feeling his way down the same dark paths that *Exotica* found, in the painful repetitions of Francis and Christina.

LuAnn is struck by how tender, firm, and loving Roger's voice is, as he calms the girl and directs the staff to take her to the hospital. He appears at the moment as a perfect father, and LuAnn is filled with admiration for his gentle manliness. The wounded girl is taken outside to a car, and driven away while Roger stands watching. LuAnn has gone outside and gotten into her own car on the dark street, where she sits smoking a cigarette, feeling the energy this violent incident has pumped into her. As Roger turns to go back inside he sees her, and walks over to the car, where he asks her through the open window for a cigarette. She looks into his eyes, and says "Join me"; and they both know she doesn't mean just for a smoke. As they fumble with their clothes and a condom, LuAnn suddenly comes to her senses, and apologizes, saying she can't do it. They part with a smile and she drives home. But the erotic energy stays with her, and she directs her passion onto Ted over the next couple days. (I find my students are often unsettled by this aspect of the story. They don't like to think that one's passion for one's spouse might be catalyzed by someone other than one's spouse. But Shakespeare's *A Midsummer Night's Dream* is built around the notion that we catch desire like a disease from other people, and everybody loves it! We'll talk about this in the last chapter.)

LuAnn is recounting this story to her friend Marsha a few days later. Marsha tells LuAnn her first marriage had broken up because she had committed adultery. The act itself had seemed almost trivial, but the hurt it caused when her husband discovered it couldn't be healed, and she still mused about what her life would have been if she had been more mature and stayed faithful. Marsha is surprised when LuAnn tells her she plans to go to a Catholic priest and confess her sin, in the sacrament of confession. "Don't ever tell Ted," Marsha says, and LuAnn agrees. The sin was not about Ted, but about herself, and about the unpredictable way erotic desire flared up in her in response to the incident at the girls' home. "Sex is like the weather," LuAnn says, as uncontrollable and variable. The story ends as she reflects on accepting forgiveness, from God and from herself, for her imperfections. "I can't take all the credit when I'm good," she says, "so I don't have to take all the blame when I fail." She is living out the traditional act of contrition that completes a sacramental confession: she resolves to amend her life with the help of God's grace, and to sin no more; even though she acknowledges she is still vulnerable to a change in the erotic weather.

I said about the Woody Allen movie *Hannah and Her Sisters* that I find something immoral about the treatment of marital infidelity there. My students have often been harsher than I was about the characters in the movie. Indeed, some expressed a desire to see them suffer for their infidelities, or at least to see them suffer more. I've found many students are angry with LuAnn when they read "The Timing of Sin"; they would really like to see LuAnn suffer, and they feel that this story lets her off too lightly. So the issue of marital infidelity is one that creates, you might say, an aesthetic problem, a tension between the aim of literature to make the truth "palpable and delightful," as Dubus put it, and the moral responsibility to show the ugliness and destructiveness of immorality. A reader like me who finds LuAnn an especially attractive character can suffer a kind of moral paralysis in the face of her attractiveness. (Was Plato paralyzed by Alcibiades? His charisma could disarm whole armies of moralists.) This can also happen with a real person whom we find attractive. So that somehow we diminish the severity of what she herself understands to be a sin. We will see these themes in Thomas Mann's *Death in Venice*, issues about how beauty can become unhinged from morality. One reason that in a book like this one, which claims to integrate philosophy and literature, philosophy is usually allowed to win, is the anxiety that when literature wins, beauty triumphs over morality. Mann has his main character live out some of the consequences of letting beauty triumph over morality, or at least over artistic discipline.

Should LuAnn suffer more for her infidelity than she does? Should I condemn this story in something like the way I criticized *Hannah and Her Sisters*? Let me say something about why I'm not tempted to do that, though I'm open to the conversation. For LuAnn Arceneaux, as we found out in "All the Time in the World," sexuality is very tightly integrated with her religiosity, with her sense particularly of the sacramental character of her own life. For LuAnn, God is not a disembodied, other-worldly person. God enters into her life through bodily practices, the way she inhabits the world as herself incarnate, as bone and flesh, to use the words of Adam of Eve. So it's not surprising a woman so vividly sensual experiences her sexuality as a big part of her everyday life. It's possible for the young and unmarried sometimes to think that marriage should, and indeed even that marriage will, eclipse the erotic attractiveness of everyone other than one's spouse. This story takes

it as a matter of course that that's false. LuAnn walks through a world of erotically interesting people. She would feel it as a diminishment of her life, of her liveliness, if that aspect of the world were to disappear. The reason that she almost commits adultery with Roger is the admiration she feels for his tenderness for these broken girls to whom he's dedicated his life. She sees him as paternal, as fatherly toward them. The violence at the home brings this admiration to a point of passion, and suddenly what was a little crush becomes a serious moral hazard, even, to use the old theological term that LuAnn uses with Marsha, an occasion of sin. The line between admiration and attraction is a very blurry one, and LuAnn being married, being happily married, being committed to her marriage, doesn't make the border any easier to police. The dishonesty of a failure to respect the line may be clear enough, but sometimes we just seem to find ourselves outside the city limits.

In a revealing moment after LuAnn has told the story to Marsha, she says, "If I ever say I know I won't do it, love me, hit me, slap me." Don't let me have a false view of my own moral strength, she is telling Marsha. I can't make erotic desire safe or tame. Sex is good, but it isn't tame, not for me. And LuAnn doesn't want her desire to be manageable, like Eryximachus would have it. LuAnn doesn't want to have safe sex. Because for her, to have safe sex is to give up what sex is, that suddenness that lets her say "My God," when she realizes that Ted Briggs might be the kind of man she wants to have sex with. But then she's got to admit that if she's unwilling to make sex safe, she'll also need help. And for her she finds that help sacramentally. And so she tells her friend Marsha she's going to confession, which Marsha finds incredibly quaint. "So wait," her friend asks, "you just about committed adultery in a car parked on a public street, and you're going to go tell a priest about this? Won't that just make you feel worse?" But that's not the way LuAnn sees it. LuAnn believes that what she needs is forgiveness. Because she thinks she has to recognize she needs help from somebody else, namely, grace from God, to put a stop to the fantasy that she's in control, that her erotic passion can be safe sex.

So the story drives us away from the notion that LuAnn confessing is a cheap or an easy way out for her, though some readers will find it so. Rather, it's LuAnn coming back to her sense of herself, seeing that she can't do it all alone. But her recognition that she can't do it all alone can look like an excuse. To her it's a taking of responsibility, taking possession of her own weakness. But from another point of view, a point of view that demands more moral self-sufficiency than LuAnn demands from herself, her acknowledgment of weakness can look like it's giving her an excuse. For me, her acknowledgment of that weakness in the sacrament of confession, when she turns her heart and mind toward some sort of redemption, prevents me from interpreting her claim to weakness as merely a cover story, as a way of letting herself off the hook. But I can understand why other readers do not respond to her that way, and think that she has taken a cheap way out, a way that doesn't demand enough from herself. I found in discussing this story with many different readers over the years that many are most offended by one particular exchange between LuAnn and Marsha. When Marsha says to LuAnn, "Don't ever tell Ted," and LuAnn says of course she wouldn't, a fair number of readers think she is betraying Ted, and believe she should not confess to God through a priest, through a sacrament, but rather confess to her husband. Such readers rely on an ideal of marriage as transparent, where the responsibility of a spouse is to let yourself be fully visible to your spouse, without secrets. Attachment to this ideal of marital transparency is of a piece with many viewers' irritation with Dave's preference for love over truth in *The Secret Lives of Dentists*. Like Alan Rudolph's movie, Andre Dubus's story disagrees with that ideal. It puts forward the prospect that even in a marriage there will always be some opacity between lovers.

What sort of demand for truthfulness is appropriate at the heart of a marriage? More generally, what kind of demand for transparency, for explicitness, should be a requirement of true repentance and of forgiveness? The theological tradition of the Catholic sacrament of confession is that it's inappropriate for the priest to demand that the person confessing a sin also confess to the person wronged. For whom would LuAnn do the confessing if she brought this to Ted? Would she do it to make Ted feel better? Or would she do it in a selfish way, to make herself feel better? When should we burden a spouse with a confession of our own faults? The issues come alive in Dubus's story, and are made most palpable, if not exactly delightful.

Chapter Seven
LOVE'S INDIGNITIES

Alcibiades ended the *Symposium* with an unsettled response to Socrates's cheerful account of the ecstasy and exhilaration of falling in love and being in love. Socrates gives such a cheering account of abandoning yourself to love because, as he says he learned from the wise woman Diotima, love is where we reach out to immortality through procreation. We give birth through intimate union with someone who loves us, whether this birth is a physical child or the spiritual offspring of poetry and a life of creative virtue. Procreation is neither merely male nor merely female. Socratic creativity is the golden thread that runs through the tapestry of the *Symposium* and binds it into a beautiful whole: the theme of creative androgyny, of the procreative integration of the masculine and the feminine.

Alcibiades did not so much reject this Socratic invitation as find it unlivable, a standing challenge to his real life in the shape of a shame-inducing ideal. "That's beautiful, but I just couldn't live that way"; any teacher worth hearing had better get used to listening to those words. The right response can't be to throw away the ideal, to accept that an ideal can't be expected to be a real measure. That would be like saying to a rich young man, "Well, you've done enough, obeying the rules; settle for that life," instead of looking at him with love and giving the awful invitation, "If you would be perfect, sell all you have and come, follow me." No surprise the students of such a teacher sometimes wish he were dead. Socrates can seem a bit like blind Martin, with a demand for purity that becomes inhumane, a cheerful Othello. His restless insistence is unforgiving, and can make us long for a restful moment just to live as we are, rather than as what we can be. Forgive us, and we will resolve to amend our lives, but don't humiliate us. Let us keep our dignity.

But when it comes to falling in love and being in love, this plea for dignity can sound like Lysias's speech from the *Phaedrus*, a plea for not exposing oneself or one's beloved to the inescapable wildness of erotic desire. Socrates had gratified the beautiful Phaedrus with his revision of this non-lover's speech, but he does not accept its words as his own. He will unveil his vision of love in his famous second speech, a vision that stretches the lover's dignity in a fine frenzy between heaven and earth.

Perhaps the greatest of all modern reflections on love's indignities is Thomas Mann's novella *Death in Venice* (published in 1905). Mann, who was awarded the Nobel Prize in Literature in 1929, tells the story of a distinguished writer, Gustav Aschenbach, who finds the experience of erotic love both cheering, as it is for Socrates, and disturbing, as it is for Alcibiades. Aschenbach's taste of the erotic unsettles his disciplined routine, and inspires his creativity at the same time it threatens to dissolve his identity and his dignity. Mann used this story to talk about himself, and to reflect on the roots of his own creativity. His story of an artist's struggle to turn his passions into disciplined writing draws directly on Plato, on the *Symposium* but especially on the *Phaedrus*.

Two more recent works of art teach me how to think about Mann's Platonic novella. "Out of the Snow" is the last of the four Ted Briggs and LuAnn Arceneaux stories from Andre Dubus's *Dancing After Hours*; and the movie *Babette's Feast*, directed by Gabriel Axel, won the American Academy Award as Best Foreign Film in 1988. (It is based on a story by Isak Dinesen.) You might say that both Dubus's story and Axel's movie are anti-Pausanias works of art. Pausanias tried to preserve the lover's dignity, and his own, by keeping heaven and earth, soul and body, as separate as they could be. Dubus and Axel challenge the division between the body and the soul, at least when it comes to romantic love. They mount this challenge through some of the religious ideas, especially Roman Catholic ideas, we considered when we thought about Aristophanes's speech and the biblical story of Adam and Eve.

Narcissus and Echo unveiled

The speech Phaedrus has in his pocket, written by Lysias, then revised and intensified in Socrates's first speech, praised the non-lover as superior to the lover, because a non-lover is still in his right mind. Strive to create relationships with people who are in their right mind, advises Lysias, and avoid people who are crazy, even if they are crazy about you. Socrates gratified Phaedrus by giving his improved, more philosophical version of Lysias's speech, but only after insisting he would keep his head veiled. He refused to own this speech, and Socrates cuts it off very abruptly, because he thinks this rationalization of erotic experience is making a mistake about love. The speech that prefers safe rationality to the dangerous wildness of erotic love suddenly feels all wrong.

What's wrong, says Socrates, is the premise that sanity is better than madness. Take the exemplary case of poetry. The best poets don't rely on their own whims and fancies. Such skill may be serviceable, but compared to the feathered wings of true poetry, mere skill is hardly more than a flying fish. Poetry, says Socrates, is inspiration, the inflowing of a god, possession, not skill. So too the lover, whose experience is not that of choosing, but of being chosen, abducted; falling not walking. The poet's life, like the lover's, is by abandonment. If self-control is the basis of dignity, then neither lover nor poet has much use for it. Socrates unveils his head and prepares to praise the lover's madness, not with an analysis, but with a myth.

Plato has been setting the scene for this famous speech, known as "the charioteer speech," since Phaedrus and Socrates first left the city. On their way to the plane tree where they will lie down, they pass near a shrine to Boreas, god of the north wind – Socrates has a more precise idea where it is than Phaedrus. Boreas, portrayed as winged and feathered in Greek art, is one of the patron gods of the city, and the shrine commemorates a myth that links him to the city's origins, a myth prominently represented in the sculpture on the city's great temple to Athena, the Parthenon. Once upon a time, the story goes, the princess of Athens, Oreithyia, was playing with her friends, out in the country, near the very stream in which Phaedrus and Socrates bathe their feet. (Plato, alone in all the versions of the myth, even gives the friend a name: Pharmacia, from the Greek word for "potion." It is dangerous to play with a potion out in the wild, and Plato squeezes every drop of magic from the name and its connections. But we can't spend the day in explanations!) Boreas fell in love with her, and swept her away, fathering children with her and so becoming a close relative of the royal line in Athens. This origin myth was remembered on the Parthenon because Boreas was said, the historian Herodotus reports, to have answered the Athenians' prayers during their war against the Persian Empire, a century before the *Phaedrus* was written, descending from the north in a violent squall that destroyed the enemy fleet. The violence of the god is both the rape of the girl and the salvation of the Athenians, neither tame nor safe, but good – if you are willing to accept being possessed by some god as a good, an unsettling invitation also on offer in *Death in Venice*.

When Socrates tells this story, Phaedrus scoffs at it, but Socrates does not. "I suppose," says Socrates, "we could reduce this myth and others like it to a naturalized, rational explanation, with the girl simply swept over a cliff by the north wind, and the rest of the story merely the product of the seething brain of some poet." (Herodotus himself is a rationalizer of myths, including the story of Boreas answering the Athenians' prayer.) But this false sophistication, Phaedrus, this impudent knowingness, in fact avoids knowledge, and especially self-knowledge. To project yourself onto the figures of myth might be the way to understand who you really are. "I, for example, am not sure what sort of wind god I might be, a chaotic and dangerous one, or a more orderly and gentler breeze." Socrates alludes to a passage from the poet Hesiod, where it is Boreas himself who is the gentle, providential breeze. He projects himself as lover onto the god, and leaves Phaedrus to accept the offer to play the beautiful abductee. The background of the Boreas story lets Socrates mean more than he explicitly says. The suggestive banter between the old man and the young beauty, about who is forcing from whom the scandalous words of Lysias's speech, with its role reversals and veiled offers, is discreetly elevated to the realm of myth.

Socrates at first had followed Phaedrus's example, and presented the management of erotic life as acceptable, even noble. But when he uncovers his head and speaks in his own voice, or at least in the voice of poetic possession, Socrates now praises a life that gives itself over to being mad, to being crazy about your beloved. Socrates recants the first speech, the rationalizing speech, in favor of the mythological charioteer speech, and so gives an example of the very advice about heeding myths he had earlier given to Phaedrus. He follows the example, he says, of an earlier recantation, by a Greek poet named Stesichorus. This poet, Socrates says, once made a mistake like the one Lysias and Phaedrus and Socrates himself have just made, slandering love. Stesichorus composed a poem about the famous Helen, and followed Homer by claiming that this great favorite of Aphrodite, divine herself, had been seduced and abducted by Paris, precipitating the Trojan War. Also like Homer, Stesichorus was struck blind for misrepresenting Helen and erotic love in this way. But unlike Homer, Stesichorus recovered his sight when he recanted and told a different story about Helen, the true story.

Helen, you see, never really went to Troy. Paris thought he had the real woman in his clutches on his ship and then in Troy, but he was deceived. The gods substituted a phantom image, a breathing likeness, while the true Helen was winged through the clouds and taken for safekeeping to Egypt. (Socrates gives only a brief allusion to the whole story, and Stesichorus's poem has not come down to us. But we do have Euripides's tragedy *Helen*, which tells the same story, and Plato probably had it in mind.) Helen's loving husband Menelaus brought the phantom with him from fallen Troy, but after some confusion, he recognized the real Helen in Egypt on the return journey. The deceptive image departed, and the true love came home. Menelaus, "the lover," rediscovered "Helen's beauty in a brow of Egypt." The pursuit of the likeness as the thing itself was the cause of all the turbulence and competition of the Trojan War. But for the true lover, the phantom turned out to be only a mnemonic of the true beloved, the divine Helen. Egypt, in Plato's imagination always a changeless, timeless land, becomes the mythic home of the real beloved.

Socrates will follow Stesichorus's example with his own myth of loss and homecoming. The soul, suggests Socrates, is deathless and restless with erotic energy, forever ascending beyond heaven and descending to earthiness, like the phoenix of love that Diotima described. No poet below, says Socrates, has ever made a sufficient hymn to this realm beyond the heavens, recalling Phaedrus's complaint that provoked the praises of love in the *Symposium*. But he will try. What the soul really is, he says, is beyond comprehension, but in a myth we can apprehend something of its nature and fate.

The soul is like a chariot covered with feathered wings, Socrates says, driven across the heavens by a charioteer who commands a team of two horses, a white horse noble and obedient, and a black horse rather sensuous and unruly. In our mythic life, we try to follow in the train of the gods, whose horses are all good, and fly in calm orderliness, as they ascend to the top of the heavens and see there the most beautiful, perfect visions. But our horses are turbulent, heavy, competitive, and at the best we get no more than fitful glimpses of those beautiful objects in which the vision of the gods can rest. We eventually fall to earthly lives, and how we live here reflects what we've seen there, and in a new cosmic cycle we try again to make the ascent back to our heavenly home.

When we had wings and soared up to the heavens, we had direct, immediate vision of divine and sacred things, and especially of the finest virtues, of justice in itself and wisdom and courage. And most wonderful of all, there on its own, without any mixture of the mere earthiness of this fallen world, was the vision of beauty itself. Even there, our vision was not calm and stable like the gods', but the glimpses of the highest and most beautiful realities are what make us truly human and distinguish us from all other living things. This direct, even if limited, experience of what exists in itself is ultimately what gives us the power of speech and cognition, since these realities are the standards by which we can categorize and navigate the imperfect things of this world.

We have fallen, according to Socrates's myth, from this direct and unmediated vision. But yet justice, courage, wisdom, all of these virtues have within them something divine, something sacred, and when we see them in our world, imperfectly embodied though they are, still we have a kind of admiration for them. But, Socrates suggests, our experience of beauty is fundamentally different, keener and more unsettling. Beauty has a special privilege in human life, Socrates insists. However much we might admire justice or courage, with beauty we are moved in our whole being. In particular, the experience of falling in love because we experience someone as beautiful is much more vivid and immediate than the experience of admiring somebody for his or her justice or temperance or courage. And Socrates suggests what makes beauty so special is the way it bridges the usual gap between the human and the divine, between our everyday world and the myth world, and so between the body and the soul. Beauty, unlike any other virtue or excellence, is perceived immediately in our sensuous life. Beauty shines through. However justice might impress us, it does not shine forth immediately in the way that beauty does. So beauty has the particular privilege of bringing us more directly back to the experience of something as sacred or divine than anything else will. Sensuous beauty is the privileged vehicle of mythic memory, and a beautiful beloved is the most sensuous beauty of all.

We may well treat people with special respect when we think them distinguished in justice or in courage or in temperance. But it's unlikely that we will ever dote on those people, dote to idolatry, as Shakespeare says lovers do. Indeed, many of us who are in love with somebody can, at least in our calmer moments, see that the person we're in love with may not be the most just or courageous or temperate person we know. Indeed, our beloved may not be especially exemplary in any of those virtues. Yet we cherish our beloved with an intensity and immediacy that goes beyond our concern for anybody else, even if we can be forced to concede those other people are better. This intense immediacy can be seen as the charioteer speech's explanation for Phaedrus's death test, the reason that, before a parent or sibling or the closest friend, a lover will die for you.

Socrates describes the experience of remembering mythic beauty through the sensuous beauty of a beloved in images as comic and touching as they are graphically sexual. The images are also as androgynous as Diotima's descriptions of erotic experience in the *Symposium*. In our fallen state, our wings have gone dormant, retracting beneath our skin. But the triggering vision of physical beauty, reviving our memory of the divine beauty of the myth world, shakes the soul to its roots and sets it throbbing. Though Socrates is composing an image of the soul, he at the same time gives a powerful description of physical sexual arousal. Our wings suddenly start to rise again, and the heat of desire melts and lubricates the whole soul as it longs to approach this image of the divine. The pricking and tickling of the emerging wing shafts drive the soul nearly to frenzy. (Socrates uses some of the same language Aristophanes had used about the violent bodily explosions that cured his hiccups.) The lover sees the beloved like a votive statue of the god – like the little statues Socrates and Phaedrus noticed near the shrine of Boreas – and can barely hold himself back from prostrating himself and offering sacrifice. Erotic desire draws him to the god by drawing him to the beloved.

With all this throbbing, erecting, and melting, lovers hardly are in a state for calm analysis of what's happening, and so falling in love first and foremost makes lovers confused, puts us at a loss, so we do not know what we should do or say. We cannot read the oracle. But at the same time, love is an experience of extraordinary exhilaration and excitement. The charioteer speech is an interpretation of this exciting erotic confusion. When we fall in love with somebody here – that special experience of appreciating a beloved's beauty, often enough a beauty that may well escape the notice of other people, that may even make us an occasion of laughter for our friends – when we experience a beloved's beauty in a way that excites us to a kind of erotic exhilaration, what's really happening is that this beloved person is for us an occasion of remembering our mythic life, something sacred and divine.

It's not that the beloved himself or herself is a god. When we fall in love with somebody, we don't think that person is a god, but we are grateful for being reminded of what a god must be. Remember Stesichorus's story of Helen in Egypt: the turbulence of the war was caused when the phantom was taken as real, and homecoming was achieved only when that phantom was turned into a reminder of the real Helen. The beloved himself or herself, Socrates suggests, is a votive statue, an occasion for our hearts and minds to turn themselves toward the gods, toward something sacred. The lover, in fact, will use this mnemonic image as a model for himself, striving to conform to it, to imitate the god that shines through. The lover treats himself, we can say, as the votive statue, shaped to the god beyond. The new self is the triumph of memory.

Falling in love is a memory aid, a mnemonic device, Socrates suggests. But the primary thing we remember through the experience of our beloved's beauty is who we really are. The beauty of the beloved and the rush of exhilaration it gives us drives us back almost into the myth world; we lose our mundane self and renew the original self, the better self with wings. (And don't we all feel like we're flying when we fall in love?) Now we understand an odd sentence Socrates uttered early in the dialogue, when Phaedrus was pretending he didn't want to share the speech he had been memorizing from Lysias. "Phaedrus, if I don't know you, I must have forgotten myself, too," Socrates says. Socrates is suggesting he knows Phaedrus's love of speeches too well to be fooled into thinking Phaedrus doesn't have a copy of Lysias's speech. But he also means something that only becomes clear now, in the charioteer speech: that his love for Phaedrus is the vehicle for his own self-knowledge. If Socrates could not understand Phaedrus, could not see the sacred beauty that Phaedrus represents as a kind of votive statue, Socrates would be unable to recover something that is truly his own, a kind of knowledge about what's most important and what's possible for human love.

Now, this all sounds as if falling in love would be a delightful, rather lighthearted thing. Why would anyone want to avoid a memory of a divine beauty, a memory that brings all the excitement of falling in love? But of course, this homecoming involves deep loss. Recovering our mythic vision will lead us to overlook a lot of what in everyday life we take to be most important. In remembering the human potential for something sacred and divine through falling in love with your beloved, you tend to become more foolish by the everyday standards of the world. You stop being respectable. You write bad poetry. You follow somebody around like a puppy dog. You look like a slave. You do all the silly things Lysias had criticized when he said it is better to be a non-lover. In short, you tend to lose your dignity. So that the very act of memory, for which the beloved is so potent a vehicle, can look from the outside like an act of forgetful foolishness. It's no surprise that there's an aspect of our personality, let's call it the dignified aspect, that resists giving itself over to the crush, to the fall. It's no wonder that we call it "falling" in love, as if we lose control and safety. We don't call it walking leisurely into love. It's something that seems to happen to us, not that we choose. Love strikes us from the outside, as if we'd been made passive, and lost something of ourselves in order to let it fall upon us. So this speech tries to capture our ambivalence toward the experience of love. There's something that's truly us that's recovered when we fall in love, but also something that we think of as really important to us, call it our dignity, that we lose when we fall in love. Menelaus rejoiced to bring home the true Helen, but he must have felt the loss of all the glory of the phantom war.

Philosophers, soldiers, doctors, writers, all have strategies for saving their dignity, their picture of their perfect soul. But the black horse is as much who we are as is the white horse, or as the charioteer. And indeed in the way Socrates tells the story, if we had no black horse, if we didn't have the restlessness of sensuality, one wonders if we would ever overcome our bashfulness and approach those beautiful people who attract our erotic interest, would ever progress from admiration to risk actual love. The charioteer and the white horse, Socrates says, pull back and resist the lascivious advances of the black horse toward the beautiful boy. They promise to approach another time, but when will that time come? Awed by the image of divine beauty, they pretend to forget their promise when the black horse "reminds" them, and act indignant about "the things of Aphrodite." In other words, Socrates makes the black horse the instrument of memory, in a myth that makes memory the work of love; and he puts charioteer and white horse on the side of the pretend non-lover of his now-recanted first speech. Nobility can be an impediment to true love. The white horse, in fact, is described with all the physical traits of an aristocrat, among which is its elegant hooked nose. The restless, beauty-hungry black horse is common as dirt, would be a barefoot hillbilly in America; and of course it is snub-nosed, Socrates says, surely with a smile, since his snub nose was as infamous and characteristic as his bare feet. As he projected himself into Diotima's account of Love as a restless, barefoot spirit, so he paints himself black in the charioteer speech, to unsettle the non-lovers in the audience.

Plato's comic set piece can't be appreciated if philosophy insists on maintaining its hook-nosed nobility even when confronted with the suggestive joking of its most famous snub-nosed commoner. Socrates is working the same ground in a comic vein that Wagner's *Tristan and Isolde* works in tragedy. Isolde's legitimate spouse, King Marke, sings of how he respected Isolde so much he could not bring himself to sleep with her: he was all white horse. The nobility of his person and his music is manifest, but so is the greater con-summation of the lover's music of Tristan. So while in some sense the black horse is a bad horse, an unruly horse, the point of the myth cannot be captured by thinking that we would all be better off if only we could unyoke the black horse and be rid of it. That was the view of Lysias that Socrates has now recanted, and like the view of Pausanias in the *Symposium*, when he elevated Heavenly Aphrodite to the exclusion of Earthy Aphrodite, until one couldn't see much point in being in love at all. The charioteer speech is the *Phaedrus*'s way of bringing back Dionysus and the flute girl.

The fundamental experience of the lover for the beloved, then, is something like this: When the lover sees the beloved's beauty, the lover is reminded of something divine and sacred that in, so to speak, mythical life we had immediate access to but that in this, our real life, we have access to only through mediation, especially the mediation of loving someone. There's a certain sense, then, in which your love for your beloved is rather impersonal. The lover's interest does not terminate with the beloved, you might say. Rather, through the beauty of this beloved person you can see something divine. One consequence of this vision is your desire to make your-self better, to conform yourself more closely to the divine exemplar now shining through your beloved.

This model or image of the lover provokes two anxieties for the beloved. First, such a lover might make a beloved feel rather, well, transparent to the lover's gaze, as if your lover is looking through you to the divine beauty he sees, or rather is reminded of. A votive statue directs worship toward the god represented by the statue, not to the statue itself. The beloved appears as an icon, an image not worshipped itself – that would be idolatry – but directing worship to the real divinity. Second, the lover takes the god beyond the statue as the standard, not just of self-fashioning, but also of fashioning the beloved. Socrates suggests a lover tries to make his or her beloved more and more like the god the lover sees repre-sented in the beloved. He compares the lover to a sculptor, forming a statue into a better and better likeness of a god. It is one thing to say you wish your beloved to become a better and better person. This aspect of the charioteer speech reminds us of Pausanias's claim in the *Symposium* that the lover is essentially an educator. True love goes along with the desire that the beloved become a better person. But when you think of yourself as the beloved, being treated by your lover like the material of a statue, the mood shifts, I think. Doesn't the image become rather creepy when the lover is making the beloved over, to fit an ideal in the lover's imagination? It's too much like the plot of Alfred Hitchcock's *Vertigo*, about as creepy a movie as there has ever been.

These two anxieties are the *Phaedrus*'s version of the anxiety Socrates provoked in Alcibiades. Alcibiades made it clear that he felt shame before Socrates, even though he was usually a shameless man. Alcibiades could feel Socrates working him like clay, trying to make him a better man, a better approximation to a likeness of god. And Alcibiades concedes that he would in fact be better, if he conformed more with Socrates's ideal for him. But is this provoca-tion to become better, to become an unattained but attainable self, what we really want from a lover? We don't always want to be bet-ter, nor, if it comes to it, do we want always to be asking our beloved to become better. "I love you just the way you are," sang an old Billy Joel song, and that can sound restful for both parties. Antoine meant to say these comforting words to Mathilde when he told her not to lose a pound or he'd throw himself under a bus (in *The Hairdresser's Husband*), and it was deadly that she heard them in the provocative spirit – Be perfect! – of teachers like Socrates, Jesus, and Emerson. But, a Platonist may counter, if I love you just the way you are, or if you demand of me that I love you just the way you are, we might end up flattening our relationship. It might well be that the best kind of love is a love in which my love for you, my beloved, creates in you aspirations to live up to this lover's image of you. Your lover sees more in you than you may see in yourself. And so this experience of the lover being a kind of refining or perfecting mirror of the beloved is also central to the myth of the charioteer.

This notion of the perfecting mirror, in which the beloved sees his better self and feels a call to become that self, is introduced most explicitly in a passage of unusual beauty, even for Plato. Toward the end of the charioteer speech, Socrates turns his attention from the experience of the lover, focused on the beloved's beauty, to the experience of the beloved. Why a lover is attracted to a beautiful beloved is at a basic level easy to understand, even if the mythic revelations of the charioteer speech are astonishing. But it is harder to account for the beloved feeling love for the lover – remember, Socrates assumes the lover is older and not especially attractive. "When the lover is filled with love for his beloved," Socrates says, "his own desire overflows back toward the beloved." Notice how Socrates has appropriated Agathon's ideal of the overflowing fullness of love. But now he does something wonderful with the idea: "Think how a breeze or an echo bounces back from a smooth solid object to its source," says Socrates, inhabiting again his mythic identity as Boreas, that enchanting wind. "That is how the stream of beauty goes back to the beautiful beloved and sets him aflutter. It enters through his eyes, which are its natural route to the soul." The lover is so filled with the beauty of the beloved, that this beauty overflows and can be felt by the beloved flowing into him. The lover's eyes, Socrates is inspired to say, reflect like a mirror the beautiful image of the beloved, and the beloved can see that self-image best exactly in the lover's eyes. The mirror of romance shows us who we are better than we could ever discover on our own.

The beloved finds something extraordinarily attractive about the beauty the lover lets him see. But the beloved is not really sure what it is that he is finding so attractive. So Socrates goes on to say, "The beloved is in love but has no idea what he loves, does not understand and cannot explain what has happened to him," says Socrates. In the terms of the myth of memory and the heavenly chariot, the beloved "forgets" that he is seeing himself, his very self, in the lover as in a mirror. Without realizing it, the beloved, through the lover, is able to experience his or her own beauty. We can't see our own beauty. It's only when somebody else loves us that our beauty comes back to us. One thinks again here of the experience of Susan Dorsey, the actress who loves Ted Briggs in Andre Dubus's story "Falling in Love." Susan could experience a kind of fullness, a kind of gratitude only when her excellence as an actress was reflected back to her with the appreciation of a lover. For Susan, a lover became a sort of echo chamber in which she could hear her own praises.

Plato has given the *Phaedrus*'s model of romantic love a mythic richness with a discreet allusion in this passage about the echo and the mirror. We noticed in the last chapter Socrates's account in the *Symposium* of love as constant death and rebirth. That passage was Plato's allusion to the myth of the phoenix, the bird that dies and is renewed. Plato did not spoil the surprise by having Socrates blurt out, "Hey, love is like a phoenix!" He let us discover the secret, introducing a subtle clue early on, when Apollodorus mentioned a certain man named Phoenix, who had known what happened at that famous party at Agathon's house. Plato likes to let us readers make such discoveries for ourselves; it makes the truth more palpable and delightful. At the risk of ruining the surprise, I want to point out that he does the same sort of thing here in the *Phaedrus*. The essential structure of this model of love: the lover sees the beloved's beauty, but responds primarily to the divine beauty that this earthy beauty merely reminds him of; and the beloved loves his own reflection, delivered to him by the lover, even though the beloved doesn't realize what he loves is just an ideal image of himself. The myth behind this model of love is, of course, Echo and Narcissus.

For readers who aren't familiar with this myth, one of the foundational myths about romantic love in Western culture, here is its basic outline. A nymph named Echo (a female fairy of the forest, so a pastoral myth befitting the *Phaedrus*) falls in love with an extremely beautiful young man, named Narcissus. But both woman and man have a peculiar trait that dooms their love. Echo lives under a curse that prevents her from starting a conversation, since she can only repeat words spoken to her. This means she can't say "I love you" to Narcissus unless he first says it to her. Narcissus, on the other hand, has accidently seen his own beautiful reflection in a brook, and not knowing the beauty is his own, he falls in love with that beautiful face. Echo is doomed never to utter an original word, but always to be mediated by the real origin that comes from outside her. Narcissus is doomed to love only himself, but in a mirror, without knowing what it is he truly loves.

Now, the earliest surviving source of this myth of Echo and Narcissus is four centuries later than Plato, in Ovid's *Metamorphoses* (which means "transformations" in Latin), from where the story has spread throughout the length and breadth of the Western literary tradition. For example, John Milton in *Paradise Lost* used it as his model for Eve innocently falling in love with herself in a stream in the Garden of Eden. But it is obvious, I think, that Plato has this very myth in mind when he writes that the lover – like Echo – only reflects back the beloved's beauty, so that without realizing it the beloved falls in love with his own beauty – just like Narcissus. In a certain mood – perhaps in most of our romantic moods, in fact – this asymmetrical model of romance can look awkward, and perhaps perverse. There's something about the beloved that we're tempted to see as narcissistic, and surely Plato's reference to the mirror here drives us toward this. You remember, too, that Phaedrus himself is a very beautiful young man. Socrates is subtly hinting that Phaedrus has something narcissistic about him, with his pride, even vanity. This puts Socrates into the position of the poor nymph Echo, who can't get her beloved to hear anything except what he has already thought and said for himself. This mythic identification with Echo helps us to understand the odd way that Socrates first gave a speech in which he was little more than a ventriloquist's dummy, intensifying Lysias's speech to try to catch the attention of Phaedrus. Every Echo runs the risk of falling in love with a Narcissus.

Plato must have realized, too, that painting Phaedrus and Socrates as Echo and Narcissus was a dangerous thing to do. If you're in an unsympathetic mood with the charioteer speech, where does this mythic projection leave you? It seems to me it leaves you in a position where you think that a Platonic love relationship, as it's described in the *Phaedrus*, is a relationship between a narcissist and a fantasist. The beloved simply likes his or her own beauty as it's reflected back from the lover. You love your lover exactly because your lover loves you. You love the puffing up, the flattery, you get from being with a lover. The lover, on the other hand, seems to love not you, not the beloved himself or herself, but what the beloved could be, the heavenly beloved that the lover is reminded of by this earthy beloved. The lover depersonalizes you, projects onto you his own fantasy of a perfected beloved. So if you, O Beloved One, are not in the mood to accept a new identity from the way that your lover idealizes you, you might think that this is the model of a spectacularly unhealthy relationship. A lot depends on what you take your true self to be. If you don't accept that the lover's idealization of you is the *real* you, a more real you than the rather petty and mundane you that most of us happen to look like every day, then it looks like the lover is just foisting a fantasy upon you. But if the real you is that divine and sacred self that the lover discovers in an inchoate experience of erotic restlessness, this projection is no mere fantasy. It is the vehicle of your self-knowledge, the ecstasy of finding yourself more truly and more strange in a mythic exemplar.

I would put the main questions of Socrates's Myth of the Charioteer this way. When as lovers, we see something in our beloveds that goes beyond anything they usually can see in themselves, is this a vision – a glimpse of a wonderful truth that usually escapes us – or an illusion – a mere wish fulfillment, in which we pretend to see what isn't there at all? When as beloveds, we appreciate our lovers' interest in us, and feel elevated by it, is this a provocation to become that better self our lovers see, or is it the merest vanity, a settling for a falsely inflated view of ourselves? Plato thinks a properly nourished love grows the wings of the soul, and lets lover and beloved soar into vision and the better self; but he haunts this cheerful picture with the myth of Echo and Narcissus, to chasten us even as he cheers. What more could we ask of a teacher?

Dionysus and Aphrodite in Thomas Mann's Venice

Thomas Mann's novella *Death in Venice* is one of the most attractive and sustained reflections on Plato's *Phaedrus* anybody has written. The novella, of course, is accessible even to someone who hasn't read Plato, but it's clear that the story takes on a special power for somebody who's coming recently from a reading of the charioteer speech. Throughout the story, Mann draws on a number of Greek sources to make his own novella into a kind of modern myth.

As a reminder, or simply as a help for readers who haven't (yet!) read *Death in Venice*, here is a bare summary of the story. Gustav Aschenbach is a writer, now in his fifties, whose work is universally admired. His books are already taught in schools, and his style is held up for emulation. In short, his books are already classics. The control and discipline that marks his work seems effortless to his readers, but it is the product of a personal regimen both demanding and seldom interrupted. The passion and sensuous beauty of his works is made possible by a severe, even ascetic, lifestyle, once described memorably by an acquaintance: "Aschenbach has always lived like this," he said, holding up his hand in a clenched fist, "and never like this," relaxing his arm and letting the wrist rest carelessly on the back of the chair. Mann bodying forth Nietzsche's famous contrast (in *The Birth of Tragedy*) between the art of Apollo, rooted in discipline and form, and the art of Dionysus, rooted in passion and movement. Throughout the story, Mann's variations on this theme, like Nietzsche's own, have been deeply influenced by Richard Wagner's opera *Tristan and Isolde*, where romantic love sweeps away all demands of nobility and honor. Wagner's sea suffuses *Death in Venice* as the image of an ecstatic loss of identity.

Aschenbach does allow himself vacations, or perhaps more precisely, extended recreations, that is, trips to allow him to rest and regain energy for his creative spirit. The story opens with Aschenbach walking in Munich, feeling restless and exhausted, ready for one of his trips. Provoked into thought by an odd man with "a distinctly foreign exotic air" he sees at the cemetery, he thinks perhaps he will go somewhere exotic – a word we have heard before in Atom Egoyan's movie *Exotica*. He has a fantasy of "going all the way to the tigers," but in the end he wants something more tame, and decides to travel to Venice: a city famous as a meeting point for Europe and the exotic East, but also a tried and true tourist destination. Even on holiday, Aschenbach maintains his classic discipline, and he is disgusted by a man, at least his own age, whom he sees traveling, dressed up in clothes more suited to his much younger companions, and who, Aschenbach realizes with contempt, has tried to hide his age with rouge and hair dye.

When he arrives in Venice, he travels to his hotel in a coffin-like gondola with a sinister gondolier, lulled by the rhythmic movements of the sea. He discovers there a Polish family, with several unremarkable daughters and one ravishingly beautiful teenage boy named Tadzio. Aschenbach first thinks of the boy as a perfect embodiment of classical Greek beauty, like a marble statue. (Another foreigner in Venice had seen his beloved as "monumental alabaster"; how did that turn out?) Once when the boy sees Aschenbach looking at him and turns away with a smile, Aschenbach sees the boy as Narcissus, pleased by his own image as reflected in Aschenbach's gaze, like lover and beloved in the *Phaedrus*. But gradually Aschenbach's attraction becomes a passionate obsession, and his interest in the boy becomes more obviously erotic and ecstatic. Aschenbach has always been able to indulge his artist's love of beauty without losing his dignity, relying on his discipline and his ability to transform passion into words. But the boy breaks down Aschenbach's accustomed control, and he feels himself losing his identity and pursuing the boy shamelessly.

Aschenbach suspects a cholera plague from the East has entered Venice (as Euripides made Dionysus and his enchanted women a dangerous and exotic import from the East). He considers alerting the Polish family, but decides he will do nothing that might make the boy leave, and of course he risks death for himself by staying as well. His suspicions are confirmed by an unlikely source, a vulgar street musician whose suggestive performance at the hotel is as fascinating to the artist as it is beneath his dignity. Utterly enslaved to his desire for the boy, Aschenbach visits the hotel barber, and undergoes his own Dionysian transformation, getting the same rouge and hair dye that had so recently seemed to him inconsistent with mature dignity. The possessed old man is imitating the most tragic of all Greek stories of Dionysus and his ecstasies, *The Bacchae* (*The Women of Dionysus*). The tragedy comes when the central character loses his grip on his tough manly identity under the influence of the god, seduced and transformed into a Dionysian reveler, dressed up in women's clothes and sent out to be destroyed in the wild. Aschenbach has a horrifying dream of being torn apart by his obsession with the beautiful boy, full of Euripides's images.

The story ends when Aschenbach dies on the beach, beckoned, he thinks, by the boy in the waves. With his failing strength he struggles to rise from his chair and follow his Dionysian beloved; and the dolphin leaps into the limitless sea. He is a victim of both the plague from the East and of erotic love – or has he been liberated by them? Love and Death embrace in Art, and the artist cannot settle with one unless he is unsettled by the other.

Readers once found Aschenbach's alleged sexual inversion a reason not to enter into the story; I now find some use his alleged pedophilia to justify their refusal. But perhaps this avoidance of Aschenbach has another root, not in his sexuality, but in what grounds his restlessness. Aschenbach is seized by a restlessness he can't fully understand, provoked by the man at the cemetery. This figure had a striking appearance: "Of medium height, thin, beard-less, and strikingly snub-nosed, the man was the red-haired type and had its milky freckled pigmentation. His lips seemed too short; they pulled all the way back, baring his long white teeth to the gums." Two other figures are characterized by the same features: the sinister boatman who rocks Aschenbach in his gondola coffin when he arrives in Venice; and the obscene musician at the hotel. To connect these episodes and these figures, Mann has made an almost mechanical symbol of all these features, the reddish hair, the pale complexion, the snub nose, the bared teeth, first noticed at the cemetery. These figures, of course, are a symbol or a representative of death. And the snub nose and the missing lips make of them a skull.

Gustav Aschenbach, when he was in his early or mid-fifties, started to be obsessed with death. *Death in Venice* is haunted by Phaedrus's death test from the *Symposium*. Of course, Mann puts this thought into the story without ever explicitly saying, "Aschenbach was obsessed with death." That would be a very flatfooted description, because it would misrepresent Aschenbach's own consciousness. Aschenbach is not obsessed with death as a topic or as an explicit thought. His mood and the forms his imagination bodies forth are where the obsession finds its habitation, without being named directly by him. Thomas Mann's novella is thinking, but it's not thinking merely by presenting you with a series of claims, with an argument. Instead it's trying to let the reader experience Aschenbach's own experience of the world, an experience that comes to him through images much more than it does through theses. So that, for example, an important part of the revelation of Aschenbach's own mental state, of his consciousness, comes through descriptions of Aschenbach's dreams. Dreams, those primordially imagistic experiences, may often on their surface, as we say, look nonsensical, or don't seem to have any meaning at all. But yet somehow, the density of those images is strangely moving to us. So Thomas Mann is not thinking like, and not writing like, the stereotypical philosopher, whose mind is in arguments not images. But that doesn't mean Mann's not being thoughtful. The thoughtfulness comes through his development of a recurring set of images that lead you farther and farther into the mind of a particular artist, of this man Gustav Aschenbach.

This man is unsettled by a particular experience at the cemetery, an experience he doesn't quite put a name on or a word to. He lets the experience remain, so to speak, an image. But it provokes in him a restlessness, a restlessness that he finds a bit awkward, indeed in a way a bit embarrassing. He thinks he has too much dignity, another word that occurs over and over again in this story, simply to have an aimless youthful restlessness to travel. So, Aschenbach accepts the challenge of this death's head he sees at the cemetery, but at the same time he resists it. He refuses to interpret the restlessness outside of his usual frame of reference. Instead he interprets it simply as a repetition of something he does anyway, to go on vacation for recreation, to do new work, new creation. Aschenbach attempts to control this restlessness. "He needed a change of scene, a bit of spontaneity." Think of how comic that is, in its way, somebody planning to be spontaneous. "I've been working too hard," you tell yourself, "I've got to schedule in some spontaneity." How spontaneous is scheduled spontaneity? But that's the way Aschenbach keeps control of his life, it's why he can create art out of the great passion that's in his life. Because he can schedule, because he can discipline (another word that appears over and over), he manages passion. He wants passion. Without it, he couldn't write. His writing would be flat and dull, it would have nothing in it of innovation, no striking images. He wants passion, but he wants to be able to manage it. "He needed a change of scene, a bit of spontaneity, an idle existence, a foreign atmosphere and an influx of new blood to make the summer bearable and productive. He would travel, then." Good, he's satisfied; he thinks he will overcome his restlessness. "Not too far, not all the way to the tigers." But it won't work, because Dionysus and Aphrodite are wild animals, and can't be made into pets. This is a story about a man who thought he could manage his passions, but in the end his passions do drive him all the way to the tigers, and the tigers are no more tame than C.S. Lewis's lion. He ends up in the jungle when he thought he was only going to Venice, the tourist's version of the exotic.

For Aschenbach, the artist's life rests on a knife-edged balance between discipline and passion. He pictures himself as a kind of hero, a deeply courageous man who in the discipline of his writing, morning after morning after morning, constantly achieves a victory over the unruly energies that would threaten to make of him nothing but an image of dissipation. Aschenbach should remind us of the non-lover who's praised in the first two speeches in the *Phaedrus*. That professed non-lover in the speech Phaedrus speaks for Lysias, is himself a writer, managing his erotic passions by writing down a speech. Socrates's reformulation of Lysias's speech revealed the secret that the writer is a secret lover, full of passion, whose beloved brought him all the way to the tigers. But yet he thinks he can present himself, through a clever bit of deception, of controlled self-presentation, as someone who's managing his erotic attraction, not as somebody who's taken over by it, who's enthused by it, who's filled with it as if he's possessed by a god, or as if he's blown over a cliff by the north wind.

Death in Venice wants to help us as readers experience something of Aschenbach's own situation, his own psychic, spiritual state, a spiritual state that is very precisely characterized. The story takes us in so deeply not because we get a psychological theory of Aschenbach, but because the images that Mann uses and goes back to over and over again immerse us in a very particular view of the world. The thoughtfulness comes in the particulars. It doesn't come in a general thesis. It's not as if we can say, "Well, here's my theory about the dangers of erotic love and I've got a really good example that will illustrate my theory: think of Gustav Aschenbach from Thomas Mann's novella *Death in Venice*." That makes the theory more important than the images of the story. It's not the way Mann works. It's the particularity of the images in this story of this man that gives us the key to our own thoughtful understanding of erotic risk – not risk for some German writer who died in 1905, like Aschenbach does in the story, but rather the risk for us here, now, of opening ourselves up to that strange trip that goes all the way to the jungle of erotic experience.

There are two passages where Mann directly takes up Plato's *Phaedrus*. In both passages, Aschenbach himself thinks about his infatuation with the boy by paraphrasing the *Phaedrus*: Plato's words become his words. Mann uses these two paraphrases from the *Phaedrus* in something like the way Plato uses the two speeches of Socrates within that dialogue: the first passage pretends that erotic love can be managed by philosophy or artistic discipline, while the second passage acknowledges that the way of love is by abandonment. In the first passage, Aschenbach still thinks he can enjoy the experience of the beloved boy without being destroyed by it. He thinks of the barefoot pastoral scene where Socrates and Phaedrus walk outside the city into the country, and muses on how much he is like Socrates, remembering a higher beauty through a particular beautiful young man. He is grateful for the special privilege of beauty to shine forth in the sensuous world, and is not unsettled by it. He expects to maintain his dignity as an artist and use the passion he feels in the presence of this beautiful boy simply to inspire himself to greater productivity. In the presence of this young boy, Aschenbach the artist expects to give birth in the beautiful, as Diotima put it in the *Symposium*. "The honey-colored hair fell gracefully in ringlets at the temples and the back of the neck. The sun glimmered in the down of the upper spine. The fine delineation of the ribs and symmetry of the chest stood out through the torso's scanty cover. The armpits were still as smooth as a statue's. What discipline, what precision of thought was conveyed by that tall, youthfully perfect physique." Aschenbach feels the sensuous beauty of the boy's flesh and blood, but thinks to treat him as a statue, and to control this sensuous experience through the discipline of artistic form. This is exactly what the lover does in the charioteer speech. The lover tries to shape and mold the beloved into a better and better votive statue to the divine, reminded of that mythic reality by the beloved's beauty. Aschenbach thinks about the boy as if he is just the raw material for the superior power of the literary artist, "the austere and pure will laboring to bring the god-like statue to light, chiseling with sober passion at the marble block of language." Aschenbach the artist will not lose his dignity and fall in love with this flesh-and-blood boy! He will instead use the boy as the occasion for a more spiritual experience, and "release the slender form he had beheld in his mind" and "present it to the world as an image and mirror of spiritual beauty." So Aschenbach looks to this beautiful young man and he thinks to himself, it's art, like mine, that really brings that beauty to its full perfection. I, the artist, with my dignity and my discipline, my "pure will," can take up this raw material, mere physical beauty, and turn it into something more spiritual, more lasting. I take this boy of flesh and blood, who will get old and wither and die and whose flesh will rot away, and I turn him into marble, to a statue, to stone that will last.

Aschenbach is confident that he can transfigure the physical, fleshly beauty of this boy into an image of a truer, spiritual beauty, a lasting beauty, an eternal beauty, in "the marble block of language." He is indulging in a fantasy of his own superiority and control over the beloved, through his ability to transfigure raw erotic passion into artistic discipline and production. But of course, Aschenbach is overconfident. We can see this immediately if we recall that this isn't the first time we've heard about marble in this story. Marble is the lasting stuff of a beautiful statue, the stuff that the sculptor works with. But marble was also the stuff at the beginning of the story from which that cemetery was made. So marble is ambiguous in this story. It is an image on the one hand of art's escape from mortality, and at the same time is an image of that mortality itself. To immortalize someone in marble is a pretty sure sign that you take the person to be dead. Aschenbach's fantasy reminds us of that horrible fantasy of Othello's, when he compares his flesh-and-blood wife to "monumental alabaster," to excuse his own murderous action upon her.

So at this point in the story, Aschenbach himself has used Plato's *Phaedrus* as the model of his own ability to combine in one life dignified artistic discipline and erotic passion. When Mann and Aschenbach – the boundary between the author and the character becomes harder and harder to maintain as the novella proceeds – return to the *Phaedrus* near the end of the story, Aschenbach has lost his confidence and his dignity. He realizes he wasn't able to keep in control, that in the end his discipline was destroyed by his experience of this beautiful beloved. Even art could not control beauty. So he starts again with the notion of beauty's special privilege, its sensuous presence. Aschenbach thinks of what he would say to the Polish boy by thinking of what a defeated Socrates would say to Phaedrus: "Beauty, Phaedrus, beauty and beauty alone is at once divine and visible. So beauty is, after all, the path of the sensuous man, little Phaedrus, the path of the artist to the intellect. But it is a dangerous and tempting path, indeed, a path of sin and delusion that must lead one astray. Now you see that we poets can be neither wise nor dignified." At last Aschenbach gives up the fantasy that his dignity and his discipline can be perfectly integrated with his abandoning himself to erotic intoxication. He says, "The magisterial guise of our style is all falsehood and folly." The potency of his writing, which can make of a raw erotic experience a beautiful story, something stylized, only hides the exhilaration and ecstasy of the author; it does not control it. Just as Socrates, in his first speech, shows that a rationalizing speech against love is a failed attempt to hide erotic passion, so too Aschenbach in the end claims that poeticizing speech about beauty is also a failed effort of control. This is a more radical statement than the statement of Socrates's first speech in the *Phaedrus*. In Socrates's first speech, it was rationalization that's a failed strategy of control. In Aschenbach's final reflections, though, the failed strategy of control includes poetry. Poetry ultimately is no more open to the raw power of dissolution, of intoxication, of enthusiasm, than was philosophy.

Thomas Mann's reflection on the themes of the *Phaedrus* finds in the end that real openness to erotic love gives up the self-image of dignity and discipline. The story leaves us with a terrible ambiguity about whether Aschenbach was defeated by love, or whether he triumphed over his identity as a mere artist. Is Aschenbach reduced below the level of a human being, drowned in love's indignities, by opening himself so much to love that he dies for it? Or is he in fact transposed, transfigured by opening himself in that way, beyond honor, beyond good and evil? Despite the narrator's tone of disapproval and even contempt for Aschenbach's letting go, the very contrast between reduction and transfiguration resounds with the ecstatic closing aria of *Tristan and Isolde*, where drowning in death is exactly what it is to be transfigured. When at the end of the story Aschenbach experiences that great sea of beauty, and erases the boundaries of the self that he's created through all those mornings of discipline as a writer, does he discover a potency he always had, but that up to this final consummation he had avoided or suppressed?

Was it a mistake for Aschenbach to go all the way to the tigers, where he was eaten alive? He's not the first lover, and I'm sure he won't be the last, to ask that particular erotic question.

The body's sacraments in Gabriel Axel's *Babette's Feast*

I want to end this chapter with two contemporary works that join Aschenbach and Socrates in thinking through the challenge of integrating discipline and passion. "Out of the Snow" is the fourth and last of Andre Dubus's stories in *Dancing after Hours* about Ted Briggs and LuAnn Arceneaux. *Babette's Feast* is a movie directed by Gabriel Axel. Both the story and the movie feature strong women who strive to be fully present at every moment of their lives. These women reject views of life that would make bodily pleasures and sufferings insignificant, as if a promised heaven could remove the value of this present earthy life. No; they want a life that sees the beauty shining in every physical blessing and curse, heaven as revealed in earth rather than heaven as a different place. You might say the story and the movie try to take the full measure of Socrates's claim that beauty has the special privilege of manifesting itself in this our sensuous world. Story and movie both explore this fundamental philosophical commitment of Plato's in a vocabulary that draws on Christian religious ideas, and more specially on Roman Catholic ideas about sacraments, the outward signs of divine grace. As with the Adam and Eve myth, this religious language is available even to non-believers, though of course it has a special authority and power for those who acknowledge such ideas at the core of their own faith. I think of *Dancing after Hours* and *Babette's Feast* as Platonic for everybody, and Catholic for a smaller but significant community.

Let me step back a little bit from the story and the movie, to say something more general about the theme of integrating discipline and passion. One of the anxieties at the heart of Plato's *Symposium* and *Phaedrus* is how falling in love and being in love is related to our nature as embodied beings. Whatever it might be like for angels to fall in love and be in love, for human beings the fact of our bodies, of bodily attraction, of sexuality, has to be integrated into our sense of what love is, of what love can be. The speakers in the *Symposium* often betray an anxiety about the fact of erotic attraction and the way it's driven by the body. In the *Phaedrus*, Phaedrus carries in his pocket a speech that makes a case for the non-lover, for somebody who's not erotically inclined. Socrates in his reformulation of that speech reveals to us that that speech itself is a lie, a cover story, because the non-lover is in fact a lover, somebody in the throes of erotic attraction. That is, Socrates shows the speech of the so-called non-lover is a speech that fails to recognize the depth and the honesty of sexual attraction. Socrates repudiates this way of responding to erotic attraction, and in the charioteer speech he makes an attempt to give a more adequate account of falling in love, one that does justice to the ecstasies and exhilarations of romantic love.

In the *Symposium*, the first two speakers, Phaedrus and Pausanias, both give accounts of erotic love – Phaedrus on behalf of the beloved and Pausanias on behalf of the lover – that seem to squeeze out of love all the sexual nature of erotic attraction. They don't trust themselves to love honestly in the face of the kind of special spark that our physicality, that our incarnation gives to our falling in love. Pausanias makes a strong claim that both story and movie will reject; it is Pausanias's cover story about sexual desire, part of his strict division between heavenly interest in souls and mere earthy desire for bodies. For Pausanias claimed no action is either good or bad in itself. Its goodness or its badness depends completely on the intentions with which we engage in that action. For example, says Pausanias, what we're doing right now, giving speeches at a drinking party, can either be good or bad. It all depends on what intentions we have when we give our speeches. Note how odd this claim is about speeches. Don't our words mean something in themselves? Pausanias seems to agree with Lewis Carroll's Humpty-Dumpty, who pompously insisted, "I am the master of my words." But the experience of careful speech is not that of mastering words or forcing them to conform to our intentions. It is the experience of finding the right word, of discovering a significance already there. Our words are not at our command; we ride upon them like horses of thought, we do not drive them like little mechanical cars. We must mean what we say, even when this meaning exceeds our intentions.

Pausanias applies his Humpty-Dumpty mastery to all our bodily actions. To him, actions are empty vehicles, and get their meaning only because we put meaning in from, so to speak, the intentional and psychic side of our lives. The soul part of us produces the meaning, not the bodily side. The soul does not partner with the body nor follow it, but controls and dominates it. Finally, he uses this mastery view to interpret sexual relationships. He suggests that the bodily expression of love in sexuality gets its meaning, good or bad, only from the intentions that motivate lovemaking. The bodily embrace itself isn't the real thing. The real thing is the psychic connection between two people. On Pausanias's view, the only real intercourse is between souls. Bodies just happen to be along for the ride. Perhaps the bodies are not even vehicles, but obstacles, as if we would be better lovers if we could stop being human and become angelic.

So in Pausanias's picture of an authentically erotic relationship, the erotic component itself disappears. It turns out, on this view, that an authentically erotic relationship is a relationship of pedagogy, of teaching, the lover teaching the beloved, initiating the beloved into a life of virtue. But Pausanias's claim for the emptiness of sexuality, his notion that sex is an empty vehicle that must be filled with meaning, comes under increasing pressure as the dialogue goes along. One of the ways in the modern world that this question has become pressing is in practices of contraception. The Catholic teaching about sexuality and contraception has consistently said that sexual intercourse itself already is full of meaning. It is not an empty vehicle that can be filled with better or worse meanings depending on your intentions. Lovemaking bears a certain kind of meaning already, a kind of language of the body, as if sexual intercourse already bears with it an interpretation. The meaning of lovemaking is no more ours to master than the meaning of the words "I love you" or of the marriage vow "I do." We may utter these words more or less thoughtfully, more or less honestly, depending on our intentions; but the words themselves mean something whether we want them to or not. It is our task to acknowledge this meaning, to soften our hard hearts and abandon ourselves to what the words mean. And so for the meaningful act of lovemaking.

This question of whether the body itself is a source of meaning, or whether in itself the body is an empty vehicle, goes to the heart of certain questions about sexuality. The way that Andre Dubus, in the story "Out of the Snow," thinks his way down into this set of questions about the body and meaningfulness is through the notion of a sacrament. In a particularly striking section of the story, Dubus has LuAnn reflect on her experience, now not primarily as a lover, but as a mother of three children. She's at a grocery store, buying food to make dinner for her children and her husband. When she was single, food shopping was a necessity, but not meaningful. "Now that she was gathering food for Julia and Elizabeth and Sam too, she saw it in the store as something that would become her children's flesh. As a girl she had learned about the seven sacraments of the Catholic Church, all of them but one administered by a priest. The woman and man gave each other the sacrament of matrimony." LuAnn is reflecting on the Catholic Church's notion that there's a public part of the sacrament of marriage, the giving of the vows at the wedding, but that the sacrament is not completed until the man and woman make love as spouses. The action of making love, the sexual intercourse itself, is the private bodily expression that completes the public verbal expression of the marriage vows. This idea that the sacrament of marriage requires both the words of the vows and the action of lovemaking is a reflection of the Catholic view of the intrinsic meaningfulness of sexual intercourse. Sex is not just a vehicle that can be filled with different meanings. It carries its significance with it, so that to express one's love sexually can be more or less honest, but the meaning is already there. "Being a mother," Dubus writes, "had taught her that sacraments were her work, and their number was infinite." Not just the seven sacraments recognized by the Catholic Church, but every act is a sacrament that elevates and manifests the grace present in the earthy stuff of a mother's life. Her experience as a mother teaches LuAnn that the physicality of life is itself what's meaningful. It's meaningful to give your children food, directly meaningful, not because of some more spiritual, more psychological, more soulful interpretation of that action. Your children are not souls who just happen to be driving around in bodies. Their animate, ensouled bodies are as real as anything could be. And so the action of giving them food, of bringing them flesh, is itself what gives meaning to her life.

LuAnn comes to understand every bodily thing she does as sacramental, sacramental in the sense that it's filled with a significance that has a sacred dimension to it. Does this mean that every time she cooks food, she performs an outward act of piety, keeping her hands folded, say, or making the sign of the cross? Of course not, no more than she mumbles a prayer or lights a votive candle in bed when she's making love with her husband. To live out this bodily existence as sacramental doesn't mean living it out as always pious, as making a kind of show of piety. As the poet and critic Dana Gioia has pointed out, "Catholic literature is rarely pious. In ways that sometimes trouble or puzzle both Protestant and secular readers, Catholic writing tends to be comic, rowdy, rude, and even violent." Gioia was probably thinking especially of Flannery O'-Connor, but the description fits Andre Dubus, too. Dubus is not trying to describe an internal piety, a piety of thinking; he is praising a more earthy Aphrodite. LuAnn's foundation in Catholicism doesn't mean that at the level of passing consciousness, she is always thinking "Well, I'm doing this for God!" Cooking dinner in a busy household, let alone making love in a hot bedroom, is not the most typical place to have all your passing thoughts be "Oh, I'm doing this for God!" But the structure of one's mundane everyday life might yet be a giving of something to God, or a recognition of something sacred in one's everyday life. So at least LuAnn lives it, so that LuAnn's practical love, her love as it's embodied in her actions, is a reflection of a certain kind of commitment to significance and to meaningfulness, one this story understands as sacramental. Does that mean that she always has the sorts of thoughts that one has in a church? Of course not. LuAnn values thoughtfulness, but she doesn't divide thought from action. Significant sacramental action is the bearer of meaning for her. Her life is not, as Pausanias would have it, a parade of empty actions waiting to be filled with meaning only by the intentions we bring to it. LuAnn's intentions find the meaning in her actions: they do not create the meaning.

LuAnn's sacramental sense of herself is worked out in this story through a threat to her body. Two terrible men follow LuAnn home from the grocery store. When they confront her in her kitchen as she puts away the food, she is very brave and very lucky. She knows they plan to rape her, and probably to kill her, too. She kicks one in the groin, and grabs a skillet from the counter and cracks the head of the other. She beats him until he is bleeding and broken, and his fellow criminal drags him out to the stolen car they came in, and they flee. The story ends with LuAnn reflecting with Ted on her own experience of fending these men off, particularly of beating one of them with a hunk of iron. LuAnn reflects on how her bodily actions in striking these men aren't well described by our normal categories of good and bad. She's certainly relieved she wasn't raped, and that she beat them off and escaped from them. But she doesn't think it's true simply to say she did something "good" in hitting them; nor does she feel she did something "bad" when she broke their noses and beat them until she might have killed them. There was some sort of basic, primal experience of her own body and its power in all this that "good" and "bad" are too mundane to describe. The word LuAnn finds for this experience beyond good and evil, as Nietzsche might have called it, is the Dionysian word "rapture." She felt a kind of rapture, a word that would be congenial to the ecstasy described in the charioteer speech in the *Phaedrus*. The rapture with which she defends her own bodily integrity surprises her, astonishes her, and leads her to try and reflect on it at the end of the story. Her rapture in her violence against these criminals reveals to her something about all of her life. Extremity is often the revelation of ordinariness. And so for her, in this story, her everyday living of sacraments is interpreted for her by her experience of self-defense as rapturous.

Ted misinterprets LuAnn's thoughtful pondering of this mystery of violent rapture. He thinks she is blaming herself for being bad, when she is really astonished with herself for being ecstatically powerful. So Ted tries to get LuAnn to let herself off the hook, to excuse herself by saying what she did was forced on her by necessity, so that she didn't really do it, or at least did nothing bad. But LuAnn would rather be abandoned to her ecstatic self than accept the excuses Ted offers for its astonishing powers. LuAnn tells Ted she tries to live her life by being present in every moment, making every moment, even the most mundane moments, something meaningful, something that reflects her larger life commitments. This notion of being present all the time in everything she does is something that comes home to her in the extremity of needing to do violence to other human beings to defend herself. She does not enjoy doing that violence, but neither does she regret it. She would not feel honest if she accepted Ted's comforting escape. So that by the time we get to the end of the story, we're led to some disquieting reflections on the way that our bodies are not empty vehicles of meaning, but are rather the source of it. LuAnn does not let herself off the hook for her body, and neither should we.

What does LuAnn's rapturous violence tell us about sexuality? A thought that comes to me at the end of this story involves the difference between our experience of evil through our bodies and the experience of good. A beating is a big, important thing, and a rape is a yet much more important thing, and the taking of a life in a murder is a bigger thing still. Why shouldn't a caress also be a big thing? And making love an even bigger, much more important thing? And the conception of a new life an even bigger thing still? Shouldn't the seriousness of our dread and revulsion of a beating, a rape, a murder, find its full complement in the seriousness of our joy and gratitude for a caress, for lovemaking, for conception of new life? We deprive our lives most perversely, when we let our bodies count so much for ill and so little for good. The laws of symmetry require the exaltation of the loving body to match the degradation of the broken one.

The movie *Babette's Feast* also focuses on this sacramental and incarnational aspect of human life. Romantic love plays a role in the movie, but only within a much larger picture of the way the body is the source of meaning, not merely an empty vehicle. The movie gives this theme a very strong religious frame. The action takes place in the 19th century, among a pious and very ascetic Christian community in an isolated little settlement in Denmark, with a special focus on two sisters, named Martine and Philippa, after two great figures of the 16th century Protestant Reformation, Martin Luther and Philipp Melanchthon. The little community was founded by the father of the sisters, a charismatic and austere minister, now long dead. The sisters spend their lives in simple service to the little flock, taking care of the sick and infirm and smoothing out the petty arguments accumulated over the decades of isolation. Their ascetic, closed life is unsettled by the sudden appearance of a woman named Babette, fleeing from political turmoil in France. Of course, Babette is a Catholic.

Grateful to the sisters for taking her in as an exile, over fourteen years Babette gradually and tactfully improves the material comforts of the little community, especially with her surprising expertise in making delicious food even from simple ingredients. The climax of the movie comes when the sisters decide to have a special celebration of their father's one hundredth birthday. Just as the planning begins, Babette receives an astonishing letter from an old friend in France: Babette has won a fortune in the lottery! Babette insists on being in charge of the celebration, and she sails back to

France to order the exotic and expensive foods she will prepare, along with the exquisite wines. She spends her entire fortune on the feast, and the sisters watch in growing anxiety as extraordinary delights arrive at their isolated port, all destined for the big evening. They fear lest they have led their flock into the bewitching sensual indulgences of a corrupt Catholic, but they let the feast proceed. With the rest of the community, the sisters make an agreement: they will all refrain from making any comment at all about the food and drink. Thus will they preserve their purity against Babette's well-intentioned but corrupting bacchanal. Their own sense of spiritual discipline requires them to forgo the sensual delights that, for Babette, are the vehicle of her artistry. And so this little group might as well have Pausanias as their patron saint, anxiously patrolling a closely guarded border between heaven and earth, soul and body.

The night arrives, and many hearts are revealed, and past regrets overcome, in the beauty of Babette's feast. We learn at the end that before her exile from France, Babette was the most famous chef in Paris, and she has at last been able to share the full range of her artistry with this simple community she loves, and which loves her. They enjoy every aspect of the feast, food and drink both, even though they have agreed not to mention their enjoyment. And their enjoyment of the meal lets them enjoy one another, too, so that all the petty disagreements and irritations built up over years of living so closely together are washed away in good feelings and generous spirits.

The movie is in part a religious meditation on the contrasting strengths of an austere, ascetical Protestantism and a much more sacramental, much more incarnational, much more sensuous experience of religion that's represented by Catholicism. But it is important to see that this religious frame – ascetic Protestants versus sensuous Catholics – is only a particular historical version of the tension between discipline and passion already explored in Plato's *Symposium* and *Phaedrus*, and at the heart of Thomas Mann's *Death in Venice*. Mann, who was ten years older than Isak Dinesen, who wrote the short story on which the movie is based, chose to give his reflection on the tension an ancient Greek mood, influenced in part by Friedrich Nietzsche. Dinesen – who came close to being awarded the Nobel Prize in Literature herself – instead chose a Christian mood, probably influenced by the Danish philosopher and theologian Søren Kierkegaard. But both stories are thinking about the discipline and passion needed to be an artist, and about how difficult it is to integrate these two forces into romantic love.

The movie shows us the issue of discipline and passion in romantic love when it flashes back to the past of the two sisters. Each, it turns out, had a serious suitor, and a chance to leave this ascetic little community through marriage into a large social world. One of the sisters, Philippa, had a fine singing voice. In this little community, she could express her artistry through little more than singing in church services. But her prospects change when a French opera star comes to visit this little bit of isolated coastland, looking to get away from it all on a vacation. Hearing her in church, he discovers Philippa has a beautiful voice, and he offers to give her musical training. The dour but very good man who is her father, the minister, allows this; in fact he has always seen to it that his daughters have been well educated. But it turns out that this musical training is inseparable from artistic sensuality, which becomes more difficult to keep separate from real life as Philippa's lessons progress and the opera star falls in love with her. A crisis comes when we hear the two of them singing a famous duet, "Là ci darem la mano" (Italian for "There we will give each other our hands"), from Mozart's opera *Don Giovanni*, the story of a famous seducer of women. The opera star sings the part of the seducer, and Philippa the part of an engaged woman, Zerlina, giving in to the seduction. It's a song about the experience of falling in love, and particularly it's a song about the possibility of leaving behind a marriage to the respectable person to whom you're committed and going off with a person who transports you with beauty and with sensuality. (Dana, the opera-loving wife in *The Secret Lives of Dentists*, probably loved it.) Philippa has the same experience as Aschenbach, and feels her disciplined artistic self being threatened by her erotic self. She makes a different decision from Aschenbach, though, and ends the lessons, along with the opera star's hopes for her love. But the opera star does not forget this good woman and her virtues. It turns out that when Babette arrived in Norway exhausted and penniless, she was bearing a letter of introduction from this very singer, and it is he who told Babette she could depend on the sisters to take her in.

The second sister, Martine, also had a youthful admirer who promised a more exciting future than the simple service that became her life. He was a young military man, talented but somewhat wild. He was being punished for some indiscretion by being exiled for a time to the estate of his aunt, who happened to be a member of the minister's little group. He falls in love with Martine, but leaves her when he decides he can't live up to the stern virtues of this community. Besides, he has ambitions to move up in the world. By the time of the minister's one hundredth birthday celebration, he has attained the rank of general. In a marvelous coincidence, on the night of the celebration, the General happens to be visiting the very aunt, now quite old, with whom he spent his youthful punishment all those years before. So he arrives as an honored guest back in the simple home of the one woman he really loved. But it is a blessing, especially to Babette, that the General is not a simple man himself. The presence of one cultivated man who can really appreciate her artistic accomplishment pleases her deeply. But yet it is not the condition of her artistry. What Babette does she does for that community, and most particularly for the sisters. It's also very important that the sisters are clearly much better educated and much more cultivated people than those they serve. The sister who could have been an opera singer, the sister who could have been the wife of a general, these are women who have had to give up something artistic in their own temperament, their own gifts, in order to live a certain kind of life of service. They can, to some extent, appreciate Babette, but they could not themselves go away and live in Paris without giving up what they've accomplished where they are.

At the dinner, the General tells a story about how when he was still a young man, he was taken by his commanding officer to a famous restaurant in France, the Café Anglais, which it turns out was Babette's restaurant. This officer gave a toast and talked about how the chef had the ability to transform the dinner into a kind of love affair, a love affair that made no distinction between bodily appetite and spiritual appetite. According to the General, the artistry of Babette's food can be like the experience of romantic love, when sensual enjoyment is not separable from spiritual union. Earthy Aphrodite and Heavenly Aphrodite give each other their hands. The spirit of Pausanias in the other diners inspires one of the women at the table to respond to the General's anti-Pausanian view. "Man shall not merely refrain from but also reject any thought of food and drink," she says, "only then can he eat and drink in the proper spirit." But the woman herself, along with everyone else at the feast, can surely not live up to the ascetic ideal of these words! As if the cost of the spirit is the body; as if the only reason we would caress our spouses would be to count their bones.

And so the movie reveals the sensuality of the food and drink is in fact what promotes reconciliation and joy in this little community that has become argumentative and tired of itself. The diners keep protesting the sensuousness, so that every time the General praises the food or the drink, somebody comments on the weather or otherwise pretends not to have noticed. But what their speech rejects, their actions accept. It's not a surprise that many of our best conversations come over our best meals. The bodily appetite and the spiritual appetite are not two things, but two aspects of one thing. Right after the General talks about the integration of bodily and spiritual appetite, the austere and ascetical words of the minister are recalled: "The only things we can take with us from this earthly life are those we have given away." And it seems that when he and his daughters and his flock gave away sensuality, they also gave away their very bodies. One's tempted to think that they've forgotten an ancient hope all Christians share, that we will experience the resurrection of the body. The Christian vision of Paradise is of a bodily paradise, an incarnate paradise. Not a paradise of souls, but a paradise of those ensouled. Babette has brought the sisters, at least, to the point of acknowledging this special privilege of beauty to lead us to the sacred through the sensuous. The experience of beauty can be a distraction from the divine, but it can also be the provocation we need to open ourselves to the divine. When the feast is over, Philippa, the singing sister, says to Babette the same thing that the opera star had said to her. "This is not the end, Babette. I'm certain it is not. In Paradise you will be the great artist that God meant you to be. And how you will delight the angels."

Babette's Feast is an attempt to be thoughtful about what it's like to live in a body, to have your love be something that is as much a bodily appetite as it is a spiritual appetite. The quality of the thought is so high because the movie loves everybody in it, the austere and the ascetical as much as the sensuous. And the movie cheers us because it holds out the invitation that in the end the dichotomy between the ascetical and the sensuous can be overcome in the sacramental. Director Gabriel Axel made an unusually Catholic movie because he made an unusually sacramental movie. But *Babette's Feast* can be so Catholic only because it is so thoroughly Platonic.

Chapter Eight
LOVE'S DREAM

There is a fine line between elevating romance and erotic desire, opening them to the sacred (as Socrates and Gabriel Axel do, for example), and falsifying them either by reducing them to the merely sexual (as Pausanias and Iago do) or substituting for them something easier and less unsettling (Pausanias again, as well as Lysias). Thomas Mann tried to hold that line, with tragic results; Shakespeare's *A Midsummer Night's Dream* walks the line like a comic tightrope act. This beloved play, the surest Shakespearean money-maker in the repertory, is as cheerful as Socrates about love.

But Shakespeare wrote no simple plays. Every comedy contains elements of tragedy, and every tragedy of comedy. So I will approach *A Midsummer Night's Dream* from both directions. Some themes in the play are most optimistic about love, seeing falling in love as a special opportunity for human beings to transcend the limits of everyday experience. Because these optimistic themes set the tone of the play – in musical terms, you could say they give the melody – we experience *A Midsummer Night's Dream* primarily as a comedy, full of hope and celebration. But I'll also bring out some of the themes that sound a more pessimistic undertone in the play, and that recognize more impediments or challenges to love than the dominant festive mood of the play would like to acknowledge. Ralph Waldo Emerson once wrote that "our moods do not believe in each other." When we accept the dominant mood of the play, when we are enchanted by its magic, we feel optimistic about love, and we see the impediments or obstacles to love as things we can always overcome. But if we resist the enchantment, if we are in a mood to be disillusioned with love, we might ask if the play's optimism is too easy. Shakespeare seems to give us the resources to criticize the mood of festive celebration, to unmask this optimistic mood, even while he tells the love story to enchant us. Shakespeare is at one and the same time both the author and the critic of *A Midsummer Night's Dream*. Like Plato in the *Symposium* and *Phaedrus*, Shakespeare provides a rather unsettling commentary on the bold claims about love he gives to his characters, if we are willing to listen behind the melody.

The Green World and the bedroom

I'd like to start from a general thought about the structure of the action in *A Midsummer Night's Dream*. This play has a rather typical comic structure. Two young lovers, Lysander and Hermia, escape from the city and flee to the country. This romantic escape is a bedrock part of the West's myth of love. It would be easy to find dozens or hundreds of examples in contemporary stories and movies of couples who flee the oppression or business of the city for a romantic getaway in the country, or perhaps at the beach or in the mountains. The myth of romantic love as escape is so strong that newly married couples, even when they have no money and little time, are expected by everyone, including themselves, to go on a "honeymoon" trip. Some couples may go to cities for this romantic getaway, but most choose to flee to somewhere "in nature," where they can, as the phrase has it, "get away from it all."

We could find this bedrock myth in many, many stories about love. Its oldest and most influential version is the story of Adam and Eve in the Garden of Eden, from the opening chapters of the Bible. In discussions of Shakespeare, this place of escape from the city to the country, from civilization to nature, is often called Shakespeare's "green world." In this play, the lovers need to leave the confines of civilization – civilization here defined as the ancient Greek city of Athens – but more particularly civilization defined by political control, the control exercised by Theseus, the king of Athens, and family control, parental control, here particularly the control exercised by Egeus, Hermia's father. Egeus has very strong ideas about whom his daughter should marry. He wants Hermia to marry Demetrius, whereas Hermia prefers Lysander. Hermia's best friend, Helena, would love to marry Demetrius, but he only has eyes for Hermia. King Theseus is on the side, generally speaking, of control and of good order, but he is in a sympathetic mood toward young love, because he is about to be married himself, to Hippolyta. It's not surprising that as king, he takes the side of the father's authority, though as lover himself and bridegroom, he tries to moderate the father's power and anger. In order to pursue their true love, Lysander and Hermia concoct a typical young lovers' scheme of running away, of eloping and going to the forest, where they won't be controlled by what appears to them to be the false strictures of convention, or of civilization. Demetrius desperately plans to follow after Hermia – after all, who knows what chances love might have in the wild forest? And of course Helena then pursues Demetrius, so all four young people, in love or pursuing love, end up in the green world. So this flight to the green world is a way of representing love as something in itself requiring a kind of freedom, perhaps even a kind of wildness.

In Plato's *Phaedrus*, Socrates and Phaedrus leave the city for the country, too, where they can give their inspired and enchanting speeches in praise of love. Socrates and Phaedrus leave the city of Athens to go out into the countryside, where they recline under a Plato tree in a natural bower, among the echoes of the gentle breeze and the cicadas' song, the cool flowing stream across their feet. This pastoral idyll is haunted by violence – the abductions of Boreas, and the ambiguous sexual forcefulness of seduction – but these two men treat such possibilities playfully. In a darker mood, Thomas Mann's *Death in Venice* tells of how the story's hero, the disciplined, indeed self-constricted writer Gustav Aschenbach, longs to flee "to the tigers," that is, to somewhere exotic, to somewhere that's a jungle, in order to open himself to the experience of love. Plato, Shakespeare, and Mann are all exploring the notion that there's an aspect of our romantic lives that can open up only when we achieve a kind of freedom from civilization, from convention. This freedom in *A Midsummer Night's Dream* is pursued by young people who want to shake off two kinds of authority: the oppressive identities that being members of families can put upon us, and the demands of citizenship. The young people are from the nobility or aristocracy, and this social status means they have some power to make their escape that ordinary people might not have. But it also means they are bound more tightly by their social identities, so that escape is more difficult. In other words, Shakespeare makes aristocrats the focus of his love story because they combine freedom and necessity in an especially striking way.

Shakespeare's play, then, is operating within a completely traditional "green world" understanding of the nature of love. But of course Shakespeare never leaves any tradition undisturbed, and he unsettles his green world. He populates it with two groups in addition to the young, aristocratic lovers the tradition expects there. On the one hand there are the "rude mechanicals," the lower-class characters, the common people that Shakespeare, using the English of his own day, refers to as "clowns." The leader of this comic crew is Nick Bottom, a weaver and enthusiastic actor. When Shakespeare refers to "clowns," he doesn't mean people dressed up with fuzzy orange hair and makeup. "Clowns" simply refers to the lower classes, to humble people who work at mechanical crafts for a living, which is why he also refers to them as "rude mechanicals." On the other hand, there are the magical, powerful, and dangerous fairies, with Queen Titania and King Oberon their leaders. Titania and Oberon are in the middle of a lovers' quarrel, but because they are queen and king, their private quarrel spills out to have public consequences. The young lovers are caught up in the comedy of the simple people's bumbling attempt to produce a play, and the danger of the powerful fairies' war with each other. Imagine a movie where a young couple's peaceful honeymoon at a forest inn is disrupted by some charmingly unsophisticated and comical local residents, and some powerful and mysterious visitors who are rather sinister and violent.

Now, as for the aristocrats, so for this group of rude mechanicals, the green world is a realm of freedom. But they are not primarily seeking a place where they can go to fall in love, or to flee from constraints on their love in the way that Lysander and Hermia want to flee. Instead, they go off to the forest because they want to practice a play. They plan to perform this play as part of the festive celebration of the wedding of Theseus and his wife-to-be Hippolyta. For this troupe of unsophisticated actors, the green world is a world of freedom, but that freedom is understood as a theatrical world, a world where they can go to put on new identities in a play. For them too, then, the green world is an escape, an escape from their everyday identities as craftsmen, as lower-class people. But the escape is into the new identities theater can offer. This play may be the finest exemplar of the theme of theater as freedom. Shakespeare makes the theme central, but we've seen it already, from Andre Dubus's actress Susan Dorsey and Alan Rudolph's operatic Dana, to the ventriloquism of Phaedrus and the role-playing at the *Symposium*'s theater party.

The parallel between these two escapes, of the common people into theater and the noble men and women into love, raises this question: Is the romantic escape that Lysander and Hermia try to achieve in the green world also a kind of theater? Are they doing something theatrical? Is there, not to put too fine a point on it, a bit of play-acting about their love? After all, Lysander famously says to Hermia early in the play, that "the course of true love never did run smooth." That is, Lysander tells Hermia, "We are a love story." And every love story has its challenges to overcome, the impediments to love that make the final consummation of the love all the more sweet. Of course, Lysander and Hermia don't say to themselves, "Hey, let's go out to the forest and we can play at being in love." Young lovers don't think of themselves as just playing a part in a script, and they would resent anyone who thought their romance was theatrical. But the parallel plot of the clowns, of the rude mechanicals, makes us ask a question about whether the freedom to pursue a certain romantic plot in one's life is itself something like theater. Might there be a kind of acting, or playing, that's necessary for the course of true love?

It's not necessary that this "playing" be thought of as faking. After all, playing isn't the same thing as faking, as being a fraud. It might be that true love requires us to tap into the energies of play without thinking of that play as something that's false. Can theater, can acting, can playing be the vehicle of romantic truth rather than an avoidance of the truth? After all, it may be that to become true lovers we have to escape from our staid, everyday identities in whatever city happens to control us. It may be we have to escape some identities that are safe for us, comfortable, to enter into the childlike playfulness of the green world, of the world of love. So we see an interesting parallel plot structure, the green world both as the world of theater and as the world of romantic love, a dual kind of freedom.

Here again we see a way in which Shakespeare is working with some themes that we've seen elsewhere. When the banquet opened in the *Symposium*, the manly party-goers sent away the wine and the flute-girl. Recall that the god Dionysus is the patron deity both of theater and of intoxication, as Aphrodite is the patroness of all that is feminine and romantic. The characters in the *Symposium* need to come to terms with a kind of transport, or a kind of giving up of identity, in order to take on a new identity in the theater of love. Their manly identity resists their romantic identity; they are more comfortable being tough guys than lovers and beloveds. And in the *Phaedrus*, Socrates praises the madness of romantic love, not the sobriety and safety of ordinary reasonableness. If we cling like Lysias to our right mind, our everyday identity, we will never experience the wild ascent of Love's chariot.

Shakespeare adds one more group to the green world, the fairies, Oberon and Titania and their attendants and servants. So we've got the aristocrats who escape the city for the freedoms of love; we have the lower class, the working class, who escape from the city for the freedoms of theater; but we've got the magical beings, the fairies, who live in the green world, who are, so to speak, the natural inhabitants of the green world. They live always and everywhere in that unconventional freedom, and their love takes on a kind of theatricality. We could say they are the perfect or extreme version of the green world's freedom and wildness, and we will want to look at ways in which Oberon and Titania, in their lovers' quarrel, mirror back to us in extreme form some aspects of the human lovers.

Lysander and Hermia run away to the forest, followed by Demetrius, followed by Helena. When all four are resting from their flight and fall asleep, Shakespeare uses what might appear to be a very silly and rather naïve device to move the plot along and create some romantic complexity: a magic love potion that confuses the young lovers' true affections. We don't need to rehearse all the twists and turns of these romantic confusions, but it is important to notice that the power of love's enchantment can be used either for good or for evil. King Oberon sends his mischievous fairy servant Robin Goodfellow, also called Puck, to use the love potion for two purposes, one mean and one intended to be generous. First, Oberon wants revenge on Titania in their quarrel, so he commands Puck to bewitch the queen and make her fall in love with some vile creature. It turns out she attaches herself to Nick Bottom, the lead actor of the rude mechanicals. To make this attachment even more absurd, Puck transforms Bottom's appearance, so that he has the head of a donkey. Second, the king pities Helena when he sees that she loves Demetrius but is rejected by him, since he is pursuing Hermia. So he commands Puck to put the love potion in Demetrius's eyes, so he will fall in love with Helena just as Titania will fall in love with Bottom. Of course, things go wrong, and Puck ends up making both young men fall deeply in love with Helena, and both lose all interest in Hermia, though desire for her is what brought them to the green world in the first place.

Puck's love potion manages to distort, but also to energize, the love affairs of the two young couples who flee to the green world. That love juice, that magic, seems to make romantic attraction, romantic love, something extraordinarily volatile, something that can change in the blink of an eye. It does not take fairies and a potion to work this magic. Suddenly our eyes may see a person as romantically interesting who, for months or years before, had only been a friend. That sudden transformation of an ordinary person into a vision of wonder, Plato suggested in the *Phaedrus*, is the distinctive power of beauty. Such transformation is also central to Shakespeare's vision of romantic love.

We see this sudden transformation in all the romantic couples in the play – the young men and women, but also the more mature characters, the kings and queens, Theseus and Hippolyta and Oberon and Titania, who cross from quarreling and fighting to loving and doting. Most comically, we see such sudden transformations or revelations of wonder and beauty enacted in the translation, the transfiguration of Nick Bottom from man to beast and back again. But throughout the play, these moments of sudden vision raise the unsettling question of whether to see someone with the eyes of romance requires something unnatural, and perhaps something theatrical. Could it be that the freedom to see someone as a beloved, as a lover, requires of us, or is at least encouraged by, a willingness to play the part of finding someone romantically attractive? Is this loving vision something that we have to be ready to rehearse, like a play in which we learn a part? Can our love and its freedom and the freedoms of theater, be put together into the magic of falling in love?

Shakespeare's green world in *A Midsummer Night's Dream* tries to bring together three strands of romantic freedom: an escape from external authority so that our romantic loves are seen as the truest expression of ourselves, undistorted by our social roles, whether in the family or in, let's say, adult civil society; but also a green world of freedom to play a part, to put on new identities and to let those identities speak through us; and finally, a freedom that in this play is figured as a magical freedom, the freedom of the realm of fairy, a freedom to transform or transfigure our everyday lives into something wondrous and strange, what in ordinary, not-in-love life we would not see, something visionary.

Let me move from these more general reflections on the green world to two particular scenes that raise a specific question about the place of the sexual aspect of romantic love. Both scenes focus on the same idea, that the intimacy of love unites two persons into one, versions of Adam and Eve and of Aristophanes's welded lovers. When Lysander and Hermia have fled to the forest, Hermia is worn out with the adventure, and night has come on. They decide to go to sleep – at least, that's how Hermia would describe it, since she is simply tired. Lysander, in whom the night provokes more ambiguous interests, perhaps would say they're going to go to bed. Here is some of what Lysander says to Hermia as they stop for the night, with some commentary from me in parentheses. "Fair love, you faint with wandering in the wood," (How sweet! He's looking out for her) "and to speak troth I have forgot our way." (How convenient! He's using a line – "I think we're lost" – boys in America used to use with their girlfriends, to suggest the couple go in for some romance in their parked car.) "We'll rest us, Hermia, if you think it good, and tarry for the comfort of the day." A tired Hermia responds, "Be it so, Lysander. Find you out a bed, for I upon this bank will rest my head." Lysander, like many young men, doesn't really listen to what his girlfriend has just said. He seems not to have heard the word "rest," and to have heard the word "bed" very loudly. So he decides to try some poetry, to test Hermia's interest in something more than sleep: "One turf shall serve as pillow for us both, one heart, one bed, two bosoms, and one troth." (Notice the emphasis on making one out of two: very romantic, but quite sexual, too. The images of making "one from two" sound like they might have been borrowed from Aristophanes's speech in Plato's *Symposium*, about the two halves of the original human beings trying to get back together.) Hermia appreciates the poetry, no doubt, but while she's quite young, she is not quite stupid. Her response politely turns down Lysander's ambiguous suggestion: "Nay, good Lysander, for my sake my dear, lie further off yet. Do not lie so near." To understand these words, we must picture what's happening on stage: Lysander is snuggling up to Hermia on the bank of the little brook, playing the romantic lover with his poetry. And they've probably kicked off their shoes. Hermia's politely declining the offer embedded in this ambiguous language. Lysander plays at being shocked that she could think he had any lustful thoughts in mind. He says, "Oh, take the sense, sweet, of my innocence. Love takes the meaning in love's conference. I mean that my heart unto yours is knit, so that but one heart we can make of it, two bosoms interchained with an oath, so then two bosoms and a single troth. Then by your side no bed room me deny, for lying so, Hermia, I do not lie." ("Bed room": Oh

Lysander, that is the worst pun on "bedroom" ever made in the English language!) Hermia firmly but gently puts an end to this flirtation when she responds. "Lysander riddles very prettily," she says, but she needs no comic god to get to the bottom of Lysander's desire. "Much beshrew my manners and my pride if Hermia meant to say Lysander lied," she says, granting him the courtesy of deniability. But Hermia keeps him at more than arm's distance, "such separation as may well be said becomes a virtuous bachelor and a maid." She really does, after all, intend to sleep.

Throughout this very funny and yet important scene, Shakespeare gives to Lysander a vocabulary richly expressive of unity and intimacy. Hermia appreciates the compliment in these words, and a skillful actress will bring out Hermia's quiet smile at Lysander's attempt to elevate his sexual desire for her to something higher, something worthy of his poetry. But Hermia can hear as well as we can that Lysander has not been wholly successful in controlling his desire; his poetry clearly has a very strong undertone, so strong it threatens to drown out the melody of his love in the bass growl of mere sexual desire. Lysander uses the language of a special, even unique intimacy, of the closest possible intercourse between two lovers. But of course such intercourse is ambiguous, and can be either spiritual and friendly, or physical and sexual. Hermia receives Lysander and his offer of intimacy as far as she can; but she cannot receive everything he wants to offer. Here in the green world, for all its freedom and wildness, the full physical expression of the promised intimacy would still be impatient and dishonest, she realizes. It is too soon to take their romance to the bedroom. For what have Lysander's words really offered? Nothing less than marriage. And within *A Midsummer Night's Dream*, the celebration of "two in one" finally comes on stage only with the marriages that end the play, between Hermia and Lysander, Helena and Demetrius, and Theseus and Hippolyta: the full expression of two becoming one, soul and body both. And the fullness of marriage is not a thing of the forest, but of the city: the wildness must be tamed again if love is to complete itself.

This flirtation between Lysander and Hermia reveals that marriage can capture the romance of the green world, even though at the beginning of the play, marriage looked like something imposed on young lovers by fathers and kings. But the scene also reveals the tension between Lysander's poetic language and his rather base sexual desire, the clash between his melody and its undertones. It is difficult to elevate sexual desire into the full "two in one" commitment of marriage. With his typical brilliant use of the device of the parallel plot, Shakespeare reveals this difficulty by constructing a scene all but quoting the Lysander/Hermia scene, but now focused on the two women. As childhood friends, before their lives were complicated by men and by sexual interest, Helena and Hermia achieved this sort of "two in one" intimacy. The very language that, when Lysander uses it with Hermia, has such strong sexual undertones, also appears in the mouth of Helena to describe this innocent, pre-sexual type of childhood friendship.

Our young lovers have escaped to the forest in pursuit of romantic freedom, and they all fall asleep for the night. Puck misapplies the love potion, and when they wake up, both young men end up falling in love with Helena, when before they both loved Hermia. Helena does not believe they really love her, and she thinks they're making fun of her when they tell her how attractive she is. Not knowing that the two men have been enchanted by the love potion, Helena naturally believes that they are only pretending to be in love with her rather than with Hermia. Hermia is as baffled as Helena by the men's sudden change, but Helena thinks her old friend is in on the joke. So Helena bitterly accuses all three, Lysander, Demetrius, and Hermia, of playing with her, and she is most angry with Hermia. Helena reminds Hermia of just how close their friendship has always been: "Is all the counsel that we two have shared, the sisters' vows, all schooldays' friendship, childhood innocence – O, is all forgot?" Helena is measuring the young lovers' present turmoil by the standard of the childhood intimacy she shared with Hermia, an innocent intimacy before the disruptions and dislocations of romantic love. Remember what it was like, Helena is asking Hermia, when we treated each other with the straightforward and simple intimacy of children, of sisters? – I'm reminded here of the fine movie *Stand by Me*, based on a Stephen

King story, directed by Rob Reiner in 1986. The movie is about boys before they reach the age where they're interested in girls. These boys become a band of brothers, their non-sexual intimacy established through a shared adventure they have in the woods, their green world. In both *Stand by Me* and *A Midsummer Night's Dream*, childhood friendship is used as the measure of adult relationships, and the question is raised whether any relationship complicated by romance and sexuality can measure up to the simple trust and mutual comfort of children, whether boys or girls. Terrence Malick's wondrous movie *The Tree of Life* (2011) uses a similar device, a boy's world slowing opening to the unwanted knowledge of his mother's sexuality.

Shakespeare intensifies this use of childhood friendship as a measure for adult romance as the scene continues. Helena uses the same language of "two in one" to describe her non-sexual relationship to Hermia that Lysander used to suggest a sexual one. Helena remembers how she and Hermia used to sit together "on one cushion," embroidering a pattern "on one sampler." They worked with their needles "like two artificial gods" to create "both one flower," as they sang together, "both warbling of one song, both in one key." This shared work and play makes the two of them one, and indeed makes them into a complete, self-sufficient being, like a god. Our childhood friendship, she says to Hermia, made us "as if our hands, our sides, voices and minds had been incorporate," that is, incorporated into one body, one corpus. "So we grew together," Helena concludes, "like to a double cherry, seeming parted but yet a union in partition, two lovely berries molded on one stem; so with two seeming bodies but one heart." So Helena is using the same "two in one" language as Lysander, a corporeal, bodily language, though she is describing the non-sexual intimacy that she sees as a standard of human relationships, a standard that she achieved with Hermia.

It is astonishing how close Shakespeare's images and ideas in Helena's speech come to Aristophanes's story of the original spherical human beings in Plato's *Symposium*. Helena sees something divine in the perfect unity she and Hermia experienced as a "two in one" being

– they are "artificial gods" – just as Aristophanes's original humans are likenesses of the celestial gods, the Sun, Earth, and Moon. Helena all but repeats the wish that Hephaestus, the blacksmith god, grants to lovers: to be melded into one body with one soul, "as if our hands, our sides, voices and minds had been incorporate." In their perfect, undivided state, Aristophanes's original human beings have no sexual desire, and their complete, non-sexual intimacy measures all sexual reunion as a second best, a partial but always imperfect, disrupted return to the original perfection. Helena, at this point in the play, also seems to wish away her adulthood, which includes her capacity for romance and sexuality. She longs once again for the simpler intimacy of childhood friendship. But Shakespeare sends no god to satisfy this longing. Helena must find a way to live with growing up.

Can these couples preserve, indeed even intensify, the intimacies of childhood friendship and yet accept the complexities of romantic love? You might say the promise, the optimism of the play, is that marriage allows the integration of the freedoms and intimacies of the green world into the complexities and the demands of a civil world, of a world of families and of fellow citizens. The movement of the plot takes the young lovers, and us, first away from false constraint in the city, to an escape to a freer world of romantic truth in the forest, but then back again in a return to marriage, and reintegration into the city. However much we may have fantasies of escaping to the wild and making up all the rules for ourselves, our real lives are in the city limits. This movement of escape followed by triumphant return is what makes *A Midsummer Night's Dream* an especially optimistic play, considered as Shakespeare's account of how marriage can be the fulfillment of romance.

Catching desire in a cynical mood

Because the mood and atmosphere of *A Midsummer Night's Dream* is festive and youthful, we are right to focus on the good news it gives of the power of romance. But we should also notice a rather different aspect of this play. If we are young, this play celebrates us; if we are not so young, it reminds of our youth. But the less youthful, whether in years or in temperament, will notice some darker clouds amid the sunniness of this play. I am afraid the only way to explore some of these darker themes is to say some things about love, and about life in general, that will sound rather cynical. So don't embrace the darkness completely! A cynical view never gives the whole truth. But it does help to get a truer view of the weather, if we notice the clouds from time to time.

I want to start from a fairly common human experience, one that at first appears to have little to do with falling in love. Because I've spent my adult life as a faculty member in a university, I've also had to attend a lot of committee meetings. When a department, like the philosophy department to which I belong, at an American university is deciding whether to hire a new faculty member, you might think the only thing we focus on is the mind of that person, on the intelligence and imagination of the man or woman who is a candidate for the job. But you'd be wrong if that's what you thought. If you were to simply record our conversations and see how much time is devoted to an actual discussion of the mind, or the writings, of this or that candidate, you'd find that discussion is only a part of what moves our decisions, and not always the most important part. A surprising part of the discussion, especially informal discussion, the sort of gossip that makes somebody into a candidate, does not focus on the candidate in himself, or in herself. It focuses instead on the perception of that candidate by other potential hirers. We're at least as likely – indeed, I suspect we're much more likely – to spend time talking or gossiping about whether any other institutions might be trying to hire that candidate.

Here is some practical advice based on my experience with hiring decisions: one way for a job candidate to make himself or herself an attractive candidate for one important institution is to somehow get the news to leak that you're also a candidate at another elite institution. Often we don't even consider somebody a candidate – they're not even "on our radar screen," as we say – until the moment we hear they're being considered by somebody else. Our desire for the candidate, then, seems to have less to do with what we could call the "self" of the candidate, than it does with the candidate considered within a network of prestige, of recognition. A candidate becomes interesting and important to us insofar as we believe the candidate is attractive to another department, especially a department we consider a rival, at least an equal and maybe better than us. You become a strong candidate, not as an isolated individual, but within a network of competitive prestige. One way to become a strong job candidate is to incite rivals to see you as an object of interest to their rivals.

Now, this way of generating interest in somebody is not usually calculated, and it's not all cynical, not by any means. A lot of what we find interesting or attractive comes through our imitation of the desires of other people, especially when we imitate the desires of people we admire, or whom we consider our rivals, people we envy. And of course, often enough those we admire are exactly the same as those we envy. It is the great French philosopher René Girard who studied most deeply the way we imitate the desires of others, and he developed an influential theory of what he called "mimetic desire." His penetrating application of the theory to Shakespeare (in *A Theater of Envy*) has unsettled my experience of this play. But you do not need to understand a theory to see the phenomenon at work. Consider this old but effective romantic strategy: if you're going to a party where you expect to see someone whose romantic interest you want to attract, NEVER ARRIVE ALONE. Arrive with an attractive person who will appear to be a rival to the person you're trying to attract. You become more attractive insofar as you're seen as the object of romantic interest by somebody who excites the admiration or the competition of other people. Make yourself attractive to someone by making that someone's rival enviable for having you.

Suppose you try this strategy and it works: the person you find attractive is now attracted to you, imitating the apparent desire of the person who came with you to the party. Does this mean that you wouldn't be loved for yourself? Well, that depends on what your "self" is. If you think your "self" is some wholly individualized thing that has nothing to do with your relationships to anybody else, with anybody who finds you attractive or anybody who finds you a rival or anything else, if you have a radically individualist conception of who you are, then you're likely to be a bit insulted, not to say outraged, if the main causal factor that draws you to the attention of somebody is that you're the object of romantic interest to somebody that this other person finds admirable, worth competing with. (That's a long sentence, but it's a complicated situation.) You may want the affection of the person you've attracted to attach directly to you, so to speak, without any mediation.

We saw a related anxiety about attraction being mediated rather than direct in Plato's accounts of love. In the charioteer speech in the *Phaedrus*, the true object of erotic desire could seem to be the divine realities of the myth world, not the beloved himself. The beloved becomes lovable, as this myth tells the story, only as a mediator between the mundane world and the beauty of that transcendent world. In the *Symposium*, Diotima described Eros himself, in a thinly veiled self-portrait of Socrates, as a spirit responsible for this mediation, and one can become anxious as one ascends Diotima's ladder of love that one is losing sight of the beloved that grounded the whole process. Plato has resources for mitigating this anxiety, especially by reforming our notions of who the "true" beloved is. Alcibiades came to understand the self others saw as a false Alcibiades, and the true Alcibiades to be the man he aspired to be only when he was with Socrates. I don't say this innovative view of the true self solves all the problems, but however limited this mitigation may be, at least the earthy beloved, on these accounts, is losing out to a heavenly beloved.

Much less tolerable to the beloved's vanity is to have one's desirability mediated, not by realities of a divine world, but merely by social realities in this world, by mimetic desire. You don't want your lovers' desire for you to be the product of their desires imitating somebody else's desires. This structure of mimetic romantic desire can look no better than what Helena in fact says it is, a contagion we catch like a disease from imitating the desires of others. This certainly sounds like a cynical view of romance. A silly but still real example of this model of desire as a contagious disease is the way it can seem a high-school kid has either no dates at all to the big dance or party, or too many dates. By some mystery of desire, some people become "datable," not just to a particular person who is attracted to them as an individual, but in an oddly impersonal way, as if they were emitting an attractive scent or something. Other people, probably just as interesting and good-looking, are somehow left out of that social network. But for those who get on the inside of that social network, there's an uncanny, impersonal aspect to their attractiveness. People on the inside can move around in their relationships, as if everyone on the inside is emitting the "Date me!" scent. And those relationships can change magically, in the twinkling of an eye.

All of this mimetic desire can leave us wondering if love of an individual is real at all. We have already seen in Aristophanes's speech in the *Symposium* the question of whether romantic desire picks out a unique individual, or just a type that many different individuals can satisfy. *A Midsummer Night's Dream* is a particularly focused investigation of this aspect of romantic interest and sexual desire – the way that we tell ourselves we want to be loved in a radically individualist way, and the way we tell those we love, that we love them in a radically individualist way. But yet, when we've looked at what happens from an outside point of view, it can often appear that it's a matter of accident whether romantic desire attaches to this or that particular person. The changeability of that attachment can make it look like our romantic desires are imitative rather than being primarily attached to individuals.

The way Shakespeare confronts us most directly with this problem in *A Midsummer Night's Dream*, I suppose, is out in the green world, in the forest under the influence of the magic potion, of the love juice. Two men, Lysander and Demetrius, who take themselves to be utterly devoted to Hermia, suddenly arise and find they're utterly devoted to Helena. The extravagant language they use to praise Helena upon awakening is precisely the same language that they earlier used to praise Hermia. The play is especially interested in this extravagant language lovers use to praise their beloveds. The lover clearly goes too far in his praises; to use Shakespeare's words, the lover "dotes to idolatry" on the beloved, projecting onto the beloved the manifestation of something divine or sacred. Socrates suggested in the *Phaedrus* that a lover is reminded of something divine by the beauty of his beloved, but Shakespeare's young lovers seem to confuse their beloved with the very god. Now, when you make the object of your romantic attention something divine or sacred, do you respond in a radically individualist way to something in that human being? Or do you in fact strip that human being of everything individual to him or to her, and praise this depersonalized object with an utterly general rhetoric of idolatry, of divinity, of beauty? Is it your beloved's beauty, or an abstract Beauty Itself, that you really praise?

When Lysander and Demetrius – two men, by the way, who we're told at the beginning of the play are virtually indistinguishable from each other – when those two men change their romantic allegiance from Hermia to Helena, they don't change their romantic rhetoric. But if their love has really changed, shouldn't their rhetoric change? It seems suspicious that the present praise of Helena sounds so much like the past praise of Hermia. Why do all lovers sound so much alike, if love is radically individualist?

One possibility is that the true self, that romantic self in the beloved that the lover attaches to, is not individualized. Perhaps the true "self" for which we would be loved is in fact something ideal, something of an idol. The lover projects onto us what is after all a fairly stock set of rhetorical gestures. That projection need not be cynical or mistaken, just because it would fit other beloveds as well as it fits us. But the fact that our lover's idolizing of us is hardly unique, indeed, that it is repeatable by other lovers and for other beloveds, may reveal to us this rather uncomfortable fact: what makes us lovable is something general or universal rather than something particular.

So *A Midsummer Night's Dream* presents us with a problem about idolatry, about doting. Why can romantic attachment be so voluble, so changeable? Why does the rhetoric of romantic attachment always claim to make a true discovery of something unique to a particular beloved individual, and yet the rhetoric is transferable from romantic object to romantic object? Those of you who've been fortunate enough to fall in love with more than one person, tell us: how different have the praises you sing for your beloved been the various times you've been in love? I don't know that you kept recordings of what you said to your various beloveds, but if you had, how different would the recordings sound? How many different pet names have you had for your beloved? Are they all "honey"? Are they all "sweetheart"? Do you always say they have beautiful eyes? How much repetition have you noticed in your romantic rhetoric? How transferable has the language of love been from one accidental object to the next?

Now, there are many excuses we can offer for why our rhetoric stays the same when our beloveds change. It might just be that you're not very creative. Or it might just be you're not very perceptive, and all the objects of your love look exactly the same to you. But does the static character of our language, given the mobile character of our desires, give us pause for thought? How radically individualist are the objects of our love?

In *A Midsummer Night's Dream*, Shakespeare has made it unusually hard to keep the characters straight. They are too much alike – Shakespeare's subtle way of raising the question of why one would be more lovable than the other. I've mentioned that the two young men are more or less indistinguishable. That is not wholly comforting from a romantic point of view. We expect a love story to sort out the *right* lover at the end. But Shakespeare seems quite happy to leave this central question undecided. Demetrius and Lysander, Lysander and Demetrius, who cares which is which? We're introduced to these characters exactly because they're indistinguishable. Lysander, when he defends himself as Hermia's rightful lover to Hermia's father Egeus, concedes what a great guy his rival Demetrius is. All Lysander can say to support his own case is, "I have as much money, my family background's just as noble, and besides that, your daughter loves me." There is nothing except Hermia's affection that makes one young man better than another. In fact, Hermia used to love Demetrius, who used to love Helena, awkward facts that leak out, so we can notice them if we're careful, but let them go if we're just festive and cheerful. Demetrius and Lysander are so much alike, and Demetrius loved Hermia before

Lysander did. Why do you think Lysander got interested in Hermia? You don't suppose he might have been imitating Demetrius's desire for Hermia, do you?

It's not just the men who are too close for comfort. The women are oddly interchangeable, too. We've thought about that touching, positive image of innocent intimacy in Helena's big speech about how she and Hermia were such close childhood friends. But now think again about the striking image Helena uses to express this closeness: two cherries, one stem. Great image; but just how different from each other *are* two cherries? I know I can't tell a whole bowl of them apart, though maybe a lover of cherries would claim to. Does it surprise you that the two women, entangled in love with two men who are so much alike we can hardly tell them apart, are hard to distinguish, too? And that Helena identifies the two women as so intimately attached that they're really one made out of two? No wonder their romantic attachments are subject to such mobility. Every cherry in the bowl will be just as sweet.

Nor is it just the relationships between men and women in this group of four young people that call for some analysis. It's also the relations between the two men and between the two women. When we think of mimetic desire, it's tempting to suggest the relationship of rivalry between Lysander and Demetrius accounts for why, as soon as one gets interested in one of the women, so does the other one. Likewise, perhaps it's the closeness of Hermia to Helena that accounts for the otherwise awkward coincidence of their romantic interests. When the cynical mood gets its hold on us, we may even believe the bonds of competitive intimacy between the same-sex couples are a deeper engine of their romantic desires than the purportedly individualist romantic bonds of the heterosexual couples.

But here perhaps the sensible reader may say, enough of such cynical suggestions! Surely rivalry and competition are not deeper than romantic attraction. The beauty and goodness of my beloved are the underlying realities that drive my desire. Shakespeare's play, which is after all a great classic of romantic comedy, cannot be suggesting that competition and rivalry are the real cause of romantic possessiveness. Surely *A Midsummer Night's Dream* does not really believe that the truth of romance is that your beloved is merely the prize, the trophy, of the competition between you and your rivals, where you all wish to possess the beloved to win victory over your rivals, rather than for any quality of the beloved herself or himself.

Is there any evidence at all that Shakespeare entertained such unromantic ideas?

The answer of course is yes, very much yes. These ideas are illustrated by the two mature couples, the two king-and-queen couples, both Theseus and Hippolyta and Oberon and Titania. Nearly the first thing we hear Theseus say, to his bride-to-be Hippolyta, is "I won you with my sword." Now of course there's a certain amount of sexual byplay on what might count as Theseus's sword. But the play begins from a report that a competitive situation, a war between Theseus's Athenians and Hippolyta's Amazons, formed the bond between Theseus and his bride. After Hippolyta is conquered, this competitive bond is transformed into a romantic bond. The notion that competition generates romance is this play's front door. Later on, when we meet the fairies, it turns out that Oberon and Titania are having a lovers' quarrel over possession of a beloved, a boy whom they both want to be their page. Why does Oberon want this boy? He wants this boy because Titania has this boy. Oberon's desires are utterly imitative. In both royal couples, human and fairy, what we see is the competitive engine of romantic desire and its imitative character. We're much less likely to notice this same structure in the desires of the young people, because we want a cheerful and festive interpretation of their love, not a cynical one. After all, we're just like Lysander and Hermia: most of what we know about love was learned from love stories.

Lysander says to Hermia, "The path of true love never did run smooth," and they run away to the green world, in search of romantic freedom and their true selves. But perhaps Shakespeare intends us also to hear something Lysander's words almost say: "Hermia, we're just acting out an established script about how things go for lovers. And if there weren't any interesting obstacles and impediments to our love, we wouldn't be in love. It's the adventure and the difficulty that actually makes us feel in love. So don't feel so bad. In fact, maybe we should scatter a few more obstacles around to get our love charged up." To create love, we may have to create a story, and to create a story, we need to create drama.

There is a well observed scene in Woody Allen's 1986 movie *Hannah and Her Sisters* that illustrates how two lovers might generate or imagine obstacles simply to keep their love sharp. We are shown an older couple, the parents of Hannah, falling into an argument that they've obviously had many, many dozens of times before. Hannah tries to calm them down, but it's clear that as they get angrier with each other, they also find each other more attractive. They're making charges of infidelity against each other. Hannah's father accuses Hannah's mother of being a shameless flirt; Hannah's mother accuses Hannah's father of sleeping with every ingenue in the actors union. This bickering is painful for their daughter to hear, but it allows the parents to recharge their own romantic energy. By accusing each other of infidelity, they also project an image of each other as still attractive, still provoking desire, and they desire each other again because they are imitating what's probably a more or less fictional rival. So Hannah's mother is saying, "You've always been so attractive to the ladies," inventing the ladies who can infect her with a renewed desire for her husband. She can feel her husband's attraction by feeling jealous; and her husband performs exactly the same projection onto her. Of course, this invented competition and rivalry leads to verbal violence, as they shout and accuse each other, much like Oberon and Titania do. But this competition, and their susceptibility to catching desire mimetically from somebody else, keeps the romantic energy in their relationship.

A Midsummer Night's Dream raises the prospect that virtually all romantic energy has within it this mimetic, this imitative component, and that the desire we think of as so basic and so focused on a particular individual, is almost always also a social desire, a placement within a network of imitation, competition, and repetition. As Taylor Swift sings to her latest lover, "I love the players, and you love the game. I've got a blank space, and I'll write your name."

One way to put this point would be to say, you could write *A Midsummer Night's Dream* with no magic at all, without the love potion, as René Girard suggested. (Just as Othello's only bewitchment was the story that let Desdemona play his manliness.) The sudden shift of these two almost indistinguishable men, Demetrius and Lysander, from one object of romantic interest to the other object of romantic interest, is completely explicable on the most natural of causes; no magic is required, unless we want to call the connection between competition, imitation, and desire magical. Thomas Mann made the same point about Richard Wagner's use of a love potion as a plot device in *Tristan and Isolde*. The two title lovers are given a love potion they mistakenly think to be a deadly poison. They both drink from the cup that holds the potion, and when they think they are dying, they at last reveal to each other the forbidden passion they feel for each other. This release of passion, Mann argued, would happen even if the "potion" was nothing but clear water. It was the freedom given to their passion by the prospect of death that accounts for their love, not any magical potency in the drink they share. Wagner's tragic opera and Shakespeare's comic play use a magical potion to reveal to us, if we are willing to see through the fairy tale, a natural cause of human passion. When we are in a romantic mood, we'd prefer not to notice or acknowledge this natural cause, and we pretend the volatility of romantic interest requires magic. It is more comforting, after all, to believe in magic than to notice how contagious desire can be, how what we see as attractive depends so much on what others find attractive. And once we do notice the volatile social aspect of romantic interest, it is hard not to fall into a cynical mood.

The grateful vision

It is Shakespeare's account of the common people, those rude mechanicals led by Nick Bottom, that rescues us from this cynical mood. These unsophisticated men, intent simply on putting on a good play, are in love with theater. Theater lets them find themselves, lets them express themselves. They do not worry that "playing a part" is doing something false or fake. Instead, they worry about how powerful they become when they play a part and embrace a new identity through theater. The aristocrats think of theater as all illusion and mask, while for the common people theater is visionary and revelatory. If with the common people we embrace the theater of love, Shakespeare seems to say, we will cure ourselves of the cynicism and arrogance of the aristocrats.

A Midsummer Night's Dream ends with the commoners putting on the play they were rehearsing in the forest. This play has an absurdly long and contradictory title: "The Most Lamentable Comedy and Most Cruel Death of Pyramus and Thisbe." The play is based on an old story of two doomed lovers. Shakespeare used this same story as the basis of his own tragedy, with the rather long title of *The Most Excellent and Lamentable Tragedy of Romeo and Juliet*. Shakespeare wrote *Romeo and Juliet*, his first great tragedy, and *A Midsummer Night's Dream*, perhaps his finest comedy, at more or less the same time. He surely had in mind *Romeo and Juliet* when he decided to have the rude mechanicals perform their own version of the same story. Shakespeare turns his own tragedy into an unintentional comedy in the performance of the bumbling workers. We have seen in *Othello* how thin Shakespeare can make the line separating comedy from tragedy.

Theseus, deciding on the evening's entertainment after his wedding and those of the young couples, reads an announcement for "Pyramus and Thisbe" that describes its "tragical mirth," in keeping with the absurd contradiction of its title as a "lamentable comedy." And yet, the mirth of the playing, the pure joy of the commoners in the performance, is exactly what Theseus is seeking for this festive evening. "Here come the lovers, full of joy and mirth," he says, to welcome the young couples to the celebration. So it befits his romantic mood to be entertained by these unsophisticated but sincere players. His bride Hippolyta is afraid the aristocratic audience will treat these well-intentioned but bumbling common folk with contempt, and she suggests they not be asked to perform, so they will not embarrass themselves. But Theseus is resolved, and promises to resist any tendency to laugh at the failures of the common players. (He and the other aristocrats do not keep this promise.) The play proceeds.

Of course, the "rude mechanicals" are as bad at putting on a play as we would expect them to be. I say "we," because Shakespeare plays a delicious trick on us. Because there is a play ("Pyramus and Thisbe") being performed within a play (*A Midsummer Night's Dream*), we are made a double audience. We watch the common players play, as if we were in the audience of aristocrats. Yet we also watch the aristocrats watch the commoners, as the audience of *Dream*. In other words, Shakespeare invites us to feel the sneering contempt for "bad" or unsophisticated theater that Hipployta feared the aristocratic audience would feel; but at the same time, he puts us in position to reflect on those aristocrats and that contempt, because the aristocrats are being played, too. We laugh at the aristocrats for the way they laugh at the commoners. Or to put it another way, we act superior to the aristocrats for acting superior to the commoners when they're acting "Pyramus and Thisbe."

I believe this rather dizzying embedding of play within play, audience within audience, is Shakespeare's way of unsettling us about love, too, as well as theater. Remember that escape to the green world was essential for both romantic freedom (for the nobles) and theatrical freedom (for the commoners). I suggested that the parallel between theater and romance in the green world raised the question of whether there is something essentially theatrical about romantic love itself, as if love calls on us to play a part, to embrace a role. Viewed in a cynical mood, the way love and theater interpret and intertwine with each other in this play looks like a critique of romance. But this cynical view is merely how theater looks to an unenthusiastic player, one intent on keeping the action on stage at a safe distance. Such a person withholds himself, shouting from the darkness of the audience, "It's only a play!" rather than leaping into Dionysus's realm, acting out the story on stage.

The character who most deeply embodies this embrace of theater is Nick Bottom the weaver. Bottom is introduced to us as an insatiable theatrical monster, one who wants to gobble up every role, to enter every possible identity the theater can offer. When we first meet the rude mechanicals, the parts in "Pyramus and Thisbe" are being distributed before their first rehearsal in the green world. Bottom wants to play every part. Every time a new part's introduced he says, Wait, I can do that one too! Pyramus, the doomed hero – yes, I can do that. I'll be great in a heroic rant or a lover's lament. But I can do the doomed heroine Thisbe, too, and "I'll speak in a monstrous little voice." Or the part of the lion, which has no spoken lines but only roaring: "Let me play the lion, too. I will roar that I will do any man's heart good to hear me." Bottom enters utterly into the play. Playing a part for Bottom is finding and expressing a part of himself. He is not *pretending* to be a hero, or a lady love, or a lion. He is seizing the opportunity to *be* these parts, as wonderful and strange as that may seem to those of us less theatrical than he is.

We see Bottom later in the play, when he is translated, or transfigured, by Puck, and has a donkey's head put on him. Now, if you or I suddenly found ourselves abandoned by our frightened friends in the middle of a forest because we had taken on the attributes of a beast, I suspect we'd be pretty upset. Our loss of identity would be terrifying. But not for Nick Bottom, monster of theater. Does he even seem nervous? No. He sits down and he thinks, Oh, that's wonderful; could someone bring me some hay? He simply inhabits the new role and enters right into it. He doesn't have any sense of falseness in the fact that he's playing. That's how he is who he is. Bottom becomes Bottom by playing a part. Donkey head, no donkey head, lion, hero, heroine, he enters each of them with an incredible exuberance. Every moment is a moment of rapture for him. For Nick Bottom, theater is not to be contrasted with some other real thing. Theater is the most real thing there is. Playing is the most real thing that there is.

Shakespeare forces us to make a choice toward the end of this play. Whose side will we take, Theseus's or Nick Bottom's? Both make a great speech that summarizes one point of view on the connection between theater and love. Theseus thinks love is an illusion – an odd thing for a man to think on his wedding day! But Theseus doesn't think his own love is an illusion. He only thinks this about other lovers, such as the young people who by now have returned to the city from the forest. Theseus thinks that these young people are really quite ridiculous in the way they fall in and out of love, their desires influenced by imitation and competition. He never thinks to apply this cynical view to himself. Theseus believes himself a man of reason, a no-nonsense person. But it never occurs to him to take up the third-person perspective on his first-person love. Like many who fancy themselves philosophers, Theseus exempts himself from his criticisms of everyone else. He is an aristocrat looking at the bumbling playing of common people, without noticing that he is caught up in the same theater of love as everyone else. Theseus doesn't realize that when he is talking about love, he is talking about himself.

Theseus's great speech comes in response to a comment of Hippolyta. Now, Theseus is like far too many men, in that he doesn't really listen to his bride's comment. He just gives an answer without trying to figure out what she in fact asked, or indeed whether she asked anything at all. Hippolyta says, "Tis strange, my Theseus, that these lovers speak of." She wants to understand better this strange tale from the green world, of romantic changes and transformations. She is not rushing to judge the young people. She just is pondering what has happened to them. Theseus doesn't pause long enough to ponder the mystery that Hippolyta is pointing to. Instead of a mystery to be pondered, he sees a puzzle to be solved, a problem to be fixed, like Ted with LuAnn's broken heel. Both men need to be more grateful for gifts, and not try to control the giving.

Theseus is impatient with the strangeness of love, and cynically denies there is anything wondrous about it. But the very words he utters mean more than he meant to say, and point past his cynicism. He dismisses his bride's comment, and gives his famous anti-theater, anti-imagination speech, vigorous and manly, one of the most quoted in all of Shakespeare. What the young lovers report of their green world transfigurations, Theseus says, is "more strange than true." The young lovers have let their imaginations trump their reason, inhabiting a ridiculous space akin to madness and make-believe. "The lunatic, the lover, and the poet are of imagination all compact," says the king, and he thinks it no good thing to be made of nothing but imagination. "The poet's eye in a fine frenzy rolling, doth glance from heaven to earth, from earth to heaven," and Theseus means this as an insult, being no friend of frenzy, though he has used words that in Plato's mouth could describe the ascent of the soul's chariot, energized by a beloved beauty. Do not trust the poetic eye, let alone the lover's, for "imagination bodies forth the forms of things un-known," and to Theseus, no form can be real unless it is knowable, knowable by standards he would be comfortable with, without mad-ness or frenzy. Worst of all for no-nonsense Theseus, people like these young lovers will try to live in their made-up worlds, deploying "the poet's pen" – and how can we not think of Shakespeare's own pen as he writes these lines? – that with its seductive power "gives to airy nothing a local habitation and a name." One might as well expect to find, he says with a snort, "Helen's beauty in a brow of Egypt," the fairness of Desdemona in the dusky visage of an Othello. The-seus, King of Athens, scoffs at those who would inhabit the Green World of love, perhaps because he is anxious to have them back in the city limits, where he can keep his eye on them.

Yet Theseus's own words give unwitting testimony to imagina-tion's gaudy power. He seems to protest too much over something that he claims is nothing, so that his rejection of emigration to the land of frenzy is translated into an invitation to it. The speech is as likely to be cited as praise of the imagination as criticism of it. And Theseus seems not to have noticed that Helen of Troy's main com-petitor for the crown of exemplary beauty is tawny Cleopatra, a "brow of Egypt" indeed. (Helena, often called simply Helen in the play, is contrasted with the "tawny" Hermia; did Theseus realize that the two men, Lysander and Demetrius, actually begin the play by preferring the dark Hermia to the light Helena?) In fact, Shake-speare pairs Helen and Cleopatra as exemplars in both *Romeo and Juliet* and *As You Like It*. The myths are leaking through Theseus's clutching hands. (The leakage is even more copious if Shakespeare knew the story of Helen in Egypt, perhaps through Italian sources such as Marsilio Ficino's translations and commentaries on the

Phaedrus.) Theseus's speech also doesn't pay any attention to the social character of romantic desire and romantic interest. He speaks as if each and every one of those young people out in the woods had made up his or her own story, when obviously the fact they were all together is essential to their experience, whether that experience was an airy nothing or something more habitable. And Hippolyta, quietly but with great precision, puts her finger on Theseus's mistake. "All the story of the night told over and all their minds transfigured so together," she responds to his rant, is testimony to more "than fancy's images, and grows to something of great constancy; but howsoever, strange and admirable." She refuses to give up the idea that there is something strange and wonderful, admirable, in love, and she thinks the wonder is somehow connected with our sociality, our togetherness. Perhaps the Queen means the reality of the young lovers needs a receptive audience, must be taken as theater to be seen for what it is.

Theseus gives the "love as illusion" speech. Shakespeare grants to Bottom the competing "love as vision" speech. Transformed with the donkey's head by Puck, loved for a while by Titania, queen of the fairies, Bottom has just come out of the enchantment, and he wakes up. He thinks he is still rehearsing "Pyramus and Thisbe" with his fellow craftsmen, so when he wakes, he says "When my cue comes, call me and I will answer. My next is 'most fair Pyramus.'" He hasn't yet realized the others have fled and the rehearsal is not still going on. Then he notices no one is there. At first he calls for them, but then it starts to come back to him, his experience of being translated to the magical and dangerous fairy world. In a speech both comic and profound, Bottom tries to describe an experience of ecstasy and transfiguration that goes beyond what words can say.

"I have had a most rare vision," he begins, "I have had a dream past the wit of man to say what dream it was." Throughout the play, there has been much playing with both "vision" and "dream." Bottom, or perhaps Shakespeare, suggests that his vision can be captured only in religious language that goes to the very boundaries of nonsense, if it does not cross that limit. In a passage very unusual for Shakespeare, Bottom closely paraphrases a passage from the New Testament (1 Corinthians 9–10, in a translation current in Shakespeare's time). In that passage, St. Paul says that what God will give to those who love him goes utterly beyond what the eye has seen or the ear has heard. To those who love, will be opened "the bottom of God's secrets." Nick Bottom's very name seems to come from this passage. The secrets opened by love take us into a divine realm, and cannot be fully expressed. Bottom transforms St. Paul's words, comically jumbling them but also giving them a new intensity: "The eye of man hath not heard, and ear of man hath not seen, man's hand is not able to taste, his tongue to conceive nor his heart to report what my dream was." St. Paul had said the secrets revealed by love go beyond what can be seen or heard, that is, beyond the power of language. Bottom goes farther, layering secret upon secret, with the image of synesthesia, that is, of intermingled senses (eyes hearing, ears seeing). Even these extraordinary perceptions would not be enough to capture the vision and the dream Bottom has experienced. Perhaps he needs an oracle.

Bottom does not think anyone could simply state or describe what he has gone through, but his exuberance for theater is ever optimistic. He says, "I will get Peter Quince [the director of the commoners' play] to write a ballad of this dream. It shall be called 'Bottom's Dream' because it hath no bottom." And so Bottom will communicate his "dream" by incorporating it, as a song, into the play they have been rehearsing. "I will sing it in the latter end of our play," he says, with no concern for how such a song would fit into the story of Pyramus and Thisbe. Bottom in his speech displays no anxiety about whether his dream, his transfiguration by the magic of love, was real or not. For him its reality is his ability to play it. He compares this, or rather Shakespeare compares it, to the reality of finding what's divine in human life. The tone or mood of this passage is a stunning combination of wonder and mirth. Some readers fancy there is parody in Bottom's religious language, but I cannot find in the passage any spirit of mockery or contempt. I think Shakespeare was on Bottom's side, and the side of love.

Theseus is a kind of philosopher. He distrusts theater, and playing. And so for him, love, if it has a theatrical dimension to it, must be something that's not real, something that's only fancy or imagination. For Bottom things are exactly the opposite way. It's because the world of love can be played, because we can find there a script, that he embraces it as real. But for Bottom "real" does not mean "can be explained in words." There is experience beyond words, and visions beyond explanations.

Who is at the bottom of *A Midsummer Night's Dream*? Is it Theseus and his philosophical authority, or is it Bottom, this man who's all theater and for whom love presents no anxieties? If we had an answer to that, we would know Shakespeare's true mind. But that seems to me as hard to know as what the eye might have heard or ear seen: not a puzzle to be solved, but a mystery to be pondered.

Near the beginning of Plato's *Phaedrus*, Socrates says something very odd to his young friend: "Phaedrus, if I don't know you, I must have forgotten myself, too." Socrates's own model, then, of self-knowledge is not that he turns inward on a radically individual self to know who he is. It's instead by looking outward in conversation, to what he can learn from Phaedrus, that Socrates learns again who he is himself. The answer to "Who is Phaedrus?" is an essential part of knowing who Socrates is. Socrates does not possess himself in secret self-sufficiency, which then he can open or close to other human beings. Indeed, it's only in his openness to other human beings like Phaedrus that Socrates discovers who he is himself. Alcibiades found out the secret Socrates, not with a magical glance into his invisible soul, but by careful listening to Socrates's words.

Of course this is not the only point of view available in the *Phaedrus*, no more than a socialized sense of desire is the only point of view available in *A Midsummer Night's Dream*. But considered from this point of view, the image of the mirror and the echo in the charioteer speech bears a striking resemblance to aspects of *A Midsummer Night's Dream*. When the lover sees beauty in the beloved, the lover does not merely attach to that specific person, that beautiful beloved. The lover also rediscovers something about himself, rediscovers something that, when he's not in love, he's in constant danger of forgetting. He returns to what's best in himself, to what's highest in himself, to something that this dialogue and *A Midsummer Night's Dream* understand as something divine, something sacred. This is why the language of idols, even of idolatry, seems so at home both in Plato's dialogue and in Shakespeare's play.

The self-knowledge the lover receives by opening himself to his beloved is not radically individualist, either in Plato or Shakespeare. The *Phaedrus*'s lover finds himself only by abandoning himself to love. Living the way of abandonment, the lover is pulled out of the particularity of place and time by the beauty of the beloved and returns to the world of myth, a world timeless and placeless. So that the self the lover remembers through love, the self he now embraces anew in the moment of falling in love, is a self that has the pettiness of the everyday stripped from it. The lover's vision of his particular beloved is at the same time the measure of what a true self would be, and the true self is never the radically individual self. The self that Socrates tries to remember in his conversation with Phaedrus is a better self than the self that he usually would see. Love makes you better than you usually are. But in making you better than you are, it also makes you more truly who you are. So that from this point of view, the social nature of love is not a threat to love. It's the necessary condition of the fulfillment of love. On this socialized view of love, a love always has in it imitation, an imitation of a self higher than what you are when you're not a lover.

As the *Phaedrus* tells the story of the mirror and the echo, the connection to someone in love with you allows you to see yourself and your own beauty. You cannot see the mountain near; only the gaze of your lover creates enough distance between yourself and your vision of yourself so that you become visible to yourself. I mentioned that Plato took the risk of making love narcissistic by making the lover the mirror in which the beloved sees his own beauty. But this Platonic Narcissus does not fall in love with his own present self; he falls in love with the self he can become, since it is this self of myth the lover reflects back to him. This picture of the provocation offered by love's vision is not selfish; it is ecstatic.

Indeed, it's very challenging, and we see at the end of Plato's *Symposium* what happens when the challenge becomes no longer tolerable. The social nature of his love of Socrates reveals to Alcibiades a better self he could have been, but that he refuses to pursue with an undivided heart. Alcibiades is ashamed by this refusal but he never gives up his love for Socrates. What Alcibiades learns from his love affair is not the secret of Socrates, but the secret of the true Alcibiades. Alcibiades is ashamed only because Socrates gives him a vision of how wonderful he could be.

A Midsummer Night's Dream looks much darker if it's read from the point of view of Theseus's concluding speech. Theseus refuses the notion that the self revealed to us when we fall in love is an aspirational self, a self that challenges us to be more than we are in the everyday world. Theseus presents the work of imitative imagination in love as a work of, you might say, mere flattery of the self. As if the poet and the lover, like the lunatic, are merely creating a world in which they can be at home and in control. That's not the way that Bottom experiences the theater of love, the playing of a part within the life of love. And it's not the way that Socrates in the charioteer speech presents the prospect of imitating, of mirroring, of seeing ourselves reflected by our beloveds.

How narcissistic in the end is the view of love, as something that we in some ways project onto our beloved? Is it all self-serving, is it ultimately selfish? It's only as selfish as trying to find your best self, as being always restlessly in pursuit of it. Whether when we fall in love with somebody we're willing to take on the project of this restlessness, this constant attempt to become more perfect, more complete; whether our beloved, our spouses will always be for us a standing challenge to improvement, to a truer self-knowledge; this is a difficult question. Perhaps instead we would prefer a view of love that's more like Aristophanes's speech, where we return to some original and much more comfortable sense of connection to another human being. Should our loves promote restlessness, should they provoke us to a certain kind of shame about where we are now, and a certain kind of exhilaration about what we can become? Or should love instead create a comfort zone, an enclosed world like the world that Antoine inhabits in *The Hairdresser's Husband*? A world where all of our needs are met, as opposed to that eroticized world Diotima and Socrates discover, where our needs are never met because every movement toward meeting our needs shows to us our needs are deeper and longer that we'd ever thought before we arrive at that new point; as if our hearts had always a further hardness to overcome, if we would be perfect.

I find myself returning over and over again to the question of need, of neediness. Is need something to be overcome, to be removed from a life? Removed most especially by finding that comfortable person whom we can love? Or is neediness itself the experience we should seek in erotic love? Not the satisfaction of desire, but the ever-new provocation of a further desire, a desire to be more than what we started as?

For myself, I find a reading of *A Midsummer Night's Dream* more exhilarating if it brings the play closer to the *Phaedrus*, and Bottom closer to Socrates. I do not think that Theseus's rather cynical view of love and its imaginative power is Shakespeare's final word. In the end, I think Plato's word is closer to our truths. But it remains to be said that both Plato and Shakespeare were great enough writers and thinkers that they embed in their own works a criticism of the optimistic reading of where erotic love can take us. If erotic love leaves us as narcissists, leaves us enclosed in a settled world that we create to hold at bay the demands of our neediness and our imperfections, then the question has to be asked, whether such comfortable love is something we should pursue, or whether perhaps it's something we should avoid; a putrid limb or a festering eye, to be cut off or burned out.

I do not think, in the end, there is an easy answer to the question of whether our narcissism, our clutching to this everyday self, is something that's challenged by love, as Plato would have it in the *Phaedrus*, or something that's reinforced, alas, by love. Will we lovers restlessly call each other to new perfections, or comfort each other in the everyday selfishness that wealth and education can bring? But even if, like Alcibiades, we are pained to have our failures revealed to us, we can be grateful for the fleeting and wonderful vision love grants of the self we could become. Philosophy begins in wonder, and ends in gratitude.

SOURCES AND ACKNOWLEDGMENTS

Sources

Throughout this book, I draw on Plato's *Symposium* and *Phaedrus*, and occasional from other dialogues. Sometimes I paraphrase more loosely than a translation would allow itself, but I take responsibility for accurately reflecting the significance of the Greek original. There are many translations of Plato's Greek texts. My favorite for the *Symposium* is by the great Romantic poet and Platonist Percy Bysshe Shelley. In fact, I liked it so much I edited it with notes and an introductory essay: *The Symposium of Plato: The Shelley Translation* (St. Augustine's Press, 2002). I do not have a particular favorite for the *Phaedrus*, so I am writing my own, also for St. Augustine's Press.

William Shakespeare's *Othello* and *A Midsummer Night's Dream* are the focus of two chapters, and I draw on these and occasionally on other plays throughout. There are many good editions of Shakespeare, and I have usually used the Pelican editions. Stories from Andre Dubus's collection *Dancing after Hours* (Vintage, 1997) appear in four chapters, and I identify the stories when they occur. The movies I discuss were all commercial successes and are readily available.

The writings of Ralph Waldo Emerson have often been in my mind, though they are never my main topic. Readers interested will notice the influence especially of "History," "Self-Reliance," "Friendship," and "Circles" from *Essays: First Series*; "The Poet" and "Experience" from *Essays: Second Series*; and "The Uses of Great Men" and the lectures on Plato and on Shakespeare from *Representative Men*. Though I quote from John Henry Newman only once (from *An Essay in Aid of a Grammar of Assent*, from the chapter on what Newman calls "the illative sense"), he too has had a pervasive influence on my sense of my task.

Among more recent scholars, I have made much use of Stanley Cavell's title essay in *Must We Mean What We Say?* (1969; Cambridge University Press, updated edition 2002) and his essay in that volume "The Avoidance of Love: A Reading of *King Lear*"; and his treatment of skepticism and *Othello* in *The Claim of Reason* (1979; Oxford University Press, new edition 1999). These latter two essays are collected with his other essays on Shakespeare in *Disowning Knowledge: In Seven Plays of Shakespeare* (1987; Cambridge University Press, updated edition 2003). René Girard's general theory of mimetic desire provokes me throughout, especially in the final chapter on *A Midsummer Night's Dream*, much influenced by Girard's *A Theater of Envy* (1991; St. Augustine's Press, 2004). More generally, my sense of the ways Shakespeare and Plato create worlds out of words is indebted to G. Wilson Knight's *Wheel of Fire: Interpretations of Shakespearean Tragedy* (1930) and William Empson's *Some Versions of Pastoral* (1950), two classics of literary criticism. Two translations of texts important to the book were revelations to me: Michael Henry Heim's *Death in Venice* (HarperCollins 2005) and Janet Smith's *Humanae Vitae* (New Hope Publishers, 1994). The quotation from Dana Gioia in Chapter Seven comes from his excellent essay "The Catholic Writer Today" in the journal *First Things*, December 2013. I wrote this book, and for decades taught the course that led to it, sharing the sense of the vocation of Catholic writers Gioia invokes at the end of his essay: "It is time to renovate and reoccupy our own tradition."

Finally, of the many works of scholarship on Plato that have been a part of my life, I would pick out five as especially in the background of my writing here. When I first started thinking about Plato's erotic dialogues, Charles Griswold's *Self-Knowledge in Plato's* – Phaedrus (Yale University Press, 1986), G.R.F. Ferrari's *Listening to the Cicadas: A Study of Plato's* Phaedrus (Cambridge University Press, 1987), and Martha Nussbaum's chapters on the *Symposium* and *Phaedrus* in *The Fragility of Goodness* (1986;

Cambridge University Press, 2nd edition 2001) showed me there was a conversation to be part of. More recently, Debra Nails' *The People of Plato* (Hackett, 2002) made many difficult things easy and some impossible things possible, for thinking about Plato's use of historical persons in his mythic projections. Finally, I found Josef Pieper's essay *Enthusiasm and Divine Madness* (1962; St. Augustine's Press, 1999), on the *Phaedrus*, in the early stages of writing this book, and it heartened me to find so generous a mind had been some of the same places I wanted to go. I have written a quite different sort of book from these authors, but I may not have written it at all without theirs.

Acknowledgments

This book grew from my lecture course "Ancient Wisdom and Modern Love" at the University of Notre Dame. A version of the course was first produced for video in 1993, by my friend Jeff Brenzel, to whom I owe the idea that the material was destined for a wider audience. In 2007, it was one of the first courses chosen for Notre Dame's contribution to the OpenCourseWare program, and the lectures were videorecorded and made available online, with some supplementary material. My thanks to the director of the program, Terri Bays, for all her help and initiative. The lectures later became available on iTunesU.

In spring 2012, the lectures became available on Chinese servers, where they became very popular, with viewer-provided subtitles. Beijing Tilin Press saw a publishing opportunity and approached me, and with the excellent help of editor Yan Cai, I began work on the manuscript. I was aided significantly by having transcripts of my lectures, and I thank Catherine Bruckbauer for producing them with efficiency and accuracy. The publisher partnered with Guangxi Normal University Press, under editor Xuting, to bring out the book in August of 2014, with the title爱是光着脚的哲学 (*Love is Barefoot Philosophy*), ISBN 978-7-5495-5588-8. Though that title sounds better in Chinese than in English, I was delighted when the editors suggested it, since it caught many central themes, especially the importance of a pastoral idyll of love, such

Sources and Acknowledgments

as the Garden of Eden, and Socrates's habit of going barefoot. The cover is a Chinese drawing of Adam and Eve, clothed in leaves, being expelled from Paradise. This English book has significant differences from the Chinese version, but I am not sure I would ever have written it without the encouragement of my Chinese editors. It is a wonder to me that my lectures and writing found an enthusiastic audience in China, and the editors, translators, and publishers have my deepest gratitude.

I am grateful to many friends who commented on the manuscript and whose conversations found their way into my writing.

Particular thanks to Steven Affeldt, especially for sharing provocations from Ralph Waldo Emerson and Stanley Cavell; Sidney Blanchet, who also saved me from confusing a beaver with a faun; Jacque Brogan, who took it all to heart; Benjamin Evans, especially for many conversations about opera; Michael Garvey, who with my wife Beth opened Andre Dubus for me; John Houston, a fellow admirer of the Earthy Aphrodite; Tom Morris and Debra Nails, constant friends and practical advisors; Beth O'Connor, especially for making Velazquez come alive for me; David Reeve, for years of shared Platonism; Henry Weinfield, especially for discussions of René Girard's Shakespeare; and to Noreen McMahan, Robert O'Donnell, and Orlando Rodriguez, whose early appreciations kept up my interest.

Among my many assistants in the teaching that led to this book, I mention especially Raymond Hain and Benjamin Huff, whose detailed comments on the manuscript were precious; Deirdre McQuade and Fr. Daniel Moloney, especially for entertaining my rather pagan Catholicism; and Phil Reed, who did excellent work preparing the online version of the course in 2007.

I am also grateful for the excellent work on the index by my student assistant, Rebecca Devine née Self. Finally, I offer sincere thanks to the College of Arts and Letters at the University of Notre Dame for a leave that helped me complete the manuscript.

And finally, with these few standing for many, to Anne Marie Comaratta, Colum Dever, Marty and Annie Foos, Nora Kenney, and Margaret Lynch, exemplary students who helped me remember who I am.

INDEX

"*Plato's Bedroom* is a marvelously engaging reading of Plato's *Symposium* and *Phaedrus*, interwoven with readings of Matthew's Gospel, Thomas Mann's *Death in Venice*, Shakespeare's *Othello* and *A Midsummer Night's Dream*, Woody Allen's *Hannah and Her Sisters*, Atom Egoyan's *Exotica*, Andre Dubus's *Dancing After Hours*, and Patrice Leconte's *The Hairdresser's Husband*, among other works. If you wanted an argument in favor of a liberal education — a real one — David O'Connor's book would be an ideal touchstone: this is what real humane wisdom looks like, this is what it can do when it sets itself to think about an issue of real importance to *people*, not just to fellow academics. Anyone will learn important lessons about love, and be given resources to think about them, by reading this wonderful and unusually well-written book."

> — C. D. C. Reeve, Delta Kappa Epsilon Distinguished Professor of Philosophy, University of North Carolina

"*Plato's Bedroom* is a call to follow Plato in his praise of love, and to replace suspicion and cynicism with wonder and gratitude. The author traces Plato's insights through literature, art, and film: the Bible, Shakespeare, Andre Dubus, Thomas Mann, *The Lord of the Rings* and *Hannah and Her Sisters*, are brought together in a profound meditation on how erotic love can open us to the sacred. This divine ecstasy, David O'Connor argues, is the natural inheritance of philosophy in Western culture."

> — Frisbee C.C. Sheffield, Director of Studies in Philosophy, Christ's College Cambridge

CONTINUED ON THE REVERSE SIDE.

"*Plato's Bedroom* will seduce its readers, an account of *love* in all its guises. It's serious, it's funny, it's moving. Ancient while surprisingly contemporary, this book points beyond itself to an array of movies, stories, plays, poems, religious texts, novels, and operas, but it always circles back to Plato. The ancient is rarely so contemporary, so immediate as we see it here. Love within the embrace of philosophy becomes deeper, more exhilarating, more passionate; it becomes irresistible. *Plato's Bedroom* is unsettling, because within the embrace of philosophy, love becomes deeper, more exhilarating, more ecstatic, brought to vivid life for the reader in encounters with Adam and Eve, Othello and Desdemona, Arwen and Aragorn, and so many other couples from movies and literature. Love is so much more than we have imagined, but not more than Plato realized. *Plato's Bedroom* lovingly interweaves literature and philosophy in surprising and enlightening ways, and David O'Connor has written the real story of Plato's *Symposium* and *Phaedrus* — a story of love cynically rejected, love shyly avoided, love as lust, love as procreative desire, love as immortal. Plato's dialogues have found their interpreter for our times."

— Debra Nails, philosopher, Michigan State University